An Inventory of Educational Improvement Efforts
in the
New York City
Public Schools

An Inventory of Educational Improvement Efforts in the New York City Public Schools

David Rogers

Teachers College, Columbia University
New York and London

Copyright © 1977 by The Educational Planning Foundation. All Rights reserved. Published by Teachers College Press, Teachers College, Columbia University, 1234 Amsterdam Avenue, New York, NY 10027

DESIGN BY STEVE SHERMAN

Library of Congress Cataloging in Publication Data
Rogers, David, 1930-
    Inventory of educational improvement efforts in the New York City public schools.

    Bibliography: p.
    1. Education—New York (State)—New York (City). 2. Educational innovations—New York (State)—New York (City). I. Title.
LA339.N5R58   371.3'09747'1   77-10481
ISBN 0-8077-2531-5

Manufactured in the U.S.A.

Contents

Foreword by Frank Riessman — vii

Preface — ix

Introduction — 1

1 Inventory of Educational Programs For Special Target Groups

Alternative Schools, 7
    Auxiliary Services for High Schools, 9
    Mini-Schools, 10
    Alternative High Schools, 14
    Special Programs for Talented Students, 22
    Alternatives in Elementary and Junior High Schools, 25
Vocational and Career Education Programs, 30
    Alternative Programs, 34
    Cooperative Education, 35
New Multi-Level Programs, 36
    Articulation Programs with Community Colleges, 37
    New Programs for the Handicapped, 39
    Comprehensive Magnet School Programs, 40
    Training Programs for Out-of-School Youth and Adults, 45

iv   Inventory of Educational Improvement Efforts

Drug Prevention and Intervention Programs, 50
   Centralized High School Programs, 53
   Decentralized, Community School District Programs, 54
   Alternative and Intervention Schools, 56
   Religious Schools, 56
   Delegate Agency Programs, 58
Bilingual Programs, 59
   Title VII Programs, 65
      Decentralized District Programs, 65
      Centralized High School Programs, 70
      Other Centralized Programs, 73
   Title I Bilingual Programs, 75
   Emergency School Aid Act, 76
   New York State of 1973, Chapter 720, 77
   City Tax Levy Programs, Unit Appropriation 30, 79
Open Education, 82
Desegregation, 85
   Desegregation Techniques, 86
   Indirect Desegregation Programs, 89
   Magnet Schools, 89
   Emergency School Aid Act (ESAA) Programs, 91
      Centralized Umbrella Programs, 94
      Decentralized District Programs (Basic), 94
      Non-Profit, Private Organizations, 101
Early Childhood, 101
Poverty Area, Low Income Students, Title I, 105
High School— College Collaboration, 107
   Cooperative Continuum of Education, 108
   College Preparatory Skills Programs, 110
   Community College—High School Articulation Career-Oriented Programs, 117
   Guidance and Counseling Services for College-Bound Students, 119
The Handicapped, 120
   Federally Funded Programs, 122
      Title I Special Services and Special Schools, 122
      ESEA Title III, Section 306, 126
      ESEA Title VI-B, Educational Services for Unserved Handicapped Children, 127
      Title VII, Bilingual Programs for the Handicapped, 133
      VEA-4B Umbrella for Secondary Handicapped Students, 134
      National Highway Traffic Safety Act, 139

Federal Health and Nutrition Act, State Food on the Table Act,
   DSEPPS Breakfast Program, 140
  Title III Mini-Grants, 140
  Contracted-Out Alternative Schools, 140

2 Inventory of General Purpose Innovative Educational Programs

Beacon Light Schools, 147
Arts-in-General Education, 148
Miscellaneous Programs, 149
Title III Programs, 150

3 Inventory of Administrative and Staffing Innovations

Teacher Training, 154
  Teacher Corps, 156
  Triple T (Training of Teacher Trainers), 159
  Urban-Rural School Development, District 12, 161
  Career Opportunities Program, 162
  Private Sector Teacher Centers, 162
Supervisor Training, 167
  Center for Educational Management, 169
  Other Programs, 172
Management Modernization and Reform, 175
  Economic Development Council, 176
  Deputy Chancellor, 178
  Management Consulting Firms, 179
  Division of Business and Administration, Board of Education, 182
  Automated Attendance Information Systems, 182

4 Inventory of Political Action, Advocacy, Consumer Rights Programs

Citywide Citizen Advocacy Groups, 185
School Breakfast and Lunch Related (Food) Reforms, 199
Coalitions of Citywide Groups, 203
Legal Agencies and Programs, 205
District, Neighborhood, and More Locally Based Groups, 209
Locally Based Programs, 216
Information and Media Programs, 221

5 Inventory of Participative, School-and District-Based Planning

6 Main Trends in Educational Improvement Efforts

Relevant Background, 231
Principal Recent Trends, 235
   Alternative Schools, 235
   Systems Approach, 236
   Cultural Pluralism, 237
   Curriculum Innovations, 238
   Organizational Development, 239
   Management Modernization, 241
   Programs for the Handicapped and Non-English Speaking, 241
   Inside and Outside Participants, 242
Changes Within the Official School System, 245
Gaps in School Reform Activity, 249

7 An Assessment of the Main Reform Strategies and Recommendations for Future Ones

Focus and Locus Strategies, 253
Affiliated and Unaffiliated Strategies, 254
Coordinating Strategies, 258
Consumer Advocacy and Politics, 261

Appendices

Street Addresses of the Public Schools Cited in the Inventories:
   Manhattan, 264
   Bronx, 269
   Brooklyn, 273
   Queens, 279
   Staten Island, 282

Foreword

Despite the pessimism of the 70s, a surprising number of innovative efforts have been directed toward the improvement of schooling in New York City in recent years. David Rogers has done a remarkable job of inventorying these efforts and providing an overview and assessment of the main reform strategies of the period.

The range of programs covered is instructive in itself: alternative schools, vocational and pre-vocational programs, bilingual programs, the handicapped, drug prevention programs, open education, early childhood, programs directed toward low-income students, high school-college collaboration programs, and the like. The inventory presents a balanced treatment as well as a clear presentation of the various reform attempts. Included are programs within traditional classroom settings and alternative schools outside, private sector initiated activities as well as public, incremental change efforts and more basic structural reforms, and top-down programs that begin at school headquarters and bottom-up ones that focus on individual classrooms and schools.

The inventory is organized in terms of four categories of innovation: (1) educational programs for both special target groups and for general purpose innovations; (2) administrative and staffing reforms; (3) political action, advocacy, and consumer rights efforts; and (4) participative school- and district-based planning. The latter, influenced by modern organizational theory, is an important field of organizational development, and Rogers gives it considerable attention and valuable exposition.

The inventory does not provide answers to the question, "Education for what?" nor a specific delineation of what actually improves learning. The reader should not look for such information here but rather will find a fine overview of the various structural and programmatic efforts at educational change which, in a sense, bypass these questions.

A particularly valuable chapter discusses trends in educational improvement efforts. What are these main trends?: (1) marked expansion of alternative schools programs; (2) more comprehensive approaches to change; (3) greater acceptance of the cultural pluralism of students; (4) a wide range of curriculum innovations including career education, bilingual programs, mini-schools, individualized instruction, environmental education, and the like; (5) an increased emphasis on organizational development techniques as a way of bringing about change in the schools and involving outside change agents in collaborative relations with the educators; (6) a shift from the broadside attacks on the school system of the 60s to a much more focused programatic effort; (7) significant attempts in management modernization at almost all levels within the system; and (8) emphasis on programs with special target groups, particularly the handicapped and non-English speaking.

This inventory will be extremely useful in any type of teacher training or supervisor training program, pre-service or in-service. In essence, it should be valuable for anyone considering problems of change in the school system in the United States today.

—Frank Riessman
Editor *Social Policy*
Professor of Education, Queens College

Preface

This inventory was commissioned by four corporations: AT&T, Citibank, Exxon, and Morgan Guaranty Trust, all of whom have been deeply involved in efforts to help improve the New York City public schools. The top urban affairs staff of these corporations have met informally for several years to try to improve their public education programs. They concluded that both the private and public sectors would benefit from having at their disposal a single compendium of the main reform efforts and subsequently funded this study.

In view of the many people and programs contacted in preparing the inventory, it would not be possible to thank publicly all those who helped. There were some, however, whose assistance was so extensive that I would like to acknowledge it here. They include Steve Telinski of the Office of Urban School Services of the State Education Department, Marvin Barondes, Ruth Phillips, Beatrice Shavit, George Quarles, Vince Troianno, Vera Hannenberg, Paul Niemi, Al Mathew, Shelly Umans, Phillmore Peltz, Noel Kriftcher, Carolyn Jones, Mike Vega, Carol Fineberg, Nola Whiteman, Sy Weissman, and Julian Washington of the New York City Board of Education, and David Seeley, Corinne Willing, Miriam Thompson, Bill Jesinkey, Charles Wilson, Louis McCagg, Florence Flast, Ellen Lurie, Diane Morales, and Kathy Goldman, all staff members of various private agencies.

I could not have completed the inventory without the assistance of Miriam Kahn and Lorraine Dauber. Miriam Kahn worked intensively on the project in its last few months. Her strong dedication to completing this work, her skills at securing information from a wide variety of people and resources, and her personal support and enthusiasm that went well beyond what one might expect are hereby acknowledged. Lorraine Dauber was particularly helpful in the early stages. Charlotte Fisher typed the entire manuscript with care and intelligence.

There are undoubtedly agencies whose programs were not included and would like them to be in later versions of the inventory, and perhaps there are others who were included but would like to see changes in the descriptions compiled here. We welcome and indeed actively seek out communications from such agencies, since the inventory will be updated regularly, probably every year, as new programs develop. Any inquiries regarding the Inventory may be sent to me at the Educational Planning Foundation, 52 Vanderbilt Avenue, New York, NY 10019.

The funding corporations and the author hope that many agencies involved in the public schools, including Board of Education officials, will find this inventory helpful. It may be used in a variety of ways—as a reference source or suggesting important areas of program development and research by indicating gaps and duplication in existing reform efforts.

—David Rogers
April 1977

Introduction

This is an inventory of the main efforts at improvement in the New York City public schools since 1970, with particular emphasis on activities of 1974-76. We have deliberately defined the subject quite broadly, so that interested agencies and citizen groups will have as inclusive a cataloging as possible of what turns out to be a very wide array of programs and projects. To give readers some sense of the scope of the inventory, we have included: educational programs and political advocacy and action efforts; programs within traditional classroom settings and alternative schools outside; public sector and outside, private sector-initiated programs; incremental change efforts and those aimed at more basic structural reforms; top down programs that begin at the school system's headquarters and bottom up ones that focus on an individual classroom or school.

Despite the deep pessimism of so many clients, critics, and even educators regarding the schools' performance, considerable activity directed at improvement remains. Much has been initiated from outside the system, but there are many educators and administrators inside with strong commitments to improvement, who would be much more productive than they have been were they provided the necessary support (particularly political) and resources. The inventory attempts to cover all their main activities.

2 Inventory of Educational Improvement Efforts

It will become apparent from a careful reading of the inventory that the private sector-initiated activities are but a shadow of the public, in terms of level of resources committed. They are, nevertheless, important in at least two ways. First, they support pilot and demonstration programs, often alternative ones, that may later be incorporated into existing public schools through the city's tax levy funds. And second, they sometimes require the school system to respond more quickly to particular citizen and client needs than might otherwise be the case. In many instances, pressure for reforms from outside private sector agencies provides legitimacy for changes some school officials want to make but may have held off on for fear that there wasn't a strong enough constituency for them. Recent efforts by the Educational Priorities Panel, a coalition of civic groups, to have education funds shifted from administrative to classroom use may be an example. An illustration of the first kind of private sector impact is the business and foundation support of alternative storefront schools in ghetto areas—e.g., street academies and Harlem Prep—many of whose components later were incorporated into existing schools under city tax levy money. Some of the same kinds of benefits also result from public sector initiatives—federal and state-funded pilot programs—and many of them are included in the inventory. One of the conclusions reached in the study is that there is such a wealth of talent and sophistication in both the private and public sectors, that there must be ways of making the schools more effective, even within the constraints of the existing budget.

The inventory has systematically avoided, wherever possible, any description of traditional school programs, concentrating instead only on those that represent innovations or supplemental services. For some programs it is not always easy to draw the line, as federal and state monies meant to foster innovations are, in fact, just used to buttress old ones that may not be working well or perhaps to gloss over or compensate for inequities in the allocation of city tax levy funds. At the risk of being too inclusive and seeming to dilute our definition of what constitutes an effort at reform, we have leaned in the direction of listing programs about which there may well be some debate. Since one of the goals of this inventory is to make available to interested parties information on the many educational improvement efforts, disregarding for the present their impacts, that seemed an appropriate strategy.

A decision was made at the outset not to attempt any evaluation of the various improvement efforts but rather to simply describe them. We were concerned, then, exclusively with *inputs* rather than *outputs.* One obviously cannot deny the importance of knowing which reform efforts were more or less successful, but it is also critical to bring together in one place as much information as possible on just what is going on by way of attempts at educational improvement. This has never been done before with regard to educational programs in New York City, though many people have commented for years on its importance. Such a cataloging is particularly needed at a time of fiscal crisis, when the private as well as the public sector is reassessing its priorities in public education. Simply by collecting information on what is going on, one begins to get a picture of some of the gaps and areas of duplication, and this in itself may help in thinking through priorities. Furthermore, it is important to know something about the *universe* of reform efforts before one begins to think about what is important to evaluate.

We have concentrated heavily on describing the programs and interventions as they have functioned in the 1975-76 school year. At the same time, however, we have pulled together information, where possible, on programs for the entire period since decentralization began. Our base year, then, is 1970 for many programs. Some that are no longer in existence have even been included, particularly in cases where they seemed to have had spillover effects reflected in new programs that are now ongoing.

The inventory is organized in terms of four main categories of innovation or intervention activities. They include: (1) education programs, either for special target groups or more general purpose; (2) administrative and staffing reforms; (3) political action, advocacy, and consumer rights efforts; and (4) participative, and school- and district-based planning. The latter was included because it seems to represent an important new trend in educational change efforts, influenced very much by the emerging field of organizational development and by its increasing application to public as well as private sector organizations. Early in the study, we made a deliberate choice to organize the study along such strategy or activity lines, rather than by type of participant or change agent. Information on the latter is included in each program description, and our summary at the end contains a further discussion of the relative roles of different private and public sector participants and how they have changed.

We collected information on a number of key characteristics of each activity, including the level and sources of funding, when the program started, where it was taking place, for whom (the target populations), under whose auspices, at what level of staffing, program emphases, and changes in emphasis, if any, over time. We also indicate what additional information, if any, is available about the program and where to obtain it. Needless to say, our data are more complete for some programs and activities than for others—for the usual reasons.

Though the inventory itself may appear fairly routine, in the sense of simply pulling together descriptive information, compiling it was an unusually arduous task. Since 1975-76 was a year of unprecedented fiscal problems, many private as well as public agencies were so involved in trying to stay afloat and fund themselves for the next year that they were not as available to provide us with information as might otherwise have been the case. Moreover, the Board of Education's budget problems and layoffs were of such a magnitude that it hadn't even compiled its annual booklet describing its federally and state funded programs since the 1973-74 school year, after having done so routinely the previous four years. That made this inventory much more difficult to compile.

The study was also done in a period of increasing public controversy regarding the Board of Education's budgeting practices. And in the final stages of compiling information, we had to contend with the fact that many top school administrators were spending a lot of time pulling together their own budget statements and sometimes had little time to spend in furnishing information for us. Many Board of Education staff, however, by far the vast majority, were very helpful in providing information. We also received considerable assistance from the State Education Department's Urban School Services office and from the regional office of the U.S. Office of Education.

We used three main techniques of data collection: (1) a mail questionnaire, (2) personal interviews, and (3) analysis from existing documents, particularly budget statements, project proposals, and reports. Most of our information came from interviews and documents, with many of the interviews conducted by phone. Some people were reluctant to give out much information over the phone, but most were cooperative. In view of the much greater efficiency in this procedure, as contrasted to personal interviews, we recommend it strongly to future researchers in the field. Several studies comparing the validity of information obtained by phone with that from face-to-face interviews indicate that it is quite high.

There are three parts to the inventory. The main part, chapters 1 through 5, reviews the many programs and interventions. That is followed by a section indicating some of the main trends since 1970. We conclude with a brief discussion of the various change strategies—their underlying assumptions, their strengths, and their weaknesses.

The appendices include borough-by-borough lists of all public schools whose programs are described. It may be useful to refer to this material when seeking further information about a program or to locate schools.

We tried throughout to be as detailed and precise as possible in describing the various programs. The reader should be cautioned, however, that the realities of the budget process and how public sector programs actually work preclude too much precision. The large number of budget modifications, the inadequacy of information, and the reluctance of some administrators to provide some kinds of data—particularly those pertaining to budget and staffing—require that information on those matters be viewed as only "ball park" estimates. The information is still useful and probably quite valid, but it should not be taken too literally.

Chapter 1

Inventory of Educational Programs For Special Target Groups

Alternative Schools

The first category of innovative or supplemental programs included in this inventory is what has come to be called alternative schools, a rather global concept that encompasses many different kinds of programs offering options and diverse educational services not provided in traditional classrooms. The particular types of alternative schools considered include: (1) auxiliary services for high schools, (2) mini-schools, (3) alternative high schools, and (4) alternative programs for talented students. A fifth category, contracted-out schools for the handicapped, will be considered in the last section of this chapter.

Since the late 1960s, many such alternative schools have developed in New York City and elsewhere. Outside private sector organizations had supported street academies in ghetto areas throughout the city, with funding from corporations, foundations, and the New York Urban Coalition, and with the New York Urban League responsible for their administration. Harlem Prep was another example of this strategy.

Meanwhile, the New York City Board of Education, at the initiative of Chancellor Harvey Scribner and the High School Office, established a task force on high school redesign in 1971 and began to encourage the development within the system of various prototype alternative schools.

There were, in addition, several other private sector-initiated alternative schools. The New York Urban Coalition's mini-school programs and various new high schools established by community groups—e.g., Park East High School, Harlem High School, and West Side High School—started in this period (since 1970). Finally, the Auxiliary Services for High Schools program was established to serve students who had dropped out, been suspended, or were otherwise unable to adjust to the traditional classroom.

The majority of alternative school programs in New York City are at the high school level, though many mini-schools now exist as well in elementary and junior high schools. There is now a separate Office of Access Programs in the Division of High Schools at school headquarters to administer programs at that level. Their main clientele are minority students who have not made it in "mainstream" high schools. Though no precise ethnic data exist, it appears from individual school data and from estimates of school administrators in the programs that up to 80% of their students are black and Puerto Rican from poverty backgrounds. At the same time, some alternative programs exist to serve talented students and to attract white middle-class students back into academic or comprehensive high schools that had been losing many of these students in recent years.

Though these alternative schools are actually quite diverse, they have common characteristics as well, including: small classes, extensive counselling and remedial services in the basic skills, an emphasis on affective development and experiential learning, a humanistic relation between students and educators, flexibility in curriculum and teaching methods, out-of-classroom learning experiences, much emphasis on vocational and career-oriented courses, and student participation (often parent and community as well) in school decision making.

In terms of aggregate numbers, the alternative schools serve roughly 15,000 of the 300,000 odd high school students, or only 5%. Yet, there are some attempts to incorporate innovations that started in these schools into traditional high schools. Furthermore, before the recent budget cuts, there had been considerable growth in numbers of alternative programs over since 1971. Their further development will depend on the extent to which an active and influential constituency emerges to support their funding efforts.

One consistent pattern has been for those alternative schools that had begun with private sector funding to get incorporated or absorbed into the existing system and funded mainly by city tax levy monies. Harlem Prep, Park East High School, and Lower East Side Prep are among such programs.

Some useful references with regard to these schools include three Board of Education publications: *Toward The 21st Century,* n.d.; *The Community as School,* April 1973; and *Humanization and Involvement: The Small-Unit Approach,* June 1975. Each follows up on the previous one, and they document the conceptual and operational development of the school system's alternative schools program.

Auxiliary Services For High Schools

STARTED: September 1969.

FUNDING: $3.5 million for 1975-76, including $2.3 million from tax levy and the rest from Ttitle VII, Elementary and Secondary Education Act (bilingual), Title I, and a special grant from New York State for a program of referral to jobs. Previous funding, from 1969-1974, over 90% of which came from federal and state sources, included State Urban Education monies in addition to Titles VII and I.

LOCATION: 5 day and 11 evening centers throughout the city, in all 5 boroughs, usually located in or on periphery of ghetto areas where there is the highest incidence of dropouts. The two main administrative centers are at 65 Court Street in downtown Brooklyn, around the corner from Board of Education headquarters, and 198 Forsythe Street in Lower Manhattan.

Day Centers: Ebbets Field School (Bkn), Forsyth Street School (Man), Jamaica Vocational Day Center (Q), 93 Street School, (Man), Roberta Clemente Center (Bx).

10   Inventory of Educational Improvement Efforts

Evening Centers: Brandeis High School (Man), Curtis High School (SI), Ebbets Field School (Bkn), J.H.S. 10 (Q), J.H.S. 180 (Q), Jamaica Vocational High School (Q), Julia Richman High School (Man), Maxwell Vocational High School (Bkn), New Dorp High School (SI), Prospect Heights High School (Bkn), Taft High School (Man).

EMPHASIS: Basic education; remediation in reading and math; extensive counselling and guidance (occupational, academic); preparation for the high school equivalency exam; job placement. Also has an extensive bilingual and English as a Second Language program, including one of the first all-bilingual schools in the city, the Roberto Clemente Center, and bilingual services for all centers. Typing and other business preparation as well.

TARGET: Roughly 12,000 students, down from a high of over 13,000 in 1973-74. Ages 16-21, mainly minority students, dropouts, suspended students, those with chronic attendance problems, and others with difficulty adjusting to traditional high schools. Vietnam veterans are also a target group.

STAFFING: 300.

AUSPICES: Division of High Schools.

CHANGES OVER TIME: Had expanded every year in numbers of students served and funding until 1975. Expanded on existing programs and added new ones: more job counselling and placement, more bilingual programs, more programs for such other special target groups as juvenile prisoners and Vietnam veterans. Has become a site for internships for teachers, counsellors, and supervisors. Has also broadened its network of schools and agencies that refer students to it and to which it refers students.

INFORMATION: Doctoral dissertation by Seymour Weissman, director, *Auxiliary Services for High Schools: A Model for Change,* 1975, Union Graduate School. Also a summary description of the program, 9pp., September 1975.

Mini-Schools

This strategy began, as indicated earlier, with a series of private sector-funded street academies, each funded and given other support services by an individual corporation.

Corporate sponsors include: Celanese, IBM, McGraw-Hill, First National City Bank, Union Carbide, American Airlines, Morgan Guaranty Trust, Roche, McCaffrey, and McCall, Time-Life, Pan American, Manufacturers Hanover Trust, Chase Manhattan Bank, Burlington Industries, Atlantic Richfield, Exxon, and American Express.

The Urban League had ultimate administrative responsibility, providing street workers—young black and Puerto Rican adults who had had many of the same experiences in adolescence as their street academy students and constituting role models and advisors. The New York Urban Coalition was the catalytic agency through which corporate support was mobilized and maintained. At the program's peak in the late 1960s, there were 14 or 15 separate academies. Ford Foundation grants were largely responsible for the original funding.

As foundation and business support dropped off, the Coalition began to incorporate many components of the academies into existing high schools. It helped establish Harambee Prep in Charles Evans Hughes High School in Manhattan and Wingate Prep in Wingate High School in Brooklyn, both in 1970. The next year, the Coalition helped restructure an entire high school, Haaren in Manhattan, into 14 mini-schools. The concept has since spread throughout the system, and there are now over 40 mini-schools in high schools in all five boroughs. They average between 75 and 125 students, accounting in the aggregate for 4,000, plus another 2,500 at Haaren.

Precise budget and funding data are unavailable, but if one assumes that staffing costs constitute roughly 75-80% of the total cost, it is likely that between $3 million and $4 million goes into these schools, excluding Haaren. There are 150 staff assigned to the mini-schools, including teachers, paraprofessionals, and school-neighborhood workers. The key program elements are the same as in most other alternative schools, as already discussed.

Inventory of Educational Improvement Efforts

Main Mini-Schools, 1975-76 School Year

Schools	Register of Students	Number of Staff
Brooklyn		
Bay Ridge	30	2
Boys and Girls	130	4
Fort Hamilton	38	2
Hale	20	1
John Jay	77	3
Jefferson	116	5
Lincoln	40	2
Madison	50	3
Maxwell	47	2
New Utrecht	90	2
Tilden	265	4
George Westinghouse	100	5
Wingate Mini	120	7
Wingate Prep	60	3
Wingate Academy	100	5
Manhattan		
Benjamin Franklin	250	5
Hughes	135	5
George Washington	76	4
J. F. Kennedy	94	2
Seward	150	6
Julia Richman	70	5
Washington Irving	107	4
Bronx		
Taft	80	3
Monroe	180	5
Stevenson	30	1
Clinton	100	6
Morris	0	0
Lehman	125	3
Queens		
Springfield Gardens	100	3
Richmond Hill	374	6
Bryant	101	3
Lewis	60	3
Jackson	89	3
Jamaica	50	1
Cleveland	100	5
Bays	72	3
Flushing	85	3

Educational Programs for Special Target Groups

Schools	Register of Students	Number of Staff
Hillcrest	315	11
Far Rockaway	28	2
Bowne	81	3
Richmond		
New Dorp	100	2
Curtis	80	1
Port Richmond	60	2
TOTALS	4,074	150

STARTED: Since 1970.

LOCATION: See the above list. Some are located within a high school; others have their own outside facility.

EMPHASIS: Small classes; informal, flexible curriculum; wide range of counselling services; much vocational and career assistance; student participation in school decision making.

TARGET: 4,000 students, most of them minority students from poverty backgrounds—potential dropouts, truants, with many academic and personal problems.

STAFFING: 150.

AUSPICES: Access Office of the Division of High Schools.

CHANGES: The number has increased every year since 1970.

INFORMATION: Summary materials from Access Office. Also, various evaluations, including Fox and Fox, Associates, *Evaluation of Wingate Prep, 1971-72,* August 1972.

Haaren High School (Man)

STARTED: 1971.

FUNDING: In addition to city tax levy money, the Urban Coalition put in $220,000 in 1973-74 and $600,000 the two previous years. It also brought in cosiderable foundation funds, including $30,000 from Van Ameringen Foundation, $200,000 from The Ford Foundation to the Board of Education for Haaren Streetworkers, $20,000 from the Fels Foundation, $60,000 from the Grant Foundation, $4,700 from the New York Foundation, $3,300 from Donaldson, Lufkin & Jenrette, and others.

EMPHASIS: A complete restructuring of the entire school into 14 semiautonomous mini-school units, each with a coordinator, grade advisor, and street worker. The model followed built on five inter-related elements: (1) mini-school structure, (2) street worker infusion, (3) teacher training and curriculum development, (4) school-business partnerships, and (5) full-service school concept that involved bringing the services of many youth-oriented agencies into the school. This last component was never implemented. By 1975 there were 10 mini-schools, each with a specialized curriculum, including emphasis on automotive, aviation, careers, college bound, English as a second language, Haaren Prep, high school equivalency, Mobile co-op, and pre-technical.

TARGET: 2,500 students, 95 percent black and Spanish-speaking.

STAFFING: 220, including 150 classroom teachers, 45 auxiliary personnel (16 of them street workers), 10 assistant principals, 12 teachers with administrative functions, and the principal.

AUSPICES: Access Office of the Division of High Schools.

CHANGES: Much more emphasis over time on participative planning that included all the main constituencies of the school.

INFORMATION: Voluminous summary materials produced by the New York Urban Coalition. Also, two evaluations by Fox and Fox, Associates: *Short-Term Evaluation of Haaren High School Mini-School Experiment,* August 1973, and *Evaluation of The Mini-School Reorganization of Haaren High School,* March 1975. Finally, James J. Morisseau, *The Mini-School Experiment,* November 1975.

Alternative High Schools

There are 11 alternative high schools, all of them now funded primarily by the Board of Education, with several receiving supplemental funds from foundations, business, and federal sources, (e.g., the Vocational Education Act). They range in size from 200 to 650 students, in staff from 11 to 45 or 50, and in budgets from $300,000 to $750,000. Again, these are gross figures, since no consolidated budget data are available for every school.

Several of these schools were started by community-based organizations alone. Others, while having community involvement, started with foundation, business, and government assistance as well. They total roughly 4,000 students,

350 staff, and about $5 million. Their present status is as recognized schools within the New York City Board of Education, whose teachers and other staff are subject to collective bargaining agreements, but without all having the rank and salaries of "mainstream" teachers and supervisors. During the recent budget cuts, many of these schools lost some of their new, young, minority teachers and received more experienced, white middle-class teachers who had been "excessed" out of traditional high schools.

Graduates of these schools receive high school diplomas, just like those granted in regular high schools.

City-As-School

Similar in many respects to the Parkway School in Philadelphia, in that students spend much of their time outside the classroom in a variety of settings, including museums, zoos, legal offices, theaters, cultural centers, day care centers, and other schools. This is the only almost completely external program among the 11 alternative high schools. It also has many more white and middle-class students than the others.

STARTED: 1973.

FUNDING: About $250,000. It received $14,000 in federal (Vocational Education Act) money to develop more learning experiences for employability. The rest is city tax levy.

LOCATION: 59 Schermerhorn Street, Brooklyn, NY 11201. Students are in a variety of external learning sites throughout the city. They also spend some time planning their program, in some academic subjects, and being counselled at the school.

EMPHASIS: Experience-based learning in outside non-classroom settings. Strong emphasis on career exploration; independent study; and highly individualized instruction. School year broken up into various learning cycles, each corresponding to a particular external experience. Students develop a contract with the school for their assignment. Teachers monitor their external activities, as do student peers.

TARGET: 290 students. 65 percent white, 35 percent black, Puerto Rican, and Chinese. Primarily 11th and 12th graders, with recent increase in 10th graders. Mainly middle-class students, very few, if any, having severe remediation problems. Many are "cultural" dropouts.

16 Inventory of Educational Improvement Efforts

STAFF: About 20: a director and assistant director, 7 teachers, 5 paraprofessionals, 3 clerical staff, 1 guidance counsellor. The Board of Education designation is 14.42 staff units.

CHANGES: Steadily increased its enrollment since 1973. Now reaching a ceiling of 300 students. Same basic program now as when started, except that it has many more external learning sites than before.

INFORMATION: Brochures and program summaries from the school. Also, a recent study by Robert Martinez, doctoral intern at Fordham University, on progress of the school's students, reported in summary form by the school.

Harlem High School (Man)

STARTED: September 1972.

FUNDING: About $300,000, all city tax levy.

EMPHASIS: Remediation in reading and math; occupational and career education; past emphasis on music and performing arts.

TARGET: 257 students from Manhattan and the Bronx. All black except 6 who are Spanish.

STAFFING: 20: 10 teachers, 1 guidance counsellor, 2 education assistants, 4 security staff, 2 secretaries, 1 dietician. 13.52 Board of Education staff units.

CHANGES: Increasing enrollment, up to 257 students. A lot of cuts, and many shop, arts, and music programs dropped during 1975-76 year. Also, less parent participation and visits by parents and teachers to homes of students with attendance problems.

Harlem Prep (Man)

STARTED: October 1967.

FUNDING: Roughly $750,000. Before it was incorporated into the Board of Education, received considerable outside funding from many foundations and corporations.

EMPHASIS: Entirely academic. College placement of all students. Shared student-staff decision making. Reciprocal student-staff evaluations. Highly structured, academic curriculum.

STAFFING: About 21: 13 teachers, 3 administrators, 3 secretaries, 2 custodians (one part-time). 16.24 Board of Education staff units.

CHANGES: By 1974 no longer able to sustain outside funding, at which time became part of the Board of Education. Now have different teachers, mostly white, and drawn from the civil service lists of the Board of Education.

INFORMATION: Brochures from the school, plus many evaluations by outside sources.

High School Redirection (Bkn)

STARTED: April 1969.

FUNDING: At least $550,000. $32,380 through the Vocational Education Act, to train child care aides. Also Title I money. Had begun with State Urban Education funds.

Both inside and outside the school. Small number of students work outside in day care centers, in other schools providing counselling to students, in city agencies on paid lines, and as volunteers in the mayor's citizen volunteer program.

EMPHASIS: Basic high school studies; remediation in reading and math; strong counselling component, with daily group sessions, conducted by teachers; non-graded classes; open zoned school; accredited off-site learning experience programs.

STAFFING: About 60: Director, 21 teachers, 25 paraprofessionals, 3 secretaries, 11 student aides. Some paid by federal funds. 28.74 Board of Education staff units.

TARGET: 530 students, almost all minority.

CHANGES: Started with a vocational and manpower training emphasis, having evolved from a Manpower Development and Training Act program in skills training (shop, business education, health careers) for truants. Evolved into a school that offered academic subjects required for high school diploma. Developed a child care program.

INFORMATION: Brochures put out by the school. Also, many evaluations by the Bureau of Educational Research at the Board of Education and by the Center for Urban Education of early programs funded under State Urban Education monies.

Lower East Side Prep (Man)

STARTED: September 1970 from an educational pilot program of Break Free, Inc., a non-profit Lower East Side community-oriented organization begun the year before.

18　Inventory of Educational Improvement Efforts

FUNDING: Roughly $350,000 from city tax levy, plus Title I funding for remedial programs in reading, math, and ESL; Vocational Education Act funds ($21,400) for career programs; plus support from Morgan Guaranty Trust through Break Free ($66,808). Total budget as an estimated $500,000.

EMPHASIS: Strong emphasis on remediation in basic skills; small group instruction; accelerated matriculation, particularly for older students; individual counselling and personal contact with staff; much emphasis on college preparation, (particularly on formal standards regarding attendance, grading, written work, use of library, homework, use of textbooks); individualized instruction; ESL for Chinese-speaking students; and a fairly extensive career program through the Office of Career Education at school headquarters.

TARGET: 355 students. 37 percent Chinese, many of them recent immigrants from Hong Kong; 33 percent black, 22 percent Puerto Rican, and eight percent other, most of them Italian from the "little Italy" community nearby. Most are dropouts or truants.

STAFFING: 44 total staff. That includes 4 administrators, 17 teachers, 7 streetworkers, 2 secretaries, 2 guidance people, 1 custodian, 4 student teachers from College of Human Services, 4 educational associates, and 2 Break Free College office staff. Outside funding supports some of them. 19.15 Board of Education staff units.

CHANGES: Become an independent agency in 1970. Came under the Board of Education in 1973. Moved to present site in 1974. Originally just tried to get students a high school diploma. In recent years has raised its standards and goals. Much more emphasis now on reading and math.

INFORMATION: Brochures and reports put together by the school. Its own educational plan for 1975-76 school year.

Middle College High School

This is the only one of the 11 alternative high schools that is linked directly to a college, in this instance, LaGuardia Community College in Queens. Middle College is a so-called campus school, located at LaGuardia, and its programs are closely articulated with it.

STARTED: Fall 1974.

FUNDING: About $200,000.

LOCATION: LaGuardia Community College, 32-10 Thompson Ave., Long Island City, NY

EMPHASIS: A 5-year program from the 10th grade through two years of college. Stress on remediation in basic skills to prepare for college and on different types of career training at LaGuardia. Students receive an Associate in Arts (AA) degree after 5 years. College faculty teach in the high school. A new house structure involving a home room teacher who does extensive academic and vocational counselling. 11th and 12th graders can take college courses, e.g., in typing, shorthand, psychology.

TARGET: 217 students, all from districts 24 and 30 in Long Island City, Astoria, and Maspeth, Queens. A wide range of students accepted in terms of school performance, with many of them truants and potential dropouts.

STAFFING: 13 on Board of Education lines and others from the college. Administrator, administrative assistant, 10 teachers, 1 guidance counsellor, 1 paraprofessional. 13.64 Board of Education staffing units.

CHANGES: Originally under LaGuardia College alone. Now no longer so. More academic than before. More remediation in reading and math. Expanded career education courses.

INFORMATION: A heavily evaluated program. Academy for Educational Development overseeing. Also in-house evaluations. Contact school.

Pacific High School (Bkn)

STARTED: September 1972.

FUNDING: At least $450,000, with some Title I funds for reading and math programs.

EMPHASIS: Basic high school subjects; remediation; many vocational and career related courses (clothing construction, typing, photography); informal atmosphere; small group and individualized instruction in academic subjects; no grades.

TARGET: 425 students, most from Brooklyn and Bedford-Stuyvesant community.

STAFFING: Administrators, guidance counsellor, 26 full-time teachers. 22.27 Board of Education staff units.

INFORMATION: School has developed summary materials.

P.M. High School

STARTED: September 1973.

20   Inventory of Educational Improvement Efforts

FUNDING: About $200,000, through the Board of Education.

LOCATION: George Westinghouse Vocational and Technical High School, 105 Johnson Street, Brooklyn, NY 11201

Also at various job and work sites—now including positions at Methodist Hospital in Brooklyn. In the past at the Bronx Zoo, Metropolitan Museum, Kings County and Downstate Hospitals.

EMPHASIS: Late afternoon and evening classes providing opportunity to study for a high school diploma. Extensive remediation in basic skills. Many career courses through work in outside settings; extensive placement in such settings. This is an alternative school in terms of its time.

TARGET: 202 students, generally minority students from poverty backgrounds.

STAFFING: 17. 10 full-time, 7 part-time staff. 11.14 Board of Education staff units.

CHANGES: More planning, more extensive in-school and out-of-school activities. Now has a wider range of students in terms of academic abilities.

Park East High School (Man)

STARTED: February 1971.

FUNDING: $500,000 from city tax levy. In addition, National Institute of Education grant and other incidental funds.

LOCATION: In and outside the classroom. Outside program in private agencies, including Mt. Sinai Hospital, Metropolitan Hospital, and Boys Club of New York.

EMPHASIS: Basic skills development; preparation for higher education and/or employment; internships in community agencies; community involvement and civic political awareness; affective development; occupational and career education; comprehensive high school course.

TARGET: 454 students and 100 adults. Almost all minority group: 40 percent black, 58 percent Puerto Rican.

STAFFING: 22 full-time, 5 part-time. 25.60 Board of Education staff units.

CHANGES: Came under the Board of Education in 1973. One of the first community founded high schools in the city, with those organizations remaining active in its operations. Grew in size over the first several

Educational Programs for Special Target Groups

years, but has now cut back on community outreach and internship programs. Much more emphasis on academic subjects and college preparedness. Selected by NIE as a prototype community high school for funding and evaluation.

INFORMATION: Brochures from school. NIE evaluations.

Satellite Academy

STARTED: 1970.

FUNDING: Roughly $740,000. Outside funding through VEA ($57,907), Tannenbaum Foundation, and Chase Manhattan Bank.

LOCATION: *Administrative Offices:* 257 West 93rd Street, New York, NY 10025

School Locations: Entry Level Academy; 2 New York Plaza, New York, NY 10004; 132 Nassau Street, New York, NY 10038; 332 East 149th Street, Bronx, New York; 91-14 Merrick Boulevard, Jamaica, NY 11432

Each academy concentrates on different types of careers. The Nassau Street one has clerical and business; the Queens one has social services; the Bronx has health services careers.

EMPHASIS: Emphasis on exploring different types of careers, but also strong concern for basic academic training in reading and math skills; emphasizes in addition the affective-emotional development of students, particularly on capacity for independent decision making regarding academic interests and careers.

TARGET: 687 students. Many are dropouts and truants come from all over the city.

STAFFING: Roughly 60 staff, with 48 from city tax levy and another 12 from outside funds. 32.81 Board of Education staffing units.

CHANGES: Put under the Board of Education in 1973. Has raised its academic standards and increased its emphasis on basic skills. Added staff, students, and schools in recent years, though cut backs and fewer city jobs for its graduates to go into in 1975-76.

INFORMATION: Brochures from the school.

West Side High School (Man)

STARTED: September 1972.

FUNDING: About $200,000.

EMPHASIS: Attempts to provide a more positive school experience for dropouts and truants, through close communication with staff and more flexible school structure and program. Preparation for New York City high school diploma through academic courses, independent study, off-site learning experiences. Basic high school subjects; remediation in reading and math. Crisis intervention and counselling for students with serious problems. Students have worked in the Executive Internship program and in Project Double Discovery at Teachers College.

TARGET: 225 students, almost all from District 3 in Manhattan. Dropouts, truants. 50% black, 25% Puerto Rican, 25% white.

STAFFING: 14: 1 director, 1 secretary, 2 paraprofessionals, and 10 teachers. 12.30 Board of Education staff units.

CHANGES: More intensive counselling with problem students.

Special Programs For Talented Students

Still another category of alternative high schools are schools with programs geared to the talented or to those with special interests. Some are programs geared toward attracting back and retaining white and, in some cases, minority middle-class students who had been leaving in large numbers. In contrast to the other three types, none of these schools started out primarily for the underachiever or the disaffected, though some such students may well be attending.

Career Development Institute

STARTED: September 1970.

FUNDING: $50,000, the equivalent of 2 teachers. Originally funded by New York Community Trust for 1 year, with $13,500 as start-up money.

LOCATION: Franklin K. Lane High School (Bkn). In and out of school. Accredited internships in city agencies and part-time employment in private industry.

EMPHASIS: A full high school course with concentration on preparation for careers in civil service. Both career education program and college preparatory. Individual counselling and instruction.

Educational Programs for Special Target Groups

TARGET: 300 students.

STAFFING: 4 part-time.

CHANGES: Had been privately funded initially, with an emphasis on a senior year of work-study in private industry. Now shift in emphasis to civil service agencies. Also decreases in staffing.

INFORMATION: Pamphlets available from school.

Executive High School Internship Program

STARTED: Fall 1971.

FUNDING: Board of Education and the Human Resources Administration.

LOCATION: 250 Church Street, Suite 902, New York, NY 10013. Students involved in internship activities all over the city, working as special assistants to senior officials in government and other public institutions, community and civic agencies, and business. Individualized internships.

TARGET: 535 students from all five boroughs. Roughly 50 percent white and 50 percent minority. Generally high achieving students, with strong verbal skills and capacity for independent study and work. Present enrollment includes 162 from Queens; 148 from Brooklyn; 105 from The Bronx; 63 from Manhattan; and 18 from Staten Island.

STAFFING: 19 teachers, 5 HRA secretaries.

CHANGES: More students and more internship sites and linkages with outside agencies. Also has spread to several other cities.

EMPHASIS: A one-semester internship experience, with full academic credit; four days with an agency and one back at the home base at the Human Resources Administration; students work as assistants to agency administrators, produce daily log of their activities, and present a project summary and analysis of those activities to other students in the program and then to their home school. Enables students to examine a particular career interest, to bridge the gap between school and work. Types of agencies selected, in order of frequency, include health and medicine, education, communications and the media, business and labor, law and law enforcement, social services, government, and science-related.

INFORMATION: On request at HRA.

Institute Of Music And Art

STARTED: September 1972.

FUNDING: No extra funding now.

LOCATION: Erasmus Hall High School (Bkn).

EMPHASIS: A full academic course with concentration on music, art, performing arts, and career awareness; originally established to provide a performing arts school in Brooklyn, for honors students, to attract more whites and more talented students to the school. Originally a mini-school. Has established linkages and affiliations with Lincoln Center, Brooklyn College Philharmonic, Metropolitan Museum of Art, Brooklyn Museum, and Fashion Institute of Technology.

TARGET: 835 students. Originally more white honors students; now more minority students with talent and interests in the arts.

STAFFING: 60 part-time.

CHANGES: Changes both in purpose and clientele as indicated above.

INFORMATION: School brochure.

Political Science Honor Institute

STARTED: September 1972.

FUNDING: None. Board of Education used to pay for field trips and extra books—$1,000-$1,500 a year. CUNY paid for summer salaries and field trip expenses—a few thousand a year.

LOCATION: Samuel J. Tilden High School (Bkn).

EMPHASIS: Full academic program with enrichment in social studies. Designed originally for Brooklyn high school students interested in the social sciences and law-related careers. Many specialized and advanced courses in social studies. Also forums, seminars, field trips, and college credit for advanced social studies courses.

TARGET: 250-300 students from Brooklyn, who are average or above-average students and have a record of excellence in social studies, English, and speech.

STAFFING: 3 full-time teachers and draw others from the school as well.

CHANGES: Branched out from an advanced honor program to career-related one that included many blue-and white-collar careers more generally. Used to attract white honors students and now geared to average and slightly below average students, more of them from minority and poverty backgrounds. Funding has decreased markedly.

INFORMATION: On request from the school.

Educational Programs for Special Target Groups

Talent Unlimited High School

STARTED: September 1971.

FUNDING: $18,000 for supplies and specialists.

LOCATION: Julia Richman High School (Man)

EMPHASIS: Training in performance and production in music, dance, and drama. Students take regular academic subjects in their home high schools in the morning and come to Julia Richman at 1:00 p.m. every day. Performance oriented. Work with repertory groups. Educational experiences in show production, scheduling, operations, public relations and finance, performance, direction, and stage craft; work under supervision of highly trained staff.

TARGET: 225 students.

STAFFING: 7 full-time.

CHANGES: Have added fine arts. More linkages with outside institutions. Program tighter and more structured.

Alternatives In Elementary And Junior High Schools

Though some of the most publicized of the alternative schools are at the high school level, and though that is where the most consolidated information is about innovative programs, largely because the high schools have remained centralized, there are many more such schools at lower levels in the system. This inventory does not by any means report all of them, but we certainly discovered many, and they are described below. Perhaps the most concentrated are the dozen-odd alternative programs or schools that have been established in the upper elementary grades and junior high schools in District 4. Their presence there in such numbers is generally attributed by educators and observers of the New York City schools to the district's innovative superintendent and to some able and experimentally-minded teachers whom he has supported in such efforts. These alternative programs are so extensive that there is a coordinator overseeing them from the district office. There are others scattered around the city, many having an open education approach, but District 4 seems to have more than other districts.

Clinton School Without Walls (Man)

Several of the Beacon Light schools to be described later, schools that the Board of Education's Learning Cooperative had singled out as innovative and thereby particularly deserving of its support, have alternative programs. One of the most pubicized is the Clinton School Without Walls.

STARTED: September 1970.

FUNDING: Mostly tax levy, at about $300,000 per year. Had outside funding in the past from VEA, foundations, and corporations.

EMPHASIS: Modeled on the Parkway School in Philadelphia. Much time spent at various learning centers. Afternoon elective component, out-of-school, enabling students to use the resources of various corporations and cultural centers throughout the city. Some of the program's linkages for its afternoon out-of-school activites have included Western Electric, Celanese, Inc., the Metropolitan Museum, the South Street Seaport Museum, G.A.M.E., the Polyclinic Hospital (course on nursing), and the Donnell Public Library.

CHANGES: After a few years, it was concluded that the split-day approach of classroom courses in the morning and field experiences in the afternoon did not allow enough time for academic work. The school then received a planning grant of $10,000 from the Board of Education to strengthen the academic component and integrate it better into the field work. Through interdisciplinary studies and a cluster approach in teaching, that is now taking place.

TARGET: 200 students, grades 7-9. Roughly 45 percent white, 40 percent black, 10 percent Hispanic, 5 percent others.

STAFFING: 10 teachers, 2 paraprofessionals. The program makes use of many outside resources for instruction. It has parents teaching courses, business people arranging for field trips, etc.

INFORMATION: From the school.

DISTRICT 4, Educational Alternatives Programs (Man)

STARTED: 1973, at the strong initiative of the superintendent.

FUNDING: Some additional funds from reimbursable grants, but the same formula is used as for regular schools in terms of per pupil costs and services. One of the objectives of the program is that alternative schools should not exceed the cost of running a regular school.

LOCATION: 11 schools in the district plus 2 optional-unzoned schools. They are listed and described briefly below:

BETA School, P.S.109
Grades: 4-7
Program: A remediation program for underachieving boys and girls who have experienced difficulty in adjustment to the regular school.

Bilingual-Bicultural Arts School, P.S.7
Grades: K-6
Program: An educational program that incorporates the arts (visual, music, drama and dance) into the general bilingual-bicultural curriculum.

Central Park East School, P.S.171
Grades: K-5
Program: An individualized academic program in which children use a wide variety of media for learning—woodwork, photography, cooking, nature study, sculpture, painting, drama, bookmaking. Classroom studies are enriched by a program of related field trips.

Children's Learning Center, P.S.171
Grades: 4-6
Program: An individualized learning program with concentrated instructions in reading, mathematics, and writing. In addition, there is a strong emphasis on a developmental physical education program.

East Harlem Block Schools, P.S.108
Grades: Nursery - 8
Program: A comprehensive educational community program characterized by total parent involvement.

East Harlem Career Academy, J.H.S.99
Grade: 9
Program: A school designed to involve students in a career exploration program in addition to the basic ninth grade curriculum. Related field trips and innovative experiences in the world of work will be provided.

28 Inventory of Educational Improvement Efforts

East Harlem Middle School, P.S. 155
Grades: 5-7
Program: A departmentalized educational approach with a heavy emphasis on acquiring basic skills through a multi-media, individualized program.

East Harlem Performing Arts School, P.S. 50
Grades: 3-9
Program: A demonstration school that uses the performing arts (dance, music, drama) as the framework for organizing students' academic experiences and development.

East Harlem School of Communications and Health Studies, J.H.S. 99
Grades: 7-8
Program: A program to help students acquire basic academic skills through a three-stage process of studying the community, interpreting it in various media, and acting upon their understanding of its problems and needs.

Harbor J.H.S. for the Performing Arts, I.S. 117
Grades: 7-9
Program: A school dedicated to advancing the academic achievement of its students and providing training in instrumental and choral music, dance, and drama. Students participate in an after-school program under the direction of Boys Harbor, Inc.

SCANT (School Community Action for a New Tomorrow) Alternative School, 447 East 115 Street
Grades: 7-9
Program: A school that seeks to remediate academic and behavioral functioning through an intensive program in the basic skills, individual and group counseling, and small class size.

Schomburg School, P.S. 101
Grades: K-5
Program: A bilingual-bicultural school designed to meet the academic, social, and emotional needs of children in a humanistic framework.

Optional-Unzoned Schools

P.S. 50
Grades: K-7

Educational Programs for Special Target Groups

Program: Open education based on experimental learning within the school community as well as in the larger community of the city. This uniquely planned school is divided into learning communities each with its own reading and math labs and media, science, and art centers.

P.S. 109
Grades: K-7
Program: School organized on a theme oriented focus: Kindergarten—Science; Grades 1-3—Reading skills; Grades 4-6—Departmentalized; Grade 7—Math/Science

EMPHASIS: All are smaller schoools within existing ones. Each has its own separate organization and parent council and reports directly to the district office, rather than to the principal. It is a separate, autonomous school-within-a-school. The program emphasis is very similar to what it is in alternative high school programs: smaller classes; remediation programs for under-achieving students; individualized learning programs; often a particular career emphasis; school organized on a particular theme; humanistic relation of school staff to children.

TARGET: 2,000 students, kindergarten-9th grade. Mostly Puerto Rican and black.

STAFFING: Each school has a director and several full-time teachers.

CHANGES: Though there is some variation among these schools in terms of how structured or "open" they are, the emphasis seems to be on more structured approaches to teaching and learning.

INFORMATION: From the District 4 office, Mr. Sy Fliegel.

The Door—A Center Of Alternatives

This new program, highly recommended by several educational and social agencies, provided no information other than its brief, 2-page brochure.

LOCATION: 618 Avenue of the Americas, New York, NY

EMPHASIS: Provides a wide variety of alternative services and programs for youth, Monday through Thursday, 2 p.m. through 10 p.m. and Friday, 1 p.m.-4 p.m. They include: (1) adolescent health center, with free health care services, nutrition, and diet counselling; (2) family planning and sex counselling services; (3) general counselling on family, emotional, and drug problems; (4) education counselling and a learning center with high school equivalency workshops, tutoring, remedial reading, creative writing workshops; (5) vocational counselling services; (6) legal counselling; (7) crisis intervention services for help with emergencies; (7) creative workshop program in the arts; and (8) gym, yoga, and martial arts program.

I.S. 38 (Bx)

FUNDING: Tax levy and Title I funding, the latter for $190,000.

EMPHASIS: The school functions as a mini-society. Students run a post office and bank there. The school has its own economy, using paper money. There is a school court, restaurant, and radio station. These simulated activities are all used as the vehicle for the development of students' cognitive skills: communications, speaking, writing, math, and their application to all subjects. Main focus on remedial math and reading.

TARGET: 230 registered students. Students volunteer for the program. Must have parental consent. They may leave at the end of the year with parental consent. Minimal screening.

STAFFING: 29. 2 assistant principals; 12 teachers (tax levy funds); 3 full-time teachers (Title I); and 10 educational assistants, one guidance counsellor, and 1 secretary (all Title I).

CHANGES: The school closed June 30, 1976 and will move into another school. It will no longer operate as a separate school.

Vocational And Career Education Programs

Many of the innovative and supplemental programs in this field either began or were strongly reinforced by the establishment of the Office of Career Education at school headquarters in 1972. That office has helped bring in substantially increased outside funding for new programs by developing proposals itself and giving technical assistance to others in the system to do the same. The programs it has developed and helped support involved: new alternative schools that expanded student options; responding to individualized student needs; providing for more efficient use of existing school plants and other resources; encouraging more continuity of programs from elementary to post-secondary (e.g., continuum and articulation programs between the schools and CUNY); and developing more coordinated and comprehensive services for particular target groups (e.g., the handicapped, out-of-school youth, and adults).

A main emphasis of this office was its strategic use of Vocational Education Act (VEA) funds for developing demonstration and pilot programs, many of which were later incorporated into the city's tax levy structure. VEA funds for New York City have grown from $900 thousand in 1968 to close to $9 million for fiscal year 1975. As the Office of Career Education's most recent annual plan indicates: "Strategic and judicious allocation of these funds, in conformity with a comprehensive plan, has produced a massive multiplier effect producing benefits with a value many times greater than the initial investment. In effect, planning has produced a symbiotic relationship between VEA seed monies and the tax levy structure, with maximum benefits to both. Many of the major breakthrough programs initiated with VEA funding have become part of the tax levy structure." (*Annual Plan,* p. 153).

Roughly 500,000 students are affected, however peripherally in some cases, by career education programs, many of them participating in exploratory and pre-vocational programs at elementary and junior high school levels. The focus of this office, like that of other career education offices throughout the country, has not been just on secondary education. More specifically, $35.5 million of the $150 million budget for occupational education programs in 1974-75, or 24%, went to elementary and junior high schools.

The following table summarizes all the main programs in the city, separating them out into different categories and indicating the main funding sources. As the table indicates, 85% of the funding comes from city tax levy monies, 6% through Vocational Education Act (VEA) programs, and the remaining 9% from other state and federal funding sources. Almost all of the latter—$12.241 million—goes to skills training and basic education programs for out-of-school youth

Summary Of Occupational Education Costs

	Costs and Funding Category		
	Tax Levy	VEA	Other Reimbursable
Elementary			
Industrial Arts	630	85	
Home Economics	36	15	
Business & Distributive Education	270	—	
	936	100	
	986*		
Junior High School/Intermediate Schools			
Industrial Arts	14,850	56	600
Home Economics	11,250	16	
Business & Distributive Education	5,750	—	
Miscellaneous Junior High School & Elementary Levels	—	197	
	31,850	269	600
	33,564*		
Secondary Level			
High School Programs	54,459	1,691	200
Alternate Programs			
Co-op Education	4,500	835	
Work Study	—	673	
Shared Inst. Services	378	296	
After School Occupational Skills Program	—	548	
Satellite Academies	675	66	
Human Services Internship		70	
Guidance Coordination	—	50	
Miscellaneous Special Programs	—	93	
	60,012	4,322	200
	63,241*		
Adult Occupational Programs	1,441	2,605	12,241
Handicapped Occupational Programs	31,500	932	142
Multi Level Programs		545	—
TOTALS	125,739	8,773	13,183
	132,503*		

*Total tax levy cost adjusted for estimated salary increase—teachers: $18,000 to $18,970; supervisors: $25,200 to $25,450.

Educational Programs for Special Target Groups 33

and adults. Those sources include the Comprehensive Employment Training Act (CETA), Adult Basic Education-Adult Education Act, and Welfare Education Plan.

To give some further indication of the scale of vocational and career education programs in the New York City public schools, there are roughly 38,000 students taking skills training courses at the secondary level. The Vocational High Schools account for over 36,500 of them, with another 1,163 in comprehensive high schools and the rest (267) in academic high schools. Stated more broadly to include out-of-school youth and adults, 74,000 of the enrollees in occupational training programs in the city's public school system in 1974-75 were expected to graduate and/or complete training, prepared for employment in five major occupational clusters: trades and technical occupations (25,935); business and distributive education (16,915); community and social services (7,783); health careers (2,787); and agriculture (33). The main sites for this training included: (now closed) evening trade schools (20,836); day secondary schools (16,172); CUNY community colleges (16,876); pre-employment programs (8,000); business and distributive education-adult (6,150); and manpower development training (2,478). Though it is not our purpose to list all the regular programs in the New York City schools or related agencies, there are many federally-funded and supplementary programs from within this listing.

We consider in this inventory several different types of innovative programs, some of which are cross-listed elsewhere, e.g., in the section on alternative programs. That cross-listing is a critical aspect of the inventory, since the same program has several components and should be viewed in that perspective. The main listings include: (1) various alternative programs; (2) new multi-level ones, (3) articulation programs with community colleges; (4) new programs for the handicapped; (5) magnet high school programs with a heavy vocational emphasis; and (6) training programs for out-of-school youth and adults.

A complete description and analysis of occupational programs in the schools is contained in the Office of Career Education's *Annual Plan (1975-76) and Long Range Plans (1976-80) for Comprehensive Occupational Education in New York City,* 1975. Another good source with program descriptions is *Directory of Services,* Office of Career Education, 1974-75.

Alternative Programs

As indicated above, many alternative programs have been supported by the Office of Career Education. It helped obtain VEA funding, for example, for several of the alternative high schools already described, each of which then added a career focus. In addition, it also supported two other important alternative programs through VEA funding—Shared Instruction and After School Occupational Skills Program—both of which increased available course offerings. In 1974, for example, more than 15,000 students who applied for enrollment in vocational high schools were turned down because of lack of space. Moreover, given the city's fiscal crisis, there is no chance that additional vocational schools will be built. Both programs thus help close a part of the big gap between available facilities and numbers of students applying for them, by providing afternoon and evening programs in those facilities. This stretching and fuller utilization of vocational high school resources represents a major improvement in the cost-effectiveness of such programs.

Alternative High Schools

Since all the schools in this category have just been described at length in the preceeding pages, we will just include information here on their career and job-related programs:

Educational Programs for Special Target Groups 35

The Satellite Academies: Have a VEA budget of $57,907 that includes a job developer and various other services.

City As School: Receives approximately $50,000 in VEA funds that support what are called career learning exploration experiences.

Lower East Side Prep: Receives $21,400 in VEA monies for its job placement activities.

High School Redirection: A school that started out with an explicit manpower and vocational training focus, gets $32,380 in VEA funds for a training program for child care aides involving Bishop Loughlin High School and a day care center as well.

Auxiliary Services for High Schools: Receives $48,000 for a program to refer its students to training schools (where such training is not available or feasible in the public sector). Approximately 170 students are involved.

Human Service Internships: Approximately 200 interns in this program are receiving job experience in public, civic, and service agencies in New York City, in preparation for careers and advanced training in service professions and occupations. These students attend public and private non-profit schools. Funding for this program (begun in 1973) is with VEA monies (approximately $93,000).

Cooperative Education

Though not a new program, this has been included in our inventory because it has expanded and developed so much over the past several years, again with the assistance of quite substantial VEA funding. Also of importance have been the strong leadership of its director and the support of an outside business group discussed later in this inventory, the Economic Development Council (see pages 176-8).

STARTED: 1915.

FUNDING: $4,742,000. $4,500,000 is from tax levy sources; $835,000 from VEA funding; $100,000 from LEAA in Washington.

LOCATION: Junior and senior students placed in alternate week or part-time employment in office and clerical jobs, civil service (city) agencies, health (nursing, nurse's aide), day care centers, and a variety of trade and technical jobs, as well as in ornamental horticulture. 400 corporations and 60 civil service agencies participate.

EMPHASIS: To introduce students to work and possible careers, thereby allowing for occupational exploration to reinforce basic skills training in high schools by improving student motivation.

TARGET: 8,500 students. Two-thirds minority students, one-third other.

New Multi-Level Programs

Another set of strategies initiated by the Office of Career Education with VEA monies relates to the establishment of "unit skills" programs and plans to develop skills centers throughout the city. The first step in that direction has been the development of the Bronx Comprehensive Career Campus. It is designed to serve as a model for a comprehensive educational system that will offer counselling, training, and job placement to in-school youth, out-of-school youth, and adults. There are plans to incorporate a skills center and satellite skills centers and to have a direct link with the main training services in the area, including adult programs and post-secondary institutions. It is also meant to be a model for other skills centers. At present one major program exists, the Bronx Career Counselling Center, that represents the first stage in the development of the campus model.

Bronx Career Counselling Center

STARTED: 1974.

FUNDING: $450,000 from VEA monies.

Educational Programs for Special Target Groups

LOCATION: 1030 Southern Boulevard, Bronx, NY 10455. In classrooms and in various community agencies and private companies.

EMPHASIS: Vocational guidance and counselling; testing, placement, and follow-up; information center on job openings; staff training; utilization of all resources within the area that will make youth and adults employable.

TARGET: About 800 disadvantaged secondary school students and adults.

STAFFING: 11 full-time, 1 part-time.

AUSPICES: Office of Career Education.

CHANGES: Establishing new linkages with outside institutions.

INFORMATION: Pamphlet from program.

Articulation Programs With Community Colleges

There have been increased efforts in recent years to establish closer linkages between secondary schools and the colleges, particularly community colleges, in the CUNY system. Greater impetus has been given to such efforts as a result of open admissions, of a growing awareness by college-bound students of the value of specialized skills training, and of increasing efforts at joint planning by top CUNY and Board of Education officials.

There are three types of articulation programs relating directly to vocational and career training, with other, more academic ones reported below in the section on high school-college collaboration. Those programs include (1) a cooperative education continuum ensuring that cooperative education students who graduate will be able to continue in uninterrupted employment while in college and will be assigned preferentially to a community college that has a cooperative education program; (2) occupational/career articulation programs; and (3) articulation for students in the technologies that represent a logical career advancement stage for students in both the multi-trade and unit trade vocational high schools. The purpose of these technology programs is to eliminate duplication and to place students in community colleges according to achievement. The main pilot programs now link students at George Westinghouse and William E. Grady Vocational and Technical High Schools with the New York City Community College and Alfred E. Smith Vocational High School and Samuel Gompers Vocational and Technical High School with the Bronx Community College. This last program focuses on plastics technology.

Summary of Articulation Programs with Community Colleges

Program Name/Description	Post-Secondary Institution	Secondary School(s)
Accounting	N.Y.C. Community College	Erasmus Hall
Accounting	Long Island University	Samuel J. Tilden
Computer Data Processing and Marketing	Bronx Community College	Theodore Roosevelt, George Washington
Supermarket Management	Kingsborough Community College	New Utrecht, Abraham Lincoln, Boys, South Shore
Retail Business Management	Kingsborough Community College	Sheepshead Bay
Retail Business (3 credits)	N.Y.C. Community College	Erasmus Hall, James Madison
Guidance	CUNY Guidance Laboratory	Bureau of Educational Vocational Guidance
Jewelry Design	Fashion Institute of Technology	George Westinghouse
Fashion	Fashion Institute of Technology	Fashion Institute of Technology
Commercial Photography	Fashion Institute of Technology	Art & Design Grade Dodge

Educational Programs for Special Target Groups

Summary of Articulation Programs with Community Colleges

Program Name/Description	Post-Secondary Institution	Secondary School(s)
Printing Trades and Graphics	N.Y.C. Community College Carnegie Tech. and Rochester Institute	N.Y. School of Printing
Food Trades	N.Y.C. Community College	Food Trades
Pre-Engineering, Technical Drafting	Staten Island Community College	Ralph McKee
Technical Electricity	Bronx Community College	Samuel Gompers
Health (Nursing Programs)	Bronx Community College Staten Island Community College	Grace Dodge Curtis

Cooperative Education Continuum

Through joint efforts with the CUNY Admissions Office, graduating Co-ops will be identified by code and assigned preferentially to a community college with an on-going Cooperative Education program. Co-op programs are in operation at La Guardia (all Co-op), Bronx, Kingsborough, Borough of Manhattan, and New York City. Thus, secondary Co-op students who elect to continue in uninterrupted employment while in college will have this option. On-going negotiations between the Cooperative Education Bureau of the Board of Education and the community colleges are also expected to produce joint cooperative education job-development efforts and joint community programs.

New Programs for the Handicapped

There are roughly 100,000 handicapped youth and adults in the city who receive some occupational and career services through the public schools. Since the establishment of the Division of Special Education and Pupil Personnel Services in 1973, school headquarters has made a concerted attempt to provide a more effective and coordinated program for these students. That Division has worked closely with the Office of Career Education to provide such services.

There are two types of innovative occupational and career programs for the handicapped. One is various new pilot programs, funded through sections 4B and 4B3 of the Vocational Education Act. These funds have supported a wide range of programs from pre-vocational exposure to intensive skills training and include such supplementary services as transportation, diagnostics, and evaluation services as well. They will be reviewed in detail in the section of the inventory on the handicapped.

Second, the various bureaus at school headquarters have also developed career-oriented programs for the handicapped from tax-levy funds. Bureaus for the mentally retarded, for emotionally handicapped, and for the physically handicapped have all participated, both through their own special schools and in newly-formed high school classes.

VEA-Funded Occupational Programs for the Handicapped

STARTED: 1968, after VEA amendments enacted.

FUNDING: $932,000.

LOCATION: In various elementary, junior high, and high schools and outside agencies for the handicapped.

EMPHASIS: Occupational training; various supportive services; assessment; job placement; transportation.

TARGET: Roughly 2,000 students.

Comprehensive Magnet School Programs

There are several phased out vocational high schools that have been designated comprehensive high schools and continue to offer a range of occupational education programs. In addition, other career-oriented high schools have opened within the past few years. Together they constitute what have been called comprehensive magnet high schools. The term "magnet" has been used because the career program in the schools was designated to make them attractive to whites and middle class students who had been leaving. Each of these schools has tended to concentrate on a particular career specialty in addition to its academic program. Aviation, oceanography, health, communications, and business are among the specialties represented. Most of the schools have been helped in the early planning stages by VEA seed money, sometimes for several years, illustrating particularly well the catalytic role that such federal funding has played to promote innovation.

August Martin High School (Q)

STARTED: 1971.

FUNDING: City tax levy; also some VEA past funds.

LOCATION: Mostly in the classroom. Also at Farmingdale Airport and various companies.

EMPHASIS: Strong emphasis on aviation (flying) and on communications; career exploration, college placement. 11th and 12th grade students pursue a college preparatory program or elect specialized programs for technical and professional careers in the air industry. Business education options include accounting, data processing, and secretarial studies. The occupational options include ground support vehicle maintenance, airport servicing, passenger servicing, and avionics. The school has seven resource centers for independent study.

TARGET: About 1,500 students.

STAFFING: 115.98 staff units.

AUSPICES: Division of High Schools.

INFORMATION: A handbook available on request by letter to the principal.

Beach Channel High School (Q)

STARTED: September 1973

FUNDING: Board of Education, city tax levy.

LOCATION: In the classroom; also on-water activities.

EMPHASIS: Comprehensive school with college program as well as vocational ones; particular specialties in oceanography and marine biology. Technical programs include design, technical electronics, and medical technology. Business options include secretarial studies and accounting. Occupational studies include marine power, plant mechanics, marine maintenance, and marine electronics. All students may also choose from among such specialized electives as oceanography, meteorology, navigation, seamanship, marine sciences, nautical astronomy, and Scuba diving.

TARGET: 3,000 students.

STAFFING: 180.23 staff units.

AUSPICES: Division of High Schools.

CHANGES: Funding and staffing increased until 1975-6; then cut back. Increased exposure to many aspects of marine life and water activities.

INFORMATION: Pamphlet on request.

Boys and Girls High School (Bkn)

STARTED: 1975.

TARGET: 3,000 students.

EMPHASIS: A comprehensive high school dedicated to providing all of its graduates with both a salable skill and the requirements for college. The school will house three highly specialized schools: urban planning, building, and management; computer data processing and management; and advanced placement.

Clara Barton High School for Health Professions (Bkn)

EMPHASIS: A comprehensive, coeducational high school, educating students for post-high school health-delivery services. Designated an option school for students coming from any area of New York City. Offers special electives in the medical sciences. Visits to many different types of health facilities are an important part of the program. Through its affiliation with hospitals and clinics, it offers the following courses, including opportunities for practical on-site training: practical nursing; dental assisting; dental technologist; medical laboratory technologist; medical business careers.

TARGET: 2,100 students.

STAFFING: 141.77 staff units.

Educational Programs for Special Target Groups

Edward R. Murrow High School (Bkn)

STARTED: September 1974

FUNDED: City tax levy.

EMPHASIS: An academic and career-bound school. Students interested in communications arts (public speaking, creative writing, drama), media arts (television, film production) and electronics-mechanical careers may apply to attend the school under the Brooklyn Educational Options Plan. As a school of volunteers, it offers a wide range of elective course offerings.

TARGET: 1,400 students; expanding to 2,500.

STAFFING: 85 teachers.

INFORMATION: Brochure from school.

Murray Bergtraum High School for Business Careers (Man)

STARTED: September 1975.

EMPHASIS: Because of its unique location, one block from City Hall in the world center for finance and trade, the school utilizes the talents of top business leaders to develop curricula reflecting the employment needs of the major businesses of the area: banking, insurance, international trade, investments, and public administration. This is a college-oriented as well as career-oriented high school. Especially interested in placing young women as well as young men in junior executive positions.

Comprehensive academic high school, with emphasis on business careers—stockbrokers, lawyers, accountants. School building came from Educational Construction Funds.

TARGET: 600 students; plans to move up to 2,500.

STAFFING: 51.20 staff units.

Norman Thomas High School for Commercial Education (Man)

STARTED: 1976.

EMPHASIS: Attracts students from all boroughs. Students have the choice of combining intensive commercial preparation with college preparatory work or of taking courses in two commercial areas. Specialties are secretarial studies, accounting, distributive education, and legal and medical stenography.

TARGET: 2,500 students.

STAFFING: 168.16 staff units.

Open Doors

STARTED: A private sector program began in 1970 as a component of the New York Urban Coalition under a grant from the Taconic Foundation. Transferred to the Public Education Association by the end of 1970 and to the Economic Development Council in 1974.

FUNDING: Economic Development Council and foundations. Also, Board of Education, N.Y. State Bar, N.Y. State Department of Education, and corporations, including Exxon.

LOCATION: 20 West 40th Street, New York, NY

EMPHASIS: It is a liaison service to encourage and facilitate cooperation between schools and the work-world. The objective is to help students learn about work and careers. It does this through conferences, workshops, visits, new curriculum materials, guides, and bulletins. Students are thereby helped to explore career options, prepare realistically for earning a living, and function as consumers and citizens. The program helps teachers learn more about the economy as well and provides an opportunity to employers to inform youth about their areas of work and to attract them to constructive careers. Voluminous materials are prepared and made available to schools all over the city on different types of occupations, industries, and careers.

TARGET: Teachers and students in 150 junior high schools and in 100 high schools. Business is also helped, more indirectly.

STAFFING: 3 full-time and 2 part-time.

Sarah J. Hale High School (Bkn)

STARTED: July 1975

FUNDING: City tax levy and Title VII.

LOCATION: Within the school, in classrooms; also in other schools for vocational training under shared-time program.

EMPHASIS: A comprehensive high school that includes a balance between preparation for college and vocational training. Experimentation in open classroom instruction; elective and alternative course selections; and career education. Career opportunities in business education, cosmetology, and health careers. Recently the cosmetology careers program designated an educational option for all Brooklyn students. Now a fourth career opportunity is developing—customer engineering. Modern shops; renovated buildings, the use of such new learning approaches as peer tutoring, a mini-school, and an active shared instruction program in which career-oriented students receive training in vocational and career areas at other high schools.

TARGET: 2,500 Hispanic students.

STAFFING: 169.69 staff units.

AUSPICES: Division of High Schools.

Training Programs for Out-Of-School Youth and Adults

By far the largest target population for occupational training and manpower services is out-of-school youth and adults. Estimates have placed this population at one-fourth of the total city population, far greater than the number that could ever be served. However, 85,000 are in fact served by various agencies related to the Board of Education. Add to that another 33,000 career matriculants in the community colleges and others receiving training in the private sector, and this brings the total receiving some services to 150,000.

The following table summarizes the costs of all the adult occupational programs, including skills training and basic education. As the table indicates, this amounts to $16,287,000, with $1,411,000 from city tax levy; $2,605,000 from VEA; $4,806,000 from CETA; and $7,435,000 from other federal, state, and city sources. The biggest amounts in the latter category are $2,950,000 from the Welfare Education Plan (federal statute), $2,000,000 from the Adult Education Act; $986,000 from Department of Labor Funded Manpower Development Training Programs; and $862,000 for a New York State-funded High School Consortium.

Summary of Adult Occupational Program Costs

Funding Sources & Costs ($ thousands)

	Tax Levy	CETA	VEA	Other Federal, State & City	Total
Evening Trade Schools	1,441			165	2,796
ETS Pre-Employment Program			1,190		
Manpower Development Training Programs		4,585		986	5,571
Adult Business & Distributive Education			253		253
Adult Consumer Education			500		500
Adult Basic Education - Adult Education Act		221		2,000	2,221
High School Consortium				862	862
Teacher-Tutor Pairs Program				138	138
N.Y. State Mental Hygiene				262	262
N.Y. State Civil Service				72	72
Welfare Education Plan				2,950	2,950
Auxiliary Services for High Schools			249		249
Adult Coordination & Special Programs			414		414
TOTALS	$1,441	$4,806	$2,606	$7,435	$16,288

Adult Basic Education - Adult Education Act

STARTED: 1968.

FUNDING: $2,771,000, of which $2,500,000 from the New York State Education Department through Title VI programs in adult educational skills and $221,000 from CETA.

LOCATION: In various public schools, community centers, churches, hospitals, industrial sites, New York City Department of Employment sites, colleges, and correctional institutions.

EMPHASIS: Remediation in reading, language arts, mathematics; English as a second language. Mostly evening classes. Also social living skills.

TARGET: 5,000 disadvantaged adults.

AUSPICES: Office of Career Education.

Adult Business and Distributive Education

FUNDING: $253,000 in VEA monies.

LOCATION: In over 40 schools and community training facilities.

AUSPICES: Office of Career Education.

Adult Consumer Education

STARTED: 1968.

FUNDING: $500,000 in VEA monies.

LOCATION: Adult consumer education centers all over the city.

EMPHASIS: Provides instruction in nutrition, budgeting, clothing, and family and child care to improve family life for the disadvantaged.

TARGET: About 7,000 disadvantaged adults.

STAFFING: No information.

AUSPICES: Office of Career Education.

Auxiliary Services for High Schools

FUNDING: $249,000 in VEA monies.

LOCATION: 15 day and evening centers of the program.

EMPHASIS: Provides special services for occupational training in private agencies, where such services are not available in the public sector; does this for disadvantaged students experiencing difficulty adjusting to the normal school setting; offers a wide variety of career-oriented programs designed to train people in a short period of time.

TARGET: 6,000 disadvantaged students.

AUSPICES: Office of Career Education and Auxiliary Services for High Schools.

Evening Trade Schools Pre-Employment Program

FUNDING: $1,190,000 from VEA monies.

LOCATION: In various evening trade schools throughout the city.

EMPHASIS: Remediation; occupational preparedness.

TARGET: 12,500.

Evening Trade Schools Skills Training

STARTED: Over 50 years ago.

FUNDING: $1,606,000, of which $1,441,000 is tax levy and $165,000 is from other federal, state, and city sources. All tax-levy funding ended January 29, 1976.

LOCATION: Evening trade schools throughout the city, including 22 vocational schools and various annexes.

EMPHASIS: Short-term training for entry level jobs; skills training in wide variety of occupational clusters. Guidance, job placement, and other supportive services.

TARGET: 27,000 adults and out-of-school youth.

STAFFING: Board of Education teachers from vocational high schools. Also people from industry with teaching certificates.

High School Equivalency Consortium

STARTED: 1973.

FUNDING: $940,000, from the New York State Department of Education under Part 165 of Adult Basic Education programs.

LOCATION: Schools and community facilities throughout the city.

EMPHASIS: High school equivalency preparation; diploma for English- and Spanish-speaking adults and out-of-school youth. Day and evening classes.

TARGET: 10,000 English- and Spanish-speaking adults and out-of-school youth age 16 and over, reading above 7th grade level, and without a high school diploma.

AUSPICES: A consortium of the Office of Career Education, Office of Continuing Education, and Auxiliary High School Services.

Manpower Development Training Programs

STARTED: 1974, with the beginning of the Comprehensive Employment Training Act (CETA) programs.

FUNDING: $4,585,000, through CETA.

Educational Programs for Special Target Groups 49

LOCATION: At various Board of Education, Manpower Development Training Program's training facilities. They include:

Brooklyn Adult Training Center
475 Nostrand Avenue
Brooklyn, NY 11216

Jamaica Adult Training Center
88-83 Van Wyck Expressway
Jamaica, NY 11435

Automotive Adult Training Center
1402 Atlantic Avenue
Brooklyn, NY 11216

Mid-Manhattan Adult Training Center
212 West 120th Street
New York, NY 10027

New York City Adult Training Center
45 Rivington Street
New York, NY 10002

EMPHASIS: Job training and basic education. 5 hours a day devoted to skills (hands-on training); 2 hours a day to basic education (job related). Prepares clients with a high school equivalency diploma on an as-needed basis. Goal is to place people in full-time, training-related, unsubsidized employment.

TARGET: New York City residents who meet the Department of Labor definition of "unemployed," "under-employed," and/or "economically disadvantaged."

STAFFING: 89 full-time staff positions.

AUSPICES: The Department of Labor is the funding source through CETA, with the Department of Employment of New York City as the designated prime sponsor. The Board of Education is the service delivery agent, having a performance contract with the prime sponsor.

New York State Mental Hygiene

STARTED: 1973.

FUNDING: $297,000.

LOCATION: 14 sites in all five boroughs.

EMPHASIS: High school equivalency for lower-level employees in state agencies.

TARGET: 500 state employees.

STAFFING: 22 teachers; one part time director.

50   Inventory of Educational Improvement Efforts

New York State Civil Service

STARTED: 1973.

FUNDING: $72,000.

LOCATION: 2 learning labs: one at the World Trade Center, the other at the Adult Education Skills Center, Arthur Avenue, Bronx.

EMPHASIS: High school equivalency for lower-level state agency employees seeking upgrading.

TARGET: 70 students.

STAFFING: 3 teachers; one part-time director.

Welfare Education Program (WEP)

STARTED: 1967.

FUNDING: $2,000,000, through Title 20 - Social Security Act.

LOCATION: Various public schools community centers, manpower centers, churches, hospitals, other community sites.

EMPHASIS: Basic literacy; to bring people to at least 8th grade reading equivalency level. Remediation in reading, language arts, and mathematics.

TARGET: 5,000 welfare recipients, mostly women.

STAFFING: Board of Education teachers or certificate teachers.

AUSPICES: Office of Continuing Education of the Board of Education.

Drug Prevention and Intervention Programs

The increasing use of drugs among youth, particularly in high schools, has led in recent years to the development of various intervention and prevention programs. There are no city tax levy, Board of Education funds for these programs. Instead they come into the city through the state, and all drug programs in the city schools are completely state-funded.

The main legislation relating to school-based drug programs is the state Mental Hygiene Law, Section 83.07

(School preventive education program). That law has been in effect since June 1973, having superseded others that were in operation before then, dating back to 1970.

Despite the fact that the programs exist in schools, the Board of Education does not have exclusive control over them. New York City's Addiction Services Agency (ASA) is the prime sponsor, and its staff are active in writing proposals, doing the program monitoring and evaluations, and engaging in most of the contract management. The Board of Education, as a sub-contractor, is responsible for managing the fiscal workings of the programs, including the facilities, leases, payroll, and personnel. It also helps develop the curriculum and establish entrance criteria for students. By and large, ASA, as the local designated agency is ultimately responsible for most policy decisions, although they are usually made in collaboration with Board of Education program staff, rather than unilaterally imposed. ASA plays a dual role in ensuring, first, that the needs of each community school district and high school are addressed and, second, that the programs follow the legal mandates and regulations promulgated by the state. This is, then, a cooperative, ASA-Board of Education program.

As of 1975-76, the New York City schools received $15.8 million through ASA for such drug programs. That includes $3.5 million for two high school-based ones; $10.3 million for district programs, another $1.2 million for religious schools, and $1 million in administrative costs, which covered $350,000 for personnel, $180,000 for auditing, and $175,000 for training. These funds have been cut from a high of $20 million in 1973-74, and they were down to $12.6 million for the 1976-77 fiscal year.

There are close to 1,100 staff involved city-wide in these programs, with 100 in the centralized high school programs, another 960 in the 32 community school districts (30 per district), and the others at ASA. ASA does a lot of training of classroom teachers in counselling, group dynamics, and other techniques.

The programs have changed a lot since their inception. At first, many emphasized the dissemination of information about drug abuse, its causes, and consequences, but when it became apparent that information alone was inadequate as a therapeutic tool, other strategies were adopted. They focused primarily on attempts to change values and feelings and to deal with personality problems contributing to drug use, including intensive individual and group counselling, "rap" groups, and encounter sessions and the like to help students with problems to improve interpersonal, academic, and other skills. Developing a sense of personal worth and competency in students has been found to be critical in rehabilitation.

The other main changes in the programs include more emphasis on family counselling, as an extension of individual and group counselling, and more referrals of particularly acute cases to outside agencies and to alternative schools. ASA has helped to open more than 15 such schools in districts throughout the city. It provides more intensive individual care than students could receive in a regular school. Indeed, as the budget has been cut back, fewer students have been served but more intensively.

Despite the increasing use of drugs among middle-class youth, the problem is much more prevalent in minority and poverty communities. The manifestations that drug problems take seem to vary among different racial and ethnic groups, depending on differences in values and life styles. The programs, while following state guidelines, attempt to be responsive to those differences. Nevertheless, a review of all the district and high school programs indicates that they have many common themes and characteristics. One of the most important is that the vast majority of staff time and other program resources are devoted to *intervention* rather than *prevention,* dealing with youth within the schools identified as already having drug problems. The general target for these programs is 5th to 12th grade students.

Educational Programs for Special Target Groups

Two particularly salient aspects of the programs are: (1) the wide variety of supportive services they involve, including remediation in basic academic skills (reading, math); and (2) in particular, an extensive referral program that sends students with severe drug problems into immediate treatment in a social agency. Much staff time is then devoted to providing continuous instruction to those students in regular school subjects.

The main categories of programs reviewed here include: (1) centralized high school programs; (2) decentralized community school district programs; (3) alternative schools developed by ASA; (4) programs for Catholic and Jewish religious schools; and (5) private agency programs.

All these programs are funded from the state, with ASA as the prime sponsor. The funds come, however, from two separate pools of money. The high schools and community school district programs are funded under one contract, related to the Young Drug Abuser Program, that provides for the alternative schools. The religious schools and private, non-profit programs are funded from an entirely separate pool and are designated as delegate agencies.

Centralized High School Programs

Peer Group

STARTED: 1970.

FUNDING: $450-500,000; $300,000 from state and some tax levy.

LOCATION: In 14 high schools.

EMPHASIS: Unlike Spark, uses one main method, namely, students helping other students.

TARGET: All students in those schools, particularly drug users. Claim to reach about one-third of the students in these schools, roughly 20,000 in all.

STAFFING: 15-16 staff members, 1 in each school.

AUSPICES: Addiction Services Agency and Division of High Schools.

CHANGES: Funding cut severe in 1975-76; half of staff dropped. Program emphasis changing from specialized concern with student drug problems to more diffuse concern with their human, personal growth, and adjustment problems.

INFORMATION: Available from program.

Spark

STARTED: September, 1971.

FUNDING: $3,000,000.

LOCATION: Now in 88 high schools throughout the city. Also in various treatment agencies.

EMPHASIS: Individual and group counselling; oriented toward changing behavior—e.g., improving student problem-solving and decision-making as related to drug use; much more emphasis on intervention (intensive counselling) than on prevention (information dissemination); much referral to other agencies and to other pupil personnel services in schools; multi-bureau approach that involves education and counselling; now working on articulation program with junior high schools. Have tried three models. One involves a single drug education specialist in the school, engaged in individual and group counselling. A second provides the specialist with a community paraprofessional. The third has a staff of up to 10 people working in a prevention center. This larger-scale approach is now in use in 10 schools.

TARGET: All students in these high schools, with emphasis on those with drug problems. Work with students who use alcohol as well as those on drugs.

STAFFING: 7 full-time staff in central office and 95-100 full-time in the schools.

AUSPICES: Addiction Services Agency and Division of High Schools.

INFORMATION: Pamphlets prepared by program. Extensive evaluation of the program by ASA.

Decentralized, Community School District Programs

As indicated above, all 32 community school districts have drug programs. When the state funds first became

Educational Programs for Special Target Groups

available in 1970, all districts were invited to submit proposals. At first some districts did not do so, but over the past several years, all have applied. With few exceptions, all intermediate or junior high schools and most elementary schools with 5th and 6th grades have such programs.

It would require too much detail to summarize each of the 32 community school district drug programs, particularly since they have so much in common. Instead we have indicated the amount of funding for each district and then summarized the common themes.

Funding of Community School District Drug Programs

District 1	$300,000	District 17	$280,000
District 2	425,000	District 18	285,000
District 3	425,000	District 19	400,000
District 4	400,000	District 20	450,000
District 5	260,000	District 21	450,000
District 6	425,000	District 22	390,000
District 7	300,000	District 23	300,000
District 8	300,000	District 24	350,000
District 9	200,000	District 25	400,000
District 10	495,000	District 26	395,000
District 11	250,000	District 27	470,000
District 12	300,000	District 28	300,000
District 13	370,000	District 29	350,000
District 14	320,000	District 30	315,000
District 15	425,000	District 31	495,000
District 16	325,000	District 32	350,000

It is clear that though there is some spread, the amounts allocated are quite similar for many districts.

EMPHASIS: The most frequent themes in the district programs are an emphasis on improving students' self-image as a basis for improving academic performance (attendance, grades, punctuality) and social behavior (coping skills to deal with life stresses); the use of peer group leaders and a searching for positive role models; increasing parents' involvement in the students' problems and in the school; providing family counselling and other services; and the extensive use of mini-schools and alternative schools to provide a more humanistic environment for students.

Alternative and Intervention Schools

The Addiction Services Agency (ASA) has opened many of what it calls "alternative schools" in recent years for students with acute problems. In 1975-6 there were 16 of them throughout the city; they are different from the alternative schools discussed earlier. Some exist within schools as special classes or mini-schools; others are outside. In some ASA provides the teachers; in others the Board of Education does. Some are heavily academic; others emphasize affective education. All have required academic hours, a good deal of individualized tutoring and counselling, and involve small classes of 15-20 students. The main target for most of these schools is students from upper grades in junior high and intermediate schools. They remain on the rolls of those schools, and one of the goals of this program is to get them back in the home school as soon as possible.

Religious Schools

Archdiocese Drug Abuse Prevention Program

STARTED: 1971.

FUNDING: $427,000. 95 percent from ASA and 5 percent from city tax levy.

LOCATION: Archdiocese of New York, 487 Park Avenue, New York, NY 10022

In 15 high schools and 6 elementary schools in Manhattan, the Bronx, and Staten Island.

EMPHASIS: Prevention program and crisis intervention. Rap sessions, peer counselling, and referrals. Family services working with counsellors at Bronx State Hospital.

TARGET: 5,500 students.

STAFFING: 4 psychologists, 2 social workers, counsellors.

Educational Programs for Special Target Groups

CHANGES: Funding increased to a high of $450,000 in 1973. Anticipated to drop 20 percent for 1976-77. A new crisis intervention program started at central office for hard core drug cases.

INFORMATION: Booklets and brochures from central office.

Catholic Schools Office, Diocese of Brooklyn

STARTED: 1970.

FUNDING: $426,500.

LOCATION: 345 Adams Street, Brooklyn, NY 11201. In 22 high schools and 98 elementary schools. Half of them are in Brooklyn and half in Queens.

EMPHASIS: A prevention/intervention program. Teachers trained to run after-school rap sessions. Provides individual assistance when needed. Program open to all students, except those who need long-range therapy; for these cases, referrals made.

TARGET: 6,000 students receiving direct services.

STAFF: 5 part-time psychologists.

CHANGES: Began working with elementary schools in 1974. Drug prevention activities at that level are very important part of the program.

Hebrew Day Schools

STARTED: September 1971

FUNDING: $350,000.

LOCATION: 299 Park Avenue South, New York, NY 10003. Any Hebrew day school in the city; there are 50 such schools.

EMPHASIS: Prevention/intervention. Family problems discussed. All problems dealt with that potential drug users feel are important.

TARGET: 3,000 students a year. 6th-12th grades.

STAFFING: 4 guidance counsellors full-time in field. 25 part-time counsellors.

CHANGES: Few changes in program. Development of more staff, including part-time psychologists and therapists.

INFORMATION: Evaluations by ASA.

58 Inventory of Educational Improvement Efforts

Delegate Agency Programs

Argus

STARTED: 1969.

FUNDING: $306,790, city tax levy.

LOCATION: 578 East 161st Street, Bronx, NY

EMPHASIS: Day care program; mini-school; drug rehabilitation center. Adult day and evening classes. Day care drug free treatment; ambulatory drug free treatment. The mini-school for youth having problems in school. A group home for girls. Also a building trades program and adult day program for teenage addicts. Counselling. Vocational aid and remedial education.

TARGET: 270.

STAFFING: About 30.

AUSPICES: Private.

CHANGES: Started out as court diversion project for adult day program. Now into drug rehabilitation as well.

Boys Harbor

STARTED: 1937. Drug component began in 1971.

FUNDING: $119,044 in state funds.

LOCATION: 19 East 94th Street, New York, NY 10028. Work mainly with the public schools in districts 2, 4, and 5; Harlem and East Harlem are main sites. Community planning districts 8, 11, and 7. Police precincts 24, and 23. Health districts 16, 17, 20, 21, 25, 28, 10, 19, 24, 26, 32.

EMPHASIS: Day care program for children 7-14 years of age. Adolescent program of alternative schools, country camp. Individual and group counselling; vocational guidance. Alcohol and drug prevention. Remedial education. Originally a camp in East Hampton, NY for recreation and remedial education for minority students.

TARGET: Reach 400-500 minority youth. 20% using hard drugs; 40% using drugs regularly; 80% using or have used soft drugs.

STAFFING: 40-50 in day care program; 12 in alcohol prevention; 10 in drug prevention, plus Boys Harbor staff.

AUSPICES: A supporting agency for many others.

INFORMATION: Pamphlets from program.

Bilingual Programs

One large special target group served by the New York City schools is their 160,000-odd non-English-speaking students. The state-commissioned Fleischmann Commission Report of 1973 estimated that close to 95,000 of these students were Puerto Rican, with the rest from other backgrounds—e.g., French, Chinese, Italian, Greek, and others. There are roughly 300,000 students of Spanish origin in the city schools, and many have severe learning problems. A recent study cited by Aspira of New York indicated that only 15% of the Puerto Rican population of the city aged 25 or over had graduated from high school in 1970, compared with 53.4% of the corresponding white population. Moreover, a recent study of bilingual education by the Community Service Society notes that Puerto Rican pupils are the lowest in reading, the weakest in general academic preparation, and the highest in dropouts of any ethnic group in New York State.

Until the New York State Bilingual Act of 1970, schools in the state were prohibited by law from providing instruction in any language other than English. As it became clear that Hispanic students were not learning in traditional classrooms, more legislation and federal and state funding followed. A critical development was the class action suit filed by Aspira of New York in October 1972, demanding that the New York City Board of Education provide instruction in their native language to all non-English speaking students. That suit resulted in a consent decree from the U.S. District Court in August 1974, requiring that the Board of Education set up such programs to meet the needs of all non-English-speaking students and as quickly as possible. Many other organizations supported Aspira in that suit, including the Puerto Rican Educational and Legal Defense Fund, Puerto

Rican Forum, Puerto Rican Community Development Project, Public Education Association, and others. Since then the Board of Education has moved ahead in an attempt to comply with the decree, closely monitored by Aspira, by the court, and by its own Bureau of Bilingual Education.

The Community Service Society studies and other more informal assessments by educators and civic groups indicate several key problems in implementation. A shortage of trained bilingual teachers, the inadequacy of university-based teacher training programs, and the need for more curriculum materials and for more funds are particularly important. To illustrate, the Fleischmann Commission recommended that there be 5,700 teachers to meet the need. Top Board of Education officials estimate that there are now about 1,400 such teachers.

The degree to which the consent decree has been adequately implemented has been a focus of considerable recent controversy. The fact that the first year of implementation was a time of such severe fiscal crisis and budget cuts had to have had a big deterring effect. A recent review by the Public Education Association of progress in implementation outlines some of the key areas of controversy. They include: the extent to which recently "excessed" or laid-off regular classroom teachers have been allowed to take new tests in Spanish that are easier than regular bilingual license examinations, thereby providing for the appointment of unqualified teachers to the programs; the extent to which eligible students were not receiving the program; the limited curriculum development, teaching materials, and textbooks in many programs; the adequacy of measures used to determine eligibility by evaluating students' language skills; the adequacy of the Board of Education's staffing for monitoring; the extent to which districts inform parents about the programs or the procedures for withdrawing a child if they so wished, as required in the terms of the consent decree. It is obviously not the purpose of this inventory to analyze in depth these controversies or to take positions on them. We are simply reporting that this set of programs, like many others in which litigation has taken place in recent years, are a focus of much controversy.

To give the reader some sense of the scope of present bilingual programs, roughly $38.5 million was spent on them in the 1975-76 school year. Just over $30 million came from state and federal sources—so-called reimbursible programs and essentially "soft" money, with the other $8.5 million coming from city tax levy funds. The state and federal money came from the following sources: $15,735,355 from Title I; $10,401,304 from Title VII; $2,426,248 through the Emergency School Aid Act; $970,017 through New York State (NY State Laws of 1973, Chapter 720); another $289,084 through New York State Funded Umbrella Programs; $179,754 through the Education Professions Development Act; $11,780 through Title III; and miscellaneous small grants from other sources.

The programs for which these monies are allocated are either (1) bilingual with instruction primarily in the native language of the students; (2) English as a Second Language (ESL); or (3) some combination. Over $21 million of the state and federal funds goes for bilingual programs, the first category, compared with about $4 million for ESL and $4.6 million for a combination of the two.

A key component in the Board of Education's compliance with the consent decree is its Language Assessment Battery (LAB), an instrument developed through its Office of Educational Evaluation to determine student eligibility for the program. That battery assesses language skills (English, Spanish) by assigning percentile ranks corresponding to raw scores on the test items.

It is very difficult to obtain any precise information on the number of students served by all these programs, mainly because the same students are in some cases counted two, three, or even four times. The reason for this is that many students are served by several different programs, each of which counts them as part of its target population. The Board of Education's data indicate 69,298 students serviced by these programs, the equivalent, according to its staff, of roughly 45-50,000 different students actually served. This is only to indicate that accounting procedures of different programs account for a big discrepancy between the numbers and how many students are actually served.

The same point holds on the number of staff serving in the program and the sites where they are located. 2,393 staff are listed—1,490 in bilingual, 544 in ESL, and 359 in combined programs. The actual numbers are probably two-thirds or one-half that amount. Likewise, 717 schools are listed as sites for all types of bilingual programs. In actual fact, the number receiving bilingual monies is probably closer to four or five hundred.

A key center for the development and implementation of bilingual programs is the Board of Education's Office of Bilingual Education, established in 1972. Its staff have been active in trying to secure more city, state, and federal funds and in providing technical assistance to the community school districts, high schools, and special education programs by helping them write proposals and develop programs; the office has also represented the school system in monitoring the implementation of the consent decree. Furthermore, the office has numerous other central services, including: a library and resource center; a bilingual Teacher Corps program; an ESL program; a teacher intern program; programs for physically handicapped and mentally retarded students; one in Auxiliary Services for High Schools; a bilingual consortium; and a training resource center. In all, there are 10 headquarters units in this office, engaged in various kinds of support activities.

Our review is organized in terms of the particular funding sources, including (1) Title VII, (2) Title I, (3) Emergency School Aid Act, (4) New York State, and (5) tax levy.

Before describing all the main bilingual programs, we thought it might be helpful to better orient the reader by presenting some summary tables. Table 1 summarizes the

Table 1: Grand Total of All 1975-76 Bilingual/ESL Reimbursable Programs

	1975-76 Bilingual/ESL Programs			
	Bilingual Only	ESL Only	Bil/ESL Combined	Grand Total
Number of Bilingual/ESL Reimbursable Programs Budgeted	113	19	8	140
Number of Pupils Serviced	50,304	9,279	9,715	69,298
Number of Staff Members Involved	1,490	544	359	2,393
Number of Sites in Which the Programs are Located	431	169	117	717
Budget of Bil/ESL Reimbursable Programs	$21,527,954	$3,992,913	$4,596,816	$30,117,683
Sources of Available Funds				
ESEA Title I	7,240,685	$3,897,854	$5,596,816	$15,735,355
ESEA Title III	108,385	3,395	0	111,780
ESEA Title VII	10,401,304	0	0	10,401,304
Education Professions Development Act	179,754	0	0	179,754
Emergency School Aid Act	2,426,458	0	0	2,426,458
N.Y.S. Laws of 1973, Chapter 720	970,017	0	0	970,017
N.Y.S. Funded Umbrella Programs	197,420	91,664	0	289,084
New York State Education Department (NYSED)	3,931	0	0	3,931

Table 2: Summary Table 1975-76 Programs
Number of Pupils Serviced by Funding Sources and Category of Bilingual Programs

	Title I	Title III	Title VII	Education Professions Development Act	Emergency School Aid Act	N.Y.S. of 1973 Chap. 720	N.Y.S. Funded Umbrella Programs	TOTALS
A. Indirect Services	—	150	130	—	—	131	—	411
B. Direct Services:								
Spanish Speaking	33,428	484	20,767	1,154	5,620	2,265	519	64,237
C. Other Direct Service Bilingual Programs:								
Hebrew	—	60	—	—	—	—	—	60
French	284	—	1,146	—	400	100	—	1,930
Chinese	667	—	390	—	—	—	87	1,144
Italian	80	14	920	—	—	70	—	1,084
Greek	50	—	135	—	—	—	—	185
Yiddish	—	—	129	—	—	—	—	129
Haitian Creole	—	—	25	—	—	—	—	25
German	—	—	—	—	—	65	—	65
Arabic	—	—	12	—	—	—	—	12
Russian	—	14	—	—	—	—	—	14
Serbo-Croatian	—	2	—	—	—	—	—	2
Total C	1,081	90	2,757	—	400	235	87	4,650
TOTAL A-B-C	34,509	724	23,654	1,154	6,020	2,631	606	69,298

Category A - Indirect Services. Any programs that provide training and support for administrators, teachers and paraprofessionals, resource centers for staff and students in bilingual education.
Category B - Direct Services. Instruction to Spanish-speaking pupils, which consists of one or more of these types: (1) Direct services that provide Spanish-speaking pupils with intensive instruction in English; (2) Direct services that provide pupils with one or more subject areas of instruction in Spanish; (3) Direct services that provide for reinforcement of the pupil's use of Spanish and reading comprehension in Spanish as needed.
Category C - Other Direct Service Bilingual Programs. This code is for all programs other than Spanish bilingual which provide direct service to pupils.

reimbursable programs, totalling $30,117,683. It includes information on the total number of individual programs budgeted, the number of pupils served, staff, sites, and budget. It does so for all the categories of bilingual programs noted above.

It is also important to know what kinds of students, by ethnic and language background, are served in these programs, and Table 2 provides that information. Note the preponderance of Spanish-speaking students among those serviced—64,237 of the 69,298 listed, or 93 percent of the total client group.

Title VII Programs

Title VII of the Elementary and Secondary Education Act (ESEA) is geared specifically for bilingual programs. There are three types: (1) those in the districts accounting for $6.5 million and in 20 of the 32 districts; (2) centralized high school programs in 14 high schools, totalling $2,698,915; and (3) other centralized programs for special education for the handicapped and for various technical assistance, staff training, and related services from the Office of Bilingual Education, totalling $1,841,899.

STARTED: 1973.

FUNDING: $11,044,589 up from $4,108,854 in 1973 and $10,497,328 in 1974.

Decentralized District Programs

Community school districts have developed their own decentralized bilingual programs under Title VII. Many districts have able bilingual coordinators who put together curriculum materials adapted to local needs. The headquarters Office of Bilingual Education provides technical assistance, but the districts and their bilingual staffs are increasingly interested in having the Office's services more decentralized, with district staff playing the technical assistance role and headquarters being more of a coordinator rather than a direct service provider.

Decentralized District Programs

District Number	Program Title	Funding	Locations	Grades	Emphasis	Target	Staffing — Classroom	Staffing — Non-Classroom
1	Bilingual Bicultural Program	$334,606	P.S. 20, 63, 134	K-6	English/Spanish	600		1 project director 1 community coordinator 1 teacher-trainer 1 curriculum developer 1 typist
3	Bilingual Program	309,545	P.S. 9, 75, 84, 87, 145, 163, 165, 166, 179, 191	3,5,6	English/Spanish	295	5 bilingual teachers 5 bilingual paraprofessionals	
4	Rafael Cordero Bilingual Program	327,510	J.H.S. 45, 13, 99 I.S. 117	7-8	English/Spanish	520	1 bilingual teachers 1 school aide	1 project director 1 media coordinator 1 teacher-trainer 1 guidance counselor 1 school secretary 1 senior stenographer
6	Bilingual Focus for the Seventies	310,844	P.S. 115, 128, 132, 192 St. Elizabeth	K-6	English/Spanish	1,482	5 bilingual teachers 10 bilingual professional assistants 1 teacher aide	1 project director 1 bilingual teacher-trainer 1 family assistant 1 supervisor steno.
7	I.S. 184 Demonstration Project	$164,707	I.S. 184 St. Peter Paul		English/Spanish	230	4 bilingual teachers 3 bilingual educational assistants	1 coordinator 1 school secretary
7	Northeast Regional Curriculum Development Center	483,000	P.S. 1, 25, 27, 31, 37, 40, 51 65, 157, 5		English/Spanish	9,171	7 bilingual teachers 5 school aides	1 project director 1 assistant director 1 curriculum coordinator 2 curriculum specialists 2 field coordinators

#	Program	Enrollment	Schools	Grades	Languages	Staff (teaching)	Staff (administrative/support)
8	Bilingual School Complex	298,200	P.S. 39, 60, 75, 130, 62 I.S. 52	K-8	English/Spanish	1 assistant coordinator	1 project director 1 general assistant 3 bilingual coordinators 1 Spanish curriculum coordinator 1 supervisor steno. 1 senior clerk 1 senior typist
10	Bilingual Mini-School Project	236,500	P.S. 59	K-5	English/Spanish	3 bilingual teachers 1 ESL teacher 6 educational assistants	1 project director 1 school secretary
11	Bilingualism Increases Excellence Now (BIEN)	271,919	P.S. 111, 83, 103, 105	K-4		2 bilingual resource teachers 8 educational assistants	1 project director 2 family assistants 1 bilingual teacher (media specialist) 1 bilingual clerk
12	C.S. 211 Bilingual School	290,065	C.S. 211	K-6	English/Spanish	5 bilingual teachers 5 educational assistants 5 bilingual professional assistants	1 bilingual senior clerk
13	Bilingual Program	311,300	P.S. 9, 20, 46 Fort Green-Vanderbilt Fort Green-Adelphi	K-5	English/Spanish	1 bilingual resource teacher 3 bilingual teachers	1 project director 1 bilingual teacher-trainer 1 bilingual guidance counselor 1 B.T.C.R. 1 senior school neighborhood worker 1 family worker

Decentralized District Programs

District Number	Program Title	Funding	Locations	Grades	Emphasis	Target	Staffing Classroom	Staffing Non-Classroom
14	Pilot Bilingual Program	308,679	P.S. 16, 17, 19, 84, 196, 250 Our Savior St. Peter & Paul Jesoda Hatorah Beth Rachel Kehilath Yaakov	K-6	English/ Spanish Yiddish	1,579		
15	Bilingual Bicultural Education Cluster	333,972	P.S. 1, 94, 58 Yeshiva Torah Vodaath of Flatbush Bnosyakov School for Girls	K-5	English/ Spanish	737	3 bilingual reading specialists 4 language teachers 2 educational assistants	1 director 1 coordinator 1 teacher-trainer 1 senior stenographer 1 family worker
17	Bilingual Education Proposal	295,000	Bilingual Center	K-3	English/ Spanish French	312	4 bilingual teachers 12 paraprofessionals	1 project director 1 assistant coordinator 1 typist 1 family assistant 1 teacher-trainer
18	Bilingual Bicultural Program	306,830	P.S. 114, 135, 208, 219, 233, 242, 244, 268 Block School J.H.S. 232, 252, 285 St. Catherine	K-9	English/ Spanish French/ Creole	800	4 resource teachers 10 paraprofessionals	1 coordinator 1 teacher-trainer 1 B.T.C.R.

#	Program	Budget	Schools	Grades	Languages	Students	Staff	
19	The Bilingual Program	368,042	P.S. 1, 345 St. Rita's St. Michael's	1-4	English/ Spanish	210	8 educational assistants	1 coordinator 1 teacher-trainer 1 family assistant 1 senior clerk
20	Elementary Bilingual Program	311,770	P.S. 140, 164, 48, 112, 176	K-5	English/ Spanish Italian	840	2 resource teachers 10 educational assistants	1 director 2 teacher-trainers 2 guidance counselors
23	District Model for Bilingual Development	287,546	P.S. 332	K-6	English/ Spanish	470	1 educational assistant	1 project director 1 bilingual school psychologist 2 language specialists 3 teaching staff developers 1 bilingual school secretary 2 paraprofessional program assistants 1 curriculum specialist 2 family workers
24	Bilingual Bicultural Education Program	312,400	P.S. 12, 13, 14, 19, 89, 132 I.S. 61 St. Aloysois Transfiguration	K-4 6-8	English/ Spanish Greek/Italian	702	18 bilingual professional assistants 8 bilingual educational assistants	1 project director 1 senior clerk
30	Bilingual Program	250,000	P.S. 11, 70, 171	K-6	English/ Spanish Greek/Italian	160	3 bilingual resource teachers 1 educational assistant	1 project director 3 curriculum specialists 2 senior clerks
32	Multilingual Program (SUBE-AVANTI-HABILE)	390,840	P.S. 75, 86, 123, 151, 274, 299 J.H.S. 162, 296 St. Brigid's	K-6 6-8 7-9	English/ Spanish Italian/French	1,000	21 bilingual educational assistants	2 coordinators 1 resource teacher 2 teacher-trainers 1 bilingual typist

Centralized High School Programs

Adlai E. Stevenson (Bx)

FUNDING: $207,000

EMPHASIS: To increase achievement levels in social studies, math, science, and Spanish language arts. Students also have an opportunity to participate in career-related programs in pre-technical and instructional arts. Seniors tutor other students. Spanish is the main language.

TARGET: 250 Spanish students at Stevenson and 30 at Monsignor Scanlan High School.

STAFFING: 6 in classroom as teachers, project director, guidance counsellor, and secretary.

Bushwick (Bkn)

FUNDING: $148,028.

EMPHASIS: Instruction in students' native language and intensive instruction in English as a second language.

TARGET: 250 Spanish students with limited English-speaking ability.

Eastern District (Bkn)

FUNDING: $217,000.

EMPHASIS: Designed to develop an integrated bilingual-bicultural program that may serve as a demonstration center. Students taught bilingually—Spanish and English—in mathematics, science, and social studies.

TARGET: 350 Hispanic students.

STAFFING: 11. 8 teachers, 3 administration.

Fort Hamilton (Bkn)

FUNDING: $143,780.

EMPHASIS: Instruction in substantive areas in native language. Also English language instruction.

TARGET: 52 Spanish, Greek, Arabic.

Educational Programs for Special Target Groups

STAFFING: 7. 5 classroom, 2 administrative.

George W. Wingate (Bkn)

FUNDING: $199,000.

EMPHASIS: Improving English language ability; developing career-oriented skills.

TARGET: 340 Haitian students.

STAFFING: 11. 6 classroom, 5 administrative.

James Monroe (Bx)

FUNDING: $192,400.

EMPHASIS: Students offered subjects in their native language and intensive instruction in English. Hispanic students take many courses with English-speaking students. Also bilingual career orientation and business skills.

TARGET: 250 non-English-speaking Hispanic students.

STAFFING: 9. 5 classroom and 4 administrative.

New Utrecht (Bkn)

FUNDING: $133,900.

EMPHASIS: Students work in their native language and move into mainstream classes in English when ready. Also, special guidance and community liaison services.

TARGET: 220 non-English speaking students who have arrived from Italy within the past two years.

STAFFING: 5. 3 classroom, 2 administrative.

Sarah J. Hale (Bkn)

FUNDING: $181,000.

EMPHASIS: Develops vocational knowledge, with special emphasis on English language skills. Integrates Spanish students into mainstream of the school.

TARGET: 150 Spanish students.

STAFFING: 12. 8 classroom, 4 administrative.

Seward Park (Man)

FUNDING: $218,460.

EMPHASIS: To enable Chinese students to acquire knowledge in math, social studies, and science; to improve their attendance and reduce dropouts; to improve professional skills of the bilingual staff in the program; and to increase parent and community participation in the education of the students.

TARGET: 350 Chinese students with limited English ability.

STAFFING: 12. 8 classroom and 4 administrative.

John Jay (Bkn)

FUNDING: $223,240.

EMPHASIS: Bilingual instruction in major curriculum areas. Second language instruction also provided. Stress on the humanities, staff development, and parent and community involvement.

TARGET: 335 students. Roughly 200 Spanish, 50 English, 25 Italian, 60 French.

STAFFING: 14. 12 in classroom, 2 outside.

Louis D. Brandeis (Man)

FUNDING: $220,000.

EMPHASIS: To develop English language skills for non-English speaking students and Spanish and French for the English speaking. Social studies, math, and science taught in students' native language.

TARGET: 500 Spanish and French students as well as English speaking.

STAFFING: 10. 6 classroom and 4 administrative.

Newtown (Q)

FUNDING: $199,500.

EMPHASIS: Students receive instruction in native language and English.

Educational Programs for Special Target Groups

TARGET: 335 Hispanic and Chinese students.

STAFFING: 12. 8 classroom, 4 administrative.

South Shore (Bkn)

FUNDING: $210,607.

EMPHASIS: Students provided intensive ESL instruction and various studies in their native language.

TARGET: 250 Spanish, French, Russian and Yiddish students at South Shore and several Jewish high schools.

STAFFING: 13. 5 teachers, 5 paraprofessionals, 3 administrative.

Theodore Roosevelt (Bx)

FUNDING: $204,000.

EMPHASIS: Intensive English language instruction as well as instruction in content subjects in Spanish or Italian. Also tries to develop self-image and ethnic pride and mutual respect among ethnic groups.

STAFFING: 12. 8 classroom, 4 administrative.

Other Centralized Programs

Bilingual Program for Children in Bureau CRMD

FUNDING: $232,860.

LOCATION: Bureau for Children with Retarded Mental Development, 65 Court Street, Brooklyn, NY 11201

EMPHASIS: Remediation in reading and math; to improve school adjustment, attendance, and classroom participation.

TARGET: 408 Spanish-speaking students.

STAFFING: 14. 9 classroom, 5 administrative.

Bilingual Program for Hearing-Impaired

FUNDING: $299,662.

LOCATION: Bureau for Hearing Handicapped Children, 65 Court Street, Brooklyn, NY 11201.

EMPHASIS: Individual and small group instruction. Improving language skills in both native language and English. Lipreading of high priority.

TARGET: 65 hard-of-hearing Hispanic children in local schools in the Bronx, Manhattan, and Brooklyn.

STAFFING: 13. 11 classroom, 2 administrative.

Bilingual Program for Physically Handicapped Students

FUNDING: $430,620.

LOCATION: Bureau of Physically Handicapped, 65 Court Street, Brooklyn, NY 11201

EMPHASIS: To improve these students' ability to communicate effectively in Spanish and English; to provide bilingual supportive services to improve attendance and classroom participation; to develop positive pride in their ethnic background; to develop new curriculum materials for this target group; to provide training for classroom teachers; to involve parents and community members in the special education of these students; and to train a corps of bilingual resource specialists and paraprofessionals.

Bilingual Teacher Intern

FUNDING: $292,552.

LOCATION: Office of Bilingual Education, 66 Court Street, Brooklyn, NY 11201

EMPHASIS: Provides community school districts with 100 bilingual teacher interns for employment in elementary and junior high schools designated at Title I schools,

TARGET: Up to 3,000 Hispanic students of limited English-speaking ability.

STAFFING: 10.

New York City Bilingual Consortium, Project Best

FUNDING: $439,267.

LOCATION: Office of Bilingual Education, 66 Court Street, Brooklyn, NY 11201.

Educational Programs for Special Target Groups

EMPHASIS: To develop a cadre of trained teachers and paraprofessionals in bilingual education; to use two languages, English and Spanish, in instruction; parent training in weekly workshops in bilingual education, second language instruction, Hispanic history and culture, and arts and crafts, so that parents become paraprofessionals in the program.

TARGET: 3,260 Spanish and English students.

STAFFING: 24. 15 paraprofessionals, 5 bilingual teacher trainers, 4 administrative.

Regional Cross-Cultural Training Center

FUNDING: $300,000.

LOCATION: Office of Bilingual Education, 66 Court Street, Brooklyn, NY 11201

EMPHASIS: A training center for teachers and paraprofessionals in the use of bilingual materials and resources; evaluation, pilot and field testing center for bilingual materials developed in the Northeast; a resource center for teams of educators to evaluate books and audio-visual materials; and orientation workshops for parents, students, and community advisory groups to participate in the Center's program.

TARGET: Educators, parents, paraprofessionals, and students.

STAFFING: 6. 3 teacher trainers, 1 coordinator, 1 researcher, 1 project director.

Title I Bilingual/ESL Programs

English as a Second Language (ESL)

STARTED: 1967.

FUNDING: $3,992,913

LOCATION: Office of Bilingual Education, 66 Court Street, Brooklyn, NY 11201

In 37 high schools throughout the city.

EMPHASIS: Intensive instruction in English, in small groups. Also music language arts and native language arts.

TARGET: All non-English-speaking students in those high schools.

STAFFING: 122 teachers, 50 paraprofessionals.

AUSPICES: ESL Department within the Office of Bilingual Education.

Emergency School Aid Act

STARTED: 1972.

FUNDING: $2,426,458.

LOCATION: In Districts 4, 5, 7, 19. Also Aspira of New York.

District 4

FUNDING: $681,192.

LOCATION: In 9 bilingual, bicultural mini-schools. (P.S. 7, 72, 96, 101, 102, 108, 121, 171, and St. Paul's).

TARGET: 1,105 students in grades K-6.

EMPHASIS: Preventing or decreasing academic retardation of non-English-speaking students; promoting better intercultural communication among different linguistic and cultural groups by developing a good bicultural program; developing an understanding of Puerto Rican and black history and culture; developing a bilingual staff, informing and training parents in the goals of bilingual programs.

STAFF: 37. 1 director, 1 curriculum specialist, 1 bilingual teacher, 21 other teachers, 8 educational assistants, 1 secretary, 1 clerk, 3 school aides.

District 5

FUNDING: $166, 297.

LOCATION: Schools in District 5.

EMPHASIS: Part of a broader project, one of five components, all designed to reduce minority group isolation and demonstrate that quality education is attainable in District 5, a segregated, minority area.

STAFFING: 14. 1 program director, 1 assistant principal, 1 school psychologist, 1 guidance counsellor, 1 teacher assigned as coordinator, teacher trainee, teacher in charge, 3 teachers, 2 school secretaries, 1 senior clerk, 1 school neighborhood worker, 30 educational assistants.

Educational Programs for Special Target Groups

District 7

FUNDING: $460,207.

LOCATION: 26 elementary and junior high schools in District 7.

TARGET: 1,300 black and Hispanic students who are either Spanish-dominant or English-dominant and are at least six months below grade level in reading.

EMPHASIS: Language development and reading, focused on increasing English language skills for all pupils, Spanish language skills for the English-dominant students, and reading skills for English-dominant students. Supplemental instruction in small groups and on an individual basis; parent involvement in school-related activities; and staff training.

STAFFING: 20. A supervisor, senior typist, and 18 teachers.

District 19, Bilingual-Bicultural Pilot Project

STARTED: 1975.

FUNDING: $866,762.

LOCATION: In 17 public and two non-public schools. The public schools include P.S. 13, 63, 76, 108, 149, 158, 159, 174, 182, 190, 202, 213, 218, 273, 328, 345, and I.S. 171. The non-public schools are St. Rita's and St. Michael's.

TARGET: 3,000 Spanish-speaking students in those schools.

EMPHASIS: To foster positive school achievement and attitude by offering an educational program in the student's native language. Services include: instruction in students' native language; bilingual teachers in school and community relations who help maintain positive relations between the schools and non-English-speaking parents; and an intensive instructional program in English through bringing in ESL teachers.

STAFFING: Director, bilingual and ESL teachers, bilingual teachers in school and community relations, bilingual paraprofessionals, and secretarial and clerical services.

New York State of 1973, Chapter 720

STARTED: 1973.

FUNDING: $970,017.

LOCATION: In 9 districts as well as auxiliary services for the high schools.

EMPHASIS: Described below for each program.

TARGET: 6,000 students, non-English and limited English-speaking.

STAFFING: 112 professional, 60 non-professional, most of them full-time.

AUSPICES: The Bilingual Education Unit, State Education Department.

CHANGES: Funding has increased each year. The program started out as a transitional one —e.g., as soon as students could function adequately in English, they became part of the regular program. Some movement toward a full maintenance program in their native language has taken place.

INFORMATION: Copies of proposals and program evaluations kept in the Bilingual Education Office at the State Education Department.

District Programs

District 3, Bilingual Program $122,600: Provides vertical expansion of existing bilingual programs to the 5th and/or 6th grade in ten participating schools. ESL for Hispanic and Italian students as well as instruction in students' dominant language. Moving toward a K-6 total bilingual program in the district. Teachers and paraprofessionals, paid through the grant, will receive formal university training and on-site training at no cost to the project.

District 4, Bilingual-Bicultural Mini-Center, $101,623: Serves 260 Spanish-speaking students in grades K-6 at a bilingual-bicultural mini-center. Also involved in curriculum development and teacher training.

District 6, Bilingual-Bicultural Learning Center, $122,304: Strengthens the existing bilingual-bicultural program at P.S. 173. The funding is integrated with Title 1 and tax levy monies to expand the program and bring bilingual services to students in grades K-3. Emphasis on native language and English language skills. Hispanic history and culture are part of regular social studies curriculum. Also emphasis on curriculum development, teacher training, and parent involvement.

District 12 Bilingual Education: A Successful Experience (BESE), $112,636; 60 pupils in 3rd and 4th grades at C.S. 61 Annex and 180 in 7th and 8th grades of JHS 98. The bilingual program operates in an open classroom setting at the annex, with bilingual interdisciplinary team teaching. Much instruction in major subjects in Spanish. In-service training for teachers and paraprofessionals.

District 13, Augmented Bilingual Staff Training Program, $40,000; The District seeks to train all personnel who come in contact with those pupils with moderate or serious language difficulties. After-school workshops, daily resource assistance, and demonstration sessions.

District 15, Bicultural Program, $55,097: 120 students have the opportunity to learn major subject areas as their first language. Daily classes in English as a Second Language. Puerto Rican history and culture. Students grouped for instruction on individualized basis.

District 19, Bilingual Program, $71,217: Serves 160 students located in P.S. 13, 149, 159, and 202. Provides for three bilingual teachers and an ESL specialist as well as supplementary books and instructional materials.

District 23, Bilingual Cross-Cultural Program, $86,540: This will expand on the District's present bilingual program in 13 elementary schools and one intermediate school. English dominant ESL teachers team teaching with Spanish teachers.

District 28, "Tap" (To Achieve Potential), $108,000: Individualized instruction in English and Spanish for 1st and 2nd grade students in an integrated classroom setting. Staff training in bilingual methods.

Centralized Programs

Bilingual Program in Auxiliary Services for the High Schools, $150,000: Provides instruction for Spanish, Haitian, Italian, and Greek high school students who need special services. Most of the program's 16 centers with these bilingual programs have mainly ESL, with only two having bilingual. This project provides the non-English or bilingual components in the ESL centers.

City Tax Levy Programs, Unit Appropriation 30

Each district has city tax levy funds for bilingual programs, amounting to about $6.3 million, based on an allocation formula related, in turn, to student scores on the Language Assessment Battery. Another $1.5 million goes to the high schools, with the remainder, roughly $400,000, to the

Office of Educational Evaluation to develop and administer the battery. The total number of students served in the districts is 31,641, 29,804 of whom are Puerto Rican and other Hispanics.

The test imposes a dual requirement for eligibility: first, that students have little command of English, and second, that they are much better in their native language. At present, 85,000 students qualify under the consent decree, though the parents of some of them have chosen not to enroll them in the programs.

The following are from summary data forms that include number and type of teachers and students:

Bilingual Programs Supported By City Tax Levy Funds

District	Number of Teachers	Number of Students*					Total Number of Students
1	17 - Sp.	P.R.	- 1,227				1,227
2	5 - Ch.	P.R.	- 480				960
	5 - Sp.	Ch.	- 470				
3	10 - Sp.	P.R.	- 1,476				2,735
	3 - Fr.	O.H.	- 1,074				
	2 - ESL	Ch.	- 19				
		Hait.	- 73				
		Other	- 93				
4	6 - Sp.	P.R. & O.H.	- 1,594				1,594
5	4 - Sp.	P.R.	- 471				721
		O.H.	- 250				
6	20 - Sp.	P.R. & O.H.	- 950				1,000
	1 - Gr.	Fr.	- 50				
7	7 - Sp.	P.R.	- 1,018				1,084
		O.H.	- 66				
8	17 - Sp.	P.R. & O.H.	- 1,080				1,080
9	3 - Sp.	P.R.	- 6,164				6,489
		O.H.	- 325				
10	21 - Sp.	P.R.	- 461				533
		O.H.	- 53				
		Ch.	- 4	Hait.	- 2		
		Ital.	- 3	Gr.	- 8		
				Other	- 2		

*O.H. designates Other Hispanic

Educational Programs for Special Target Groups

Bilingual Programs Supported By City Tax Levy Funds

District	Number of Teachers	Number of Students*			Total Number of Students
11	2 - Sp.	P.R.	- 107		163
	1 - It.	Ital.	- 54	Other - 2	
12	10 - ESL	P.R.	- 1,985		2,000
	8 - Sp.	O.H.	- 15		
13	6 - Sp.	P.R.	- 345		397
	2 - ESL	O.H.	- 52		
14	21 - Sp.	P.R. & O.H. - 562			562
15	15 - Sp.	P.R.	- 734		960
		O.H.	- 81		
		Chin.	- 19	Hait. - 15	
		Ital	- 67	Greek - 6	
				Other - 38	
16	4 - Sp.	P.R. & O.H. - 240			240
17	8 - Sp.	P.R.	- 345		397
		O.H.	- 52		
18	1 - Sp.	P.R.	- 47	Other - 105	191
	1 - Russ.	Hait.	- 39		
19	15 - Sp.	P.R.	- 360		360
20	7 - Sp.	P.R.	- 200	Ital. - 80	310
	6 - Ital.	O.H.	- 30		
21	4 - Sp.	P.R.	- 140		208
	2 - Ital.	Ital.	- 68		
22	0	P.R. & O.H. - 100		Hait. - 50	200
		Chin.	- 50		
23	5 - Sp.	P.R.	- 741		756
		O.H.	- 15		
24	6 - Sp.	P.R.	- 243		4,855
		O.H.	- 4,612		
25	2 - ESL	P.R. & O.H. - 200			200
26	1 - ESL	P.R.	- 9		144
		O.H.	- 29		
		Chin.	- 15	Hait. - 6	
		Ital	- 20	Greek - 6	
				Other - 59	
27	8 - ESL	P.R. & O.H. - 501			501
28	7 - Sp.	P.R. & O.H. - 204			204
29	3 - ESL	P.R. & O.H. - 240			240
30	3 - Sp.	P.R. & O.H. - 120			320
	2 - Greek	Ital.	- 80		320
	1 - Ital.	Greek -	120		

Bilingual Programs Supported By City Tax Levy Funds

District	Number of Teachers	Number of Students*				Total Number of Students
31	3 - Sp.	P.R. - 202		Ital. -	22	290
		O.H. -	4	Greek -	38	
		Chin. -	11	Other -	13	
32	18 - Sp.	P.R. - 580		Ital. - 80		720
	4 - Hait.	O.H. -	20	Hait. - 40		
	2 - Ital.					
TOTALS:	300	31,641 = 29,804 P.R. & O.H. students 1,837 students of other language groups				31,641

Open Education

An important recent development in the New York City schools, reflecting a national trend, is the movement toward open education. This involves significant departures from the traditional classroom organization—both physically and institutionally—and a complete recasting of teacher-student relations. Instead of following standardized and preconceived curricula and instructional methods within existing classrooms, the approach is much more informal. Classrooms are often grouped around a corridor that serves as a common space for teachers and students. There is a strong emphasis on students working independently and in small groups and on improving their capacity for problem-solving and the learning of concepts through working with materials that are made available. Teachers play more a role of active catalyst, stage manager, and orchestrator than in the traditional classroom, building on the interests of students and on the materials and experiences in which students become immersed.

---

*O.H. designates Other Hispanic

The emergence of open education programs in elementary schools and a few junior highs parallels in many respects that of alternative high schools at the secondary level. Originally developed in England in the 1930s, open education later spread to the United States. Joseph Featerstone's articles in *The New Republic* (August 19 and September 2 and 9, 1967) were the first to attract notice. Charles Silberman, through his book *Crisis in The Classroom* (Random House, 1970), and Dr. Lillian Weber, Professor or Elementary Education at the School of Education, City College of New York, (CCNY), were two Americans who visited England and were most responsible for encouraging the adoption of open education concepts and techniques here.

Since the late 1960s, Weber and her many colleagues and disciples have introduced open corridor and open classroom techniques into elementary schools throughout the city. Her work has concentrated in Districts 2, 3, and 5 in Manhattan, but she has recently worked in District 13 in Brooklyn as well. The programs are mainly in elementary schools and involve extensive teacher training. In addition, Weber has helped develop teacher trainers from among the teachers she has trained, so that their schools will have an internal capability to continue and expand on their open education programs without having to be perpetually dependent on outside assistance. Many teacher centers are run in this open education mode; and Weber herself has an Advisory Service to Open Corridors and a Workshop Center, both at City College, to further train teachers. Those programs will be reviewed in Section B-1 below.

In addition to Weber's work, there are open education programs in Queens, supported by a faculty group from the Department of Education at Queens College. District 4's many alternative schools are a further example, with one of Lillian Weber's former students working there; and there are undoubtedly many other open education programs that we have not listed.

CCNY, Open Corridors Programs

STARTED: 1967.

FUNDING: Federal, state, Board of Education, foundation funding, and many other sources. Partial list includes:

New York State Urban Education
1968-69 Open Corridor in P.S. 123	$17,528
1969-70 Open corridor in P.S. 123	35,000

Board of Education*
- 1971 District 3, 3-1/2 advisors full-time and supplies
- 1972-75 District 3, 3 advisors full-time   54,000
- 1973-74 Chancellor's Fund. $20,000 for staff position at Workshop Center and $60,000 to support development of open corridor in schools. Three teachers released for advisory training $80,000
- 1974-75 3 teachers released on school time and for part-time advisor work
- 1972-74 District 5, 1 full-time advisor   18,000
- 1972-74 District 2, 3 advisors   54,000
- 1974-75 District 2, 2 full-time advisors   40,000
- 1972-74 Learning Cooperative of the Board of Education, 1-½ advisors   23,000 yrly

Ford Foundation
1970-71 Advisory development	56,000
1971-72 Advisory development	173,135
1972-73 Advisory development	76,852
1973-74 Advisory development	62,505

LOCATION: *District 3:* P.S. 75, 84, 87, 144, 145, 163, 166, 191, 9. I.S. 44, J.H.S. 118; *District 2:* P.S. 3, 40, 41, 42, 190, 158, 26; *District 31:* P.S. 12 in Manhattan, and *Districts* 4, 5, 6, 13, 30, and 31 in Staten Island.

Also, City College Advisory Service to Open Corridors and Workshop Center for Open Education, 6 Shepard Hall, CCNY, Convent Avenue and 140th Street, New York, NY 10031.

TARGET: Students and teachers in those schools. 3,960 children were involved in open corridors by spring 1975.

STAFFING: Weber's CCNY staff include 3 full-time and 2 part-time at Workshop Center for Open Education and 7 full-time and 2 part-time at City College Advisory Service to Open Corridors. 156 teachers and 45 paraprofessionals involved in open corridors schools in spring 1975.

---

*Does not include former advisors who have assumed positions on regular Board of Education lines.

EMPHASIS: As indicated above. The main changes have been to develop parallel supports for open corridor programs at CCNY and in the schools themselves. This has involved obtaining more Board of Education funding, training advisors in the schools who would carry on the training themselves, and having many advisors move up into supervisory and administrative posts in the school system to provide further support. The CCNY commitment increased to include released time support for part of Weber's time, assignment of three faculty members assigned to the Workshop Center, a summer institute, a master's degree concentration, and conferences. Weber's group at CCNY has established many more contacts with districts and schools within New York and elsewhere.

INFORMATION: City College Advisory Service to Open Corridors.

Queens College-Supported Programs

LOCATION: *Manhattan:* The Learning Community, 1701 York Avenue, New York, NY 10028, and P.S. 171. *Queens:* P.S. 14, 79, and 120.

Desegregation

Though school desegregation is not nearly as contested a political issue now in New York City as it was in the 1950s and early 60s, or as it is now in such cities as Boston and Detroit, much Board of Education activity is still related to it. Chancellor Irving Anker's detailed analysis of the New York City schools' desegregation experience, written in January 1976, and supporting the school system's eligibility for assistance under the Emergency School Aid Act, reviews all this activity. The most controversial of the schools' desegregation efforts are several high school rezonings in recent years in Brooklyn and Queens, many having been initiated in response to court order and/or to rulings by State Education Commissioner Ewald Nyquist. Anker strongly urges metropolitan desegregation plans similar to those developed in many other urban areas, though little support seems to exist at present for such proposals.*

---

*Anker's paper is drawn on in this section.

86   Inventory of Educational Improvement Efforts

The desegregation-related activities of the New York City schools reviewed here include: (1) the main programs and techniques that have been used; particularly (2) the magnet school approach; and (3) programs under the federally funded Emergency School Aid Act (ESAA), the act passed to counter the trend toward racial isolation in big cities and to minimize the effects on minority students of remaining in segregated schools.

Other than these activities, school desegregation is no longer a citywide political issue in New York, and civil rights and other desegregation-oriented groups no longer regard it as a major reform strategy. It is still very important, however, for those people directly affected by the implementation of particular plans, and it is also a component of many other school programs, some of which are not always viewed in that context.

Desegregation Techniques

Among the various desegregation techniques used in New York and elsewhere, *zoning* is by far one of the most important. There are many continuing efforts now in this direction: open zoning for some high schools, whose students may cross district or borough lines; non-contiguous "skip zoning;" getting the Transit Authority to establish new bus routes; and open enrollment are among the many zoning techniques used. These techniques have been implemented much more in Brooklyn and Queens, where desegregation possibilities still exist, than in the other boroughs. Many intermediate and high schools have participated in such efforts.

Grade reorganization is another technique followed. This includes new intermediate (middle) schools (grades 5-8 or 6-8) whose location and zoning might enable them to draw on a diversified (racial, ethnic, economic) population; 4-year comprehensive high schools that might do the same; and educational parks comprised of schools at all levels (elementary, intermediate, high school) that would have integrated pupil populations by drawing from a wide area. It is not the purpose of this inventory to comment on the extent of implementation of these techniques or on political and other forces affecting it.* Suffice it to say that there are such schools, that they were designed and adopted, at least in part, to promote desegregation, and that they have probably done so to some limited degree.

Since both Brooklyn and Queens have been sites of extensive zoning plans and controversies, some resulting from court and State Education Department decisions, we will review them briefly.

Brooklyn High School Zoning

STARTED: March 1974, with a high school zoning plan that was then modified for the 1975-76 school year.

EMPHASIS: There are three stated goals: (1) to achieve a minimum 30% minority enrollment in every Brooklyn high school by 1977; (2) to rezone where necessary for better utilization of high schools throughout the borough; and (3) to extend educational options by expanding the number and variety of career choices available to students.

The first goal of 30% minority enrollment is approached by enabling students from heavily minority north and central Brooklyn to attend integrated schools in South Brooklyn, sections of Queens, and Manhattan under various Open Admissions and Choice of Admissions programs. 6 Brooklyn and 5 Queens schools are involved: New Utrecht, Franklin D. Roosevelt, Madison, Lafayette, Sheepshead Bay, and Grady High Schools in Brooklyn; Bryant, Cleveland, Forest Hills, Newtown, and Edison in Queens. In addition, to prevent overutilization in Franklin D. Roosevelt,

---

*The author has written a lengthy book, *110 Livingston Street* (Random House, 1968), that already does that.

88 Inventory of Educational Improvement Efforts

New Utrecht, the new Boys and Girls High School, and Erasmus Hall, rezonings involving them have taken place.

Finally, educational options have been extended to several schools with a particular career concentration, many of whose programs have been already reviewed above (see pages 38-9):

> Beach Channel - oceanography
> Boys and Girls High - building planning construction and management
> Clara Barton - health professions
> Eastern District - health careers, pre-engineering, communications, electronics
> Edward R. Murrow - communications
> Erasmus Hall - performing arts
> John Bowne - agriculture and ornamental horticulture
> John Dewey - experimental school; flexible, modular scheduling; independent study
> John Jay - criminal justice
> Murry Bergtraum - banking and finance
> Tilden - law, politics, and community affairs

Queens High School Rezoning

STARTED: 1975.

EMPHASIS: Reduction of overcrowding at several schools; choice of admissions zone; educational options, magnet programs, and in-school magnet programs; and expansion of special education programs for handicapped students into most Queens high schools.

There is a rezoning of Franklin K. Lane High School resulting from a federal court decision. The 5 Queens and 6 Brooklyn high schools mentioned above as receiving schools under open admissions and choice of admissions receive students formerly zoned into Franklin K. Lane. In compliance with Federal District Judge John Dooling's decision, the Board of Education directed 600 minority students from Lane to these 11 high schools on an optional assignment basis. For the school year 1975-76, no new admissions were accepted in 9th and 10th grades at Lane. Instead, these students were reassigned to the 11 schools. In 1976-77, 9th and 10th grade students entered Lane from a new school zone designed to produce an improved ethnic balance in the student body.

Other illustrative cases include:

District 17 Optional Alternate Junior High School Assignment Program: Has given an option to students graduating from eight elementary schools in District 17 to transfer to thirty-four schools in Districts 20, 21, and 22, to the extent that space was available. Was designed to alleviate severe problems of overutilization in the middle schools of District 17, and 185 students were transferred in the 1975-76 school year.

District 18 Canarsie: Long an area of desegregation controversies. In 1973, the Chancellor agreed to a plan submitted by District 18 to improve integration at JHS 68. Under the plan, minority group students were rezoned from JHS 285 and 211 to 68. 176 students have transferred under the plan.

Educational Park: There is now the Northeast Bronx Education Park in the Co-Op City area of the Bronx, with specifications by the Board of Education that schools comprising the park should have integrated pupil populations.

Again, past experience has indicated all the obstacles to effective implementation of such techniques, and those obstacles haven't disappeared since major studies that documented them were made. Nevertheless, there is desegregation-related activity.

Indirect Desegregation Programs

There are, in addition, school programs that may include desegregation as one of their benefits, either planned or otherwise, and they also merit some brief review. One is alternative high schools, some of which provide an integrated learning environment. Another is the open corridor program already described that provides opportunities for many students to work in an integrated school program based on heterogeneity of ability and background. Still others are the various bilingual programs and schools, many of which, through increasing students' competency in English and their native language, "mainstream" them back into integrated classrooms.

Magnet Schools

The programs of the different categories of magnet schools—alternative schools for the talented and various high schools with specialized career programs—have already been reviewed. One other magnet school that received a lot of publicity in 1975-76 is Mark Twain Junior High School, JHS 139.

Mark Twain Junior High School (Bkn)

In the case of Hart vs. Community School Board 21 and the New York City Board of Education, Justice Weinstein accepted a Board of Education plan for the establishment of a magnet school at J.H.S. 139 for 1975-76. That predominantly black school is in the process of increasing quite substantially its white student enrollment. It resulted in the desegregation of that school, though it drew so many whites from other schools in the district that it effectively made them into segregated schools, thus contributing to greater ethnic imbalance throughout the area. That has always been the limitation of piecemeal desegregation plans.

STARTED: September 1975.

FUNDING: City tax levy, plus Titles III and VII.

EMPHASIS: A wide variety of programs for gifted and talented students to attract more whites into the school under a voluntary busing plan initiated by court order to have school represent neighborhood black-white ratio. Academic program geared to various talent areas; mini-schools, each with interdisciplinary teacher team. Referred to as cluster teams, usually including 4 classroom teachers, each with training in a special field (language arts, science, math, reading), and about 100 students. Flexible programming into 20-minute modules; accelerated studies option; enrichment program option in traditional academic areas as well as creative and manual arts; special emphasis on basic skills, on integration of subject areas, and on utilization of community resources. This is, in brief, a new showcase school.

TARGET: 570 students from the area, being phased into full operation as a school over a three-year period, with a register of more than 1,000 students.

P.S. 101, Forest Hills (Q)

This is a magnet school that has voluntarily bused in 30% of its student body from South Jamaica, a poverty area, and in the process raised its reading scores 12%. Its active parent association helped initiate and support this effort. The school has also instituted several pilot programs that have been picked up by schools throughout the district.

STARTED: 1970.

FUNDING: City tax levy, plus some outside funding from Rockefeller Brothers Fund for $21,314 for 1975-76.

EMPHASIS: Has developed a series of programs to retain the white middle class, while meeting the needs of a minority student population. They include peer tutoring by 6th graders; individualized instruction; modified open classroom in 1st grade; departmentalized 5th grade; contract performance program in 6th grade. Until September 1975, school housed a teacher training center for the district. Dealt with such questions as how one teaches effectively in a multi-ethnic setting; how one best trains teachers to function in an individualized program; what kind of organizational structure is required in such a program. Also has a learning disability program, funded by Rockefeller Brothers Fund, focussing on 1st grade.

TARGET: 590 students.

STAFFING: Principal, 24 teachers.

Emergency School Aid Act (ESAA) Programs

The Emergency School Aid Act (ESAA), passed in 1972, provides funding to (1) help eliminate minority group segregation and discrimination; (2) encourage the *voluntary* elimination, reduction, or prevention of minority group isolation; and (3) aid students in overcoming the educational disadvantages of minority group isolation. In brief, these funds are meant to aid school districts in effectively desegregating and to improve educational opportunities and programs for those minority students in impacted ghetto schools where there are few realistic prospects for desegregation. There are three designated categories of programs: pilot, basic, and bilingual, as well as "set-asides" to fund special reading projects, bilingual education projects, metropolitan area grants, and educational TV programs. Programs are designated basic when they involve grants for nonminority schools into which minority students are bused. The money is usually for remediation for those minority students to bring them up to grade level, integrate them into the school, and prevent the white middle class in the school from leaving. In brief, it provides compensatory services and attempts to stabilize newly desegregated schools. Pilot projects, by contrast, are for schools that are overwhelmingly minority and are straight compensatory education programs. In this respect, they are much like the many other federally-funded, compensatory programs of the past decades, particularly Title I.

The first year of ESAA grants was 1973-74 when New York City received $14,544,487. The next year the federal government cut off all the Board of Education's central funds, and the amount decreased to $11,613,673. In 1975-76 they were restored, and the city's total grants went up to close to $20 million.

Centralized Umbrella Programs

New York City has several centralized ESAA programs, amounting to over $6 million. There is one for early childhood integration centers, one for open enrollment support centers that provide services for minority students who transfer out to predominantly white schools, an outreach program of reading and mathematics remediation for chronic absentee high school entrants, and another high school program, easing student adjustment, to enable minority students transferring out of a segregated high school, Franklin K. Lane in Brooklyn, to adjust to their new school.

Early Childhood Integration Centers (Basic and Pilot)

STARTED: 1973.

FUNDING: $2,181,376.

LOCATION: In public elementary schools in Districts 5, 9, 16, 21, 22, 23, and 29. One school per district. Each school has a center, with a maximum of 40% reverse open enrollment.

Educational Programs for Special Target Groups

EMPHASIS: To reduce racial isolation and combat prejudice. All classes organized by non-graded heterogeneous groups and taught by open, individually-directed methods. Stress academic achievement in the basic skills; teachers released from their classrooms for special training programs; much parent and community involvement. A community representative works full time in each school, to ensure full cooperation between the school and the full community. Parent meetings held in each school, and there are intervisitations between the different schools in the program. 200 parent volunteers. Workshops, community surveys, seminars on the cultures of different ethnic groups.

TARGET: 2,100 students, 5-8 year olds, K-2. Each center serves about 300.

Open Enrollment Support Centers (Basic)

STARTED: 1975.

FUNDING: $1,494,162.

EMPHASIS: Extensive remediation, particularly in reading for minority students now in an integrated setting under open enrollment. Diagnostic reading clinics; staff development centers. Participating colleges involved in the staff development. Much emphasis on parent training—to assist their children by helping in their reading development.

LOCATION: Districts 18, 20, 21, 22, 24, 25, 26, and local universities. Non-public schools in those districts also.

TARGET: 4,348 public school, 673 non-public school students.

STAFFING: 106. A coordinator, 2 assistants, 7 center heads, 28 staff developers, 28 reading clinicians, 7 school psychologists, 7 stenographers, 7 school neighborhood workers, and others.

Outreach Program (Pilot)

STARTED: 1975.

FUNDING: $388,294.

EMPHASIS: To help 9th grade students reverse their pattern of school absenteeism, improve their basic skills, and enter "mainstream" classes. Individual counselling of students and/or parents; group counselling; assistance from various youth and family serving agencies and school staff on problems. Outreach program of home visitation by attendance teachers and family assistants, in an attempt to improve attendance. A satellite center where remediation in reading and math skills through multi-media equipment, audio-visual aids, etc.

LOCATION: Boys/Girls High School, Bushwick High School, Eastern District High School, and Franklin K. Lane High School (all Bkn).

TARGET: Roughly 450 chronic absentee 9th and 10th grade pupils from these four segregated home schools. The program operates from a Community Satellite Center for students who have been absent 30-50 days for the previous five months and who are performing two or more years below level in reading and mathematics.

STAFFING: 23. 14 teachers, 4 family assistants, 5 educational assistants, and 1 secretary.

AUSPICES: Bureau of Attendance of the Board of Education.

CHANGES: Became bigger—added a school and one resource teacher in each school.

Easing Student Adjustment (Basic)

STARTED: 1975.

FUNDING: $2,733,972.

LOCATION: 13 high schools. Those mentioned above as receiving high schools under open enrollment in Brooklyn and Queens and 2 in the Bronx. The ones in Queens and the Bronx are for remedial reading only.

EMPHASIS: To enable minority students coming from segregated schools to adjust to new predominantly white schools. Also remedial help provided to students in receiving high schools as well as to new minority students coming in. Tutorial services, guidance.

TARGET: 2,000 students.

STAFF: 60 teachers, 22 guidance counsellors, 35 paraprofessionals, 4 clerical staff—all full time.

Decentralized District Programs (Basic)

District 3, Basic Reading Program Centers

STARTED: 1974.

FUNDING: $1,218,953.

LOCATION: 12 elementary schools (P.S. 9, 75, 84, 113, 145, 163, 165, 166, 179, 191, and 199), 2 junior high schools (54 and 118), 1 intermediate school (44), 2 non-public schools.

TARGET: Approximately 3,425 students, grades 2-8.

EMPHASIS: Provides in-service training of the regular staff as well as project staff. Parents of program participants invited to attend these training sessions in addition to parent workshops conducted at the schools.

STAFFING: 1 director, 1 curriculum trainer, 36 reading teachers, 1 clerk, 5 math teachers, 41 paraprofessionals, in addition consultants, instructional, and audio-visual supplies and materials.

District 4, Open City Project (Basic)

FUNDING: $800,000.

LOCATION: 8 elementary schools (P.S. 7, 50, 96, 101, 112, 155, 171, and St. Pauls).

TARGET: 600 children, grades K-2.

EMPHASIS: Achievement by strengthening student control over language, social behavior, and mathematical concepts by expanding the experimental base of all students in the program through a series of carefully planned enrichment activities at sites outside District 4 in New York City and through encounters with a wide range of visiting artists who visit the school sites within District 4.

STAFFING: 1 director, 1 resource teacher, 18 teachers, 34 educational assistants, 2 school secretaries; in addition, instructional supplies and materials, audio-visual equipment, transportation, admission tickets, evaluation, consultants, and parental involvement.

District 4, Bilingual Bicultural Mini-School

FUNDING: $681,192, 1975-76.

LOCATION: 9 bilingual bicultural mini-schools (P.S. 7, 72, 96, 101, 102, 108, 121, 171, and St. Pauls).

TARGET: 1,105 children, K-6 grades.

EMPHASIS: Preventing or decreasing scholastic retardation of non-English speaking children: promoting better intercultural communication among different linguistic and cultural groups by developing a good bicultural program; providing for enrichment of all pupils by developing an understanding of Puerto Rican and black history and culture; and developing a bilingual staff, who have teaching skills and language competency in both languages; and informing and training parents in the goals of bilingual programs.

STAFFING: 1 director, 1 curriculum specialist, 1 bilingual teacher, 21 teachers, 8 educational assistants, 1 secretary, 1 clerk, 3 school aides.

District 5, Center For Educational Solutions (Basic)

FUNDING: $1,193,403, 1975-76.

EMPHASIS: This is a basic project comprised of five components designed to reduce minority group isolation and to demonstrate that quality education is attainable in District 5. Following are project titles: Upper School Component, $377,483; Bilingual School Component, $166,297; Open Door Component, $179,469; Early Childhood, $182,994; and Lower School Component, $287,160 (total $1,193,403).

STAFFING: 1 program director, 1 assistant principal, 1 school psychologist, 1 guidance counselor, 1 teacher assigned as coordinator, teacher trainee, teacher in charge, 3 teachers, 2 school secretaries, 1 senior clerk, 1 school neighborhood worker, 30 educational assistants paid at an hourly rate of $4.50 for a total amount of $39,960, consultants paid at the rate of $100 per day for 85 days, in addition educational equipment, audiovisual equipment.

District 7, Upgrading Basic Skills Through Environmental Education (Pilot)

STARTED: 1975.

FUNDING: $210,279.

LOCATION: 26 public schools in District 7 and four non-public school classes in grades 4-5.

EMPHASIS: Provide students with year-round, on-site basic skills advancement activities, including five-day environmental, recreational, and camp-living experience. Camp site component aimed at fostering better relations among students and providing environmental experiences to enrich the curriculum during the school year. Goal is also to have camp experience provide increased student motivation, resulting in improved attendance and learning. To improve human relations skills, reading of

Spanish, English language proficiency, and provide teacher in-service training. Camp experience used as springboard for remediation programs in reading, mathematics, science, and other subjects.

TARGET: 2,000 students, grades 4-6 from 26 public schools and 4 non-public school classes, grades 4-5.

STAFFING: Project director, senior clerk, consultants.

District 7, Language Development And Reading Program (Basic)

STARTED: 1975.

FUNDING: $460,207.

LOCATION: 26 schools in the District.

EMPHASIS: To increase English language skills for all students, Spanish language skills for English dominant students, and reading skills for them. Supplemental instruction in small groups and on an individual basis. Parent involvement in trips and special events. Staff training.

TARGET: 1,300 black and Hispanic children who are either Spanish-dominant or English-dominant and are at least 6 months below grade level in reading.

STAFFING: 18 teachers, supervisors, senior typist, and consultants.

District 8, Achievement Academy For Uninterrupted Education (Pilot)

STARTED: 1975.

FUNDING: $556,232.

LOCATION: C.S. 238(Bx).

EMPHASIS: Provides an alternative education program for students in grades 4-9 who are demonstrating difficulty in school, including disruptive behavior and reading and math scores 1.5 years or more below level. Academic skills presented to students in a framework of career education and human relations.

TARGET: 250 students.

STAFFING: Supervisor, teachers, resource teachers, part-time psychologist, guidance counsellors, social worker, human relations teachers, educational assistants, school secretary at the site, and clerk at the district office.

District 11, Pals: Pupils Achieve Learning Skills (Pilot)

STARTED: 1974.

FUNDING: $1,515,296.

LOCATION: P.S. 2, 21, 68, 76, 87, 97, 103, 121, and Our Lady of Grace.

EMPHASIS: To improve reading and mathematics skills by providing early childhood developmental activities and laboratory approaches to reading and mathematics. Parent participation in parent-school activities. Ongoing teacher training in laboratory techniques. Reading and mathematics laboratories provide diagnostic testing and individual prescriptions for each student to improve basic skills through the learning center approach. Health interns administer vision, hearing and perceptual tests to diagnose potential obstacles to learning. A school-home liaison center to enhance parent-school activities.

TARGET: 5,100 students.

STAFFING: Project director, 40 teachers, 24 educational assistants, 12 health interns, 11 family workers, teacher assigned as mathematics coordinator, psychologist, clerk, and consultants.

District 17, Overcoming Academic Retardation Caused by Minority Isolation (Basic)

STARTED: 1973.

FUNDING: $1,163,591.

LOCATION: P.S. 138, 191, and I.S. 210.

EMPHASIS: To provide individualized, diagnostic-prescriptive instruction and supportive guidance services to students with reading, math, and English-speaking problems.

TARGET: 4,000 students in grades 1-8 in those schools.

STAFFING: Assistant principal as supervisor, 14 reading teachers, 4 math teachers, 3 teachers of English as a second language, 3 teacher trainers, 4 guidance counsellors, 3 psychologists, 3 attendance teachers, 3 school secretaries, 21 educational assistants, 3 family assistants, 1 typist.

District 18, Instructional Support System In Mathematics, Reading, And Bilingual Program (Basic)

STARTED: 1974.

Educational Programs for Special Target Groups

FUNDING: $1,047,960.

LOCATION: At the District's block school and at selected elementary and junior high schools.

EMPHASIS: To foster positive school achievement in language and attitudes by offering an instructional program based largely on students' native language skills. To provide English competency for Spanish- and French-speaking students and French and Spanish competence for monolingual English-speaking students; will intensify the integration of all parts of the community by providing an avenue for constructive contact between pupils, parents, teachers, and the community at large.

STAFFING: Teachers, guidance counsellor, school secretary (part-time), educational assistants, school aide, and coordinator of research (part-time).

District 19, School for the Gifted in Science and Mathematics (Basic)

STARTED: 1974.

FUNDING: $204,936.

LOCATION: P.S. 182, and St. Malachy School.

EMPHASIS: To foster better understanding among minority and nonminority students by creating programs in which there is a true integration of students.

TARGET: 70 students, grades 4-5, who are identified as gifted.

District 19, Bilingual-Bicultural Pilot Project (Pilot)

Already described above in bilingual section, see p. 66.

District 21 Project Arrive (Basic)

STARTED: 1975.

FUNDING: $1,054.380.

LOCATION: P.S. 99, 238; J.H.S. 43, 96, 228, 239, 281, and 303.

EMPHASIS: To foster acceptance, understanding, and harmonious relationships among diverse ethnic groups of students, teachers, parents, and community groups of all secondary schools in District 21. Concentrates on human relations and includes workshops for staff, students, and parents. Second component is a diagnostic-prescriptive approach to the remediation of reading and mathematics difficulties for those students who exhibit the adverse educational effects of racial isolation. Provision for curriculum development. In-service training program to ensure that these activities will be maintained.

TARGET: 4,800 students in grades 7-9, drawn from eligible schools listed above.

STAFFING: Teacher coordinators, guidance counsellors, reading and math teachers, paraprofessionals, senior typist, per session teacher-in-charge and teachers, assistant accountant, consultants.

District 24, Diagnosis and Treatment of Reading Disabilities (Basic)

STARTED: 1973.

FUNDING: $591,594.

LOCATION: Diagnostic/Prescriptive reading centers at P.S. 12, 13, 14, 68, 71, 87, 153, 229, St. Bartholomew, St. Leo, Our Lady of Sorrows, St. Mary Help for Christians, and St. Teresa. Four high-intensity reading centers at J.H.S. 73 and 125, two in each school.

EMPHASIS: To encourage school desegregation. Diagnosis and treatment of reading disabilities in a highly structured, individualized program, conducted in an integrated setting.

TARGET: 715 students in the elementary schools, 600 in the junior high schools. Students reading at least one and one-half years below grade level.

STAFFING: In elementary schools, a reading specialist teacher, assisted by a bilingual paraprofessional for each center. In junior high schools, a reading specialist and bilingual professional assistant, working in conjunction with the language art teacher in each center.

District 32, Staff Development Program (Basic)

STARTED: 1975.

FUNDING: $159,485.

LOCATION: 11 public and 1 non-public elementary schools in the district.

EMPHASIS: Provides an in-service training program in each school and/or cluster. Each has a group leader to conduct specific workshop activities to upgrade teaching skills of staff. Substitute teachers used to release regular teachers to be trained on school sites through workshops and demonstration lessons related to the individual school's needs. Pertinent teacher-made instructional materials developed with related training in their development and use. Parent workshops also provided.

TARGET: 80 regular teachers and 2,400 students who are performing less than 2 years below grade level in grades 3 and 4.

STAFFING: 1 part-time coordinator; 12 teacher team leaders, 720 per diem teacher days and half-time stenographer.

Non-Profit, Private Organizations

ESAA authorizes grants to non-profit organizations that support school district desegregation programs. This provides community-based support for those programs. These include:

St. Matthew's and St. Timothy's	$33,460
New Future Foundation	119,614
Comm. for a Comprehensive Education	107,498
Aspira of New York	325,848
Young Filmmakers Foundation	46,078
Aviation Development Council	289,453
Mt. Sinai School of Medicine	380,339
Broad Jump	137,072
Harlem Parents School-Community Center	185,295
New York Urban Coalition	156,219
Total	$1,780,876

Early Childhood

Since the development of the Headstart and Follow Through programs and the increasing interest in upgrading the educational skills of minority students by reaching them as early as possible, there has been some consistent effort to improve the city's early childhood programs. The New York City Board of Education has a Bureau of Early Childhood that is now part of its Center for School Development, and all the publicly funded early childhood programs are run or conducted from there. They include: (1) Early Childhood Integration Centers, funded under the Emergency School Aid Act, described in the foregoing section; (2) New York State Experimental Pre-Kindergarten Program; and (3) Follow Through, funded under Title I.

The New York State Experimental Pre-Kindergarten Program

STARTED: 1967-68.

FUNDING: $3,146,756. 89% state funded; 11% city.

LOCATION: In 27 schools in the following nine districts: 1, 2, 3, 4, 5, 8, 9, 23, and 28.

EMPHASIS: Health, nutrition, and social as well as cognitive development.

TARGET: 2,100 students.

Follow Through

STARTED: 1967.

FUNDING: $1,485,224, Title I.

EMPHASIS: A research and development program for young children (K-3) from low income families that builds on the gains made in Head Start or similar pre-school programs. The research component involves the study of learning models and their impact on children. The development component adapts to the growth patterns of individual children and the needs of families and communities.

LOCATION: District 2 P.S. 33, District 3 P.S. 76, District 5 P.S. 92, 113, East Harlem Block School, Guardian Angel, St. Columbia, and St. Paul the Apostle (Man); District 12 P.S. 6, 77, (Bx); District 16 P.S. 243 and District 23 P.S. 137 (Bkn).

The program in each school exists within the context of a comprehensive network of educational, health, nutritional, social service, psychological, and training activities for children, parents, and staff.

> *P.S. 243 (Bkn):* Chose the Bank Street College of Education as its sponsor. Many Bank Street methods and goals had been incorporated into the school's program before Follow

Educational Programs for Special Target Groups 103

Through started there in 1968. Uses the school as a total learning environment to enable each child to build positive image of him or herself as a learner. Program organized into centers of learning, including writing, mathematics, reading, housekeeping, language development, science, audio-visual, creative arts, snack bar. Has been used as a laboratory school for other Bank Street programs.

P.S. 6, 77 (Bx): Use the Behavior Analysis Model of the University of Kansas, Lawrence, Kansas. The approach places heavy emphasis on basic skills of reading, writing, and mathematics through a theory of positive reinforcement. Uses behavior modification techniques of specifying and reinforcing desirable behaviors and not reinforcing undesirable ones. The ultimate goal is the creation of environments that promote individual success and self-management.

Behavior analysis combines many techniques including programmed instruction, team teaching, individualized teaching, and rote learning. Its application to disadvantaged minority students is new.

STAFFING: Project coordinator; staff trainer who trains professional and paraprofessional staff and parents. The approach also includes a classroom teacher in charge of the instructional team, a cluster teacher responsible for all subjects other than reading, math, spelling and writing, educational assistants, and parent trainees.

P.S. 92 (Man): Follows the Cognitively Oriented Curriculum developed by the High/Scope Educational Research Foundation, Ypsilanti, Michigan. The model derives its curriculum from the research and theories of Jean Piaget and his colleagues on how children think and on how their minds develop. Content materials in science, mathematics, social studies, language and other subjects serve as vehicles to develop basic thinking operations including classification, seriation and number, spatial relations, time and causality.

Guardian Angel Schools, St. Columbia, and St. Paul the Apostle, (Man): These three non-public schools have all chosen the Hampton Institute Nongraded Model. It provides for multi-age groups of children in a flexible type of school organization where children progress according to their individual abilities. Stress on individualization of curriculum and instruction. Progress determined by individual mastery of skills rather than by age, years in school, or performance in competition with other children.

P.S. 133 (Man): This school follows the Home-School Partnership model, sponsored by Clark College, Atlanta, Georgia. The assumption underlying the approach is that home and parents are such a vital force in the child's education that parent involvement is heavily stressed. The primary focus is not on curriculum or classroom instruction but on enlisting parents in the learning process. Goals are to establish realistic and positive attitudes toward a home-school partnership from parents and teachers; to make the school setting relevant to the home situation and thereby more relevant to children; to encourage maximum utilization of parents as resource persons in the education of their children both at home and school; and to facilitate self-improvement and self-realization on the part of parents.

P.S. 76 (Man): Follows the Interdependent Learning Model, under the sponsorship of the City University of New York. Based on the assumption that education is a preparation for life and so necessitates experiences that foster interaction with peers, family, and school staff. Structured small group activities in the classroom, especially of the games variety, further peer involvement, and gradually lessen dependence on the teacher.

P.S. 33 (Man): The Follow Through Program here, in operation since 1967, follows the Self-Sponsored Model based on a child development philosophy. The curriculum is organized to answer the total needs of the child—physically, intellectually, and socially. Focus is on the individual child. Staff develop specific sequential learning experiences for each child. Parental support and initiative developed to provide two bilingual classes to meet child needs in a changing community.

P.S. 137 (Bkn): Follows the Systematic Use of Behavioral Principles Program based on behavior analysis and modification. Bereiter and Englemann have developed the procedures embodied in this program, derived from experimental research. Sponsor is the University of Oregon, Department of Special

Education. Basic principle is that behavior is influenced by its consequences (reinforcement or non-reinforcement). Program focuses on academic objectives—skill development in reading, writing, and mathematics.

Every Follow Through project has a Policy Advisory Committee (PAC), over one-half of whose members are elected by the parents. The remaining members, chosen by the parents already elected, with the advice of project staff, are drawn from agencies, community groups, and individuals with a concern for children. There has also been a city-wide Policy Advisory Council.

The program has a "troika" design that includes the Office of Education, the local schools, and outside sponsors. The Office of Education establishes guidelines and program models. The sponsors, usually early childhood specialists and university-based psychologists, apply their models in particular Follow Through schools. The local schools as participants include the school board, the Policy Advisory Committee, employed staff, and community representatives.

TARGET: 3,800 students.

STAFFING: Supervisors, teachers, guidance, paraprofessionals, clerical, nurse.

AUSPICES: Center for School Development, formerly the Bureau of Early Childhood Education.

Poverty Area, Low Income Students, Title I

Many of the programs reviewed in this inventory are for students from low income backgrounds. That is certainly the case for many of the state and federally funded ones. The program that provides the city the most funds, accounting for more than half of all federal funding, is Title I. It provides for financial assistance to school districts with the explicit mandate that the money be used for the education of students from low income families. Indeed, there are explicit eligibility criteria that must be rigorously applied. In 1975-76, over 570,000 New York City public and non-public school students were deemed eligible for Title I monies, the majority of them public school students.

Unfortunately, the Board of Education's Title I office has not kept a directory of Title I programs since the 1973-74 school year. Given the vast amounts of money and the many programs involved, it would have been impossible to develop extensive summary information as we have for all other programs. Instead, we have some brief data, focused mainly on budgets.

Scholars and school critics who have studied how Title I monies have been spent in New York City and elsewhere raise serious questions about the adequacy of many of the programs. They are often described as simply more of the same, meaning by that that federal money comes in to perpetuate programs and administrative and staffing practices that hadn't worked well in the past and simply spreads them so they may work poorly on a bigger scale. These observers would certainly hesitate to include these programs in an inventory on innovative and supplementary programs, and yet we are mentioning them here. Our main reason is that while the critics are probably right for many Title I programs, they are probably wrong for many others. Some teachers and schools do creative things with Title I monies, even while others do not. In the absence of any data that permits us to separate out the one from the other, we decided to include this brief general section on Title I as a clearly supplemental if not too often an innovative program.

STARTED: 1965.

FUNDING: Went up every year from 1965-66 through 1974-75, from just over $65 million to over $154 million. In 1975-76 the total allocation was closer to $118 million.

LOCATION: In every district in the entire public school system and in non-public schools.

EMPHASIS: Compensatory, remedial programs, particularly in reading, math, and bilingual. Follow Through is also funded under Title I.

TARGET: All eligible students in public and non-public schools. Board of Education estimates put that at 570,031 students.

STAFFING: No aggregate data available.

INFORMATION: Title I office.

High School—College Collaboration

It has become increasingly apparent that one important strategy for improving the public schools is to establish closer linkages and collaborative relations with the colleges. If teaching is to become more of a profession, in the sense of having a more codified body of knowledge and practice than in the past and having a training experience (pre- and in-service) that reflects this, it will have to develop the kinds of close relations with colleges and universities that such other professions as medicine and law have. Furthermore, since increasing numbers of students go on to college, it is important to develop better ways of articulating the curricula of elementary, secondary, and higher education. Significant reforms in the public schools may well come about as a result of such articulation and linkage efforts.

Some time in the early 1970s, top administrators and policy-makers of the City University of New York (CUNY) and the New York City Board of Education, including their respective Chancellors, began meeting on how they could collaborate more on common programs. Since an estimated 80% of the teachers in the New York City schools are trained in the senior colleges of the City University—Brooklyn, Queens, Hunter, CCNY, and Lehman—and since open admissions has brought to the City University so many graduates of the public schools who are poorly prepared for college, each agency had an interest in developing such relations. Many private colleges and universities—e.g., Teachers College, NYU, Fordham, and Bank Street College of Education—have done the same and have developed collaborative programs with the public schools in recent years. The main articulation and collaboration efforts, however, have been between the Board of Education and CUNY.

Several types of collaboration have emerged, including (1) efforts at improving the continuity of curricula from high school to college; (2) improving teacher training through increasing use of public schools as sites for apprenticeship experiences for teachers-in-training in undergraduate education programs at the universities; and (3) remedial programs for academically deficient students.

The meetings of top Board of Education and CUNY officials of a few years back eventually resulted in the establishment of an office in the Division of High Schools and a corresponding one at CUNY to oversee and support such articulation efforts. Both offices have limited resources, however. The Board of Education administrator had many other responsibilities as well and the one from CUNY was "excessed" out in the fall of 1975, reflecting its concern with other priorities, in the face of its massive fiscal cutbacks. There has been a new administrator since then, but she is responsible for only a small segment of the total articulation efforts of the two agencies.

One significant new program that merits particular attention is the Cooperative Continuum of Education on Staten Island, which includes both private and public universities, has parochial as well as public school students, and includes elementary and junior high school students as well. After reviewing that individual program in some detail, which is by far the most developed of any of the articulation efforts, we review the following other four categories of programs: (1) college preparatory skills; (2) community college-high school articulation career-oriented programs; (3) guidance and counselling services for the college-bound student; and (4) campus high schools.

Cooperative Continuum of Education

STARTED: May 1974.

FUNDING: $355,000 from the Carnegie Corporation, Ford Foundation, and Hazen Foundation of New Haven for 1974-77, plus support from the following participating agencies in amounts designated: Board of Education, $150,000; Board of Higher Education $100,000; Community School District 31, $30,000; Archdiocese of New York, $30,000; Staten Island Community College, $60,000; and Wagner College, $30,000.

LOCATION: All over Staten Island, in over 100 educational institutions as well as in local businesses, churches, and civic offices.

EMPHASIS: The establishment of a comprehensive, multi-agency consortium of over 100 institutions, serving youth and adults from kindergarten through graduate school, and including 44 parochial, 10 private, and 52 public schools; 1 private, 1 Catholic, and 2 public colleges. These institutions pool their resources to provide a more open, flexible, and efficient continuum of educational experiences for students enrolled in the participating schools and colleges. Particular programs include:

Bridge: 400-500 high school students go to college each semester, while still attending school. 25-30 intermediate school students are also attending college. Most are at Staten Island Community College, with a small number at Wagner, Richmond, and St. Johns. Roughly 50% of the students are talented and the other 50% are either average or below.

Diagnostic Reading Center: At Wagner College, supported by Community School District 31. 8-week cycle, with 60-75 3rd to 5th grade students per cycle; 10 hours of individualized diagnosis, 10 hours of initial remediation.

Learning Exchange: Courses in personal finance, languages, arts and crafts, economics, social sciences, and hobbies; taught by community members; in offices, homes, and schools all over Staten Island; at any given time, there are 10-12 courses running, with an average size of 10 "students."

Classroom Assistants Program: Graduate and undergraduate students working in elementary and secondary schools, high school students working in elementary schools—as tutors, teacher aides, counselling and administrative assistants—as part of their own training. From 220-250 "classroom assistants" work each semester in schools throughout Staten Island.

Math Skills Centers: Located in 5 high schools and 2 junior highs; jointly staffed by school and college personnel. Provide tutorial and remediation for an average of 600 students per week.

English Skills Center: Located at Curtis High School; jointly staffed by high school and college personnel. Provides tutorial and remediation in basic reading and writing skills for 75-125 students a week. Used as a base for teacher training for junior and senior high school teachers.

Curriculum Coordination & Articulation: Teachers from colleges, high schools, and lower schools collectively re-examine the curriculum as a K-16 entity, removing gaps and duplication, exploring the most efficient means of student progression, and developing collaborative programs to foster a continuum concept. Over 400 educators have been involved in producing curriculum guides, indexes for sharing teaching resources, guidebooks in particular subject areas, and establishing a central Educational Resources Library at Richmond College.

TARGET: Students of all age groups, educators, and all the participating educational agencies.

STAFFING: 10 full time professionals; 20 part-time professionals, all of the latter being regular employees of member agencies, plus the equivalent of two secretarial employees.

AUSPICES: The Cooperative Continuum, a non-profit corporation whose board includes top officials from the Board of Education, the colleges, the archdiocese, the community school district, and the United Federation of Teachers.

CHANGES: Funding has peaked, with private and foundation funding running out over the 1977 year. Programs and numbers of participating agencies have expanded rapidly since 1974 when 125 students were involved.

INFORMATION: A general description booklet, reports, and press clippings, all available from the Staten Island Cooperative Continuum, 715 Ocean Terrace, Staten Island.

College Preparatory Skills Programs

As of September 1975, there were 14 high schools and 7 colleges involved in such collaborative projects, ranging from a self-referred tutorial center to a comprehensive program involving student teaching; in-service education; and curriculum development, implementation, and evaluation. The total amount of funding for this was roughly $450,000 from the Board of Education and another $300,000 from the Board of Higher Education for the 1975-76 school year.

These collaborative programs have engendered significant interest and activity among the involved participants, resulting in many joint efforts by high school and college faculty to improve the teaching of math, expository writing, and reading. There has been some confusion regarding the population to be served. College personnel see their efforts at developing curriculum materials, instructional methods, and procedures as leading to the elimination of the need for remediation at the college level. That has, of course, been a serious problem since open admissions. High school personnel think of the "remedial" population in different terms. In some high schools, the program has been viewed as a school-wide activity that may affect large numbers of students and staff. In others, where the conception of remedial is limited, it exists on a smaller scale.

There are, in addition, 3 mini-schools connected with high schools that have the same kind of collaborative relationship with a college.

Andrew Jackson And Queens College

STARTED: 1974.

FUNDING: $85,721: Board of Education $36,070; Board of Higher Education, $49,651.

LOCATION: Andrew Jackson High School (Q). Flushing, NY 11367.

EMPHASIS: Remediation of students in math and English. An attempt to increase student motivation through changing the 9th-12th grade curricula in math and social studies. To encourage middle class parents in the community to maintain enrollment of their children in Andrew Jackson. Queens College undergraduate and graduate students tutor Jackson students in many subjects. Many supportive services from the college.

TARGET: The majority of students in the school (2,700) at all grade levels.

STAFFING: 7 faculty part-time from the college and 1 full-time from the high school. 3.2 staff units from the Board of Education.

August Martin And York College

STARTED: January 1975.

FUNDING: $20,556: Board of Education, $10,820; Board of Higher Education, $9,736.

LOCATION: August Martin High School (Q).

EMPHASIS: Tutoring of selected college-bound high school students in reading and writing skills.

TARGET: 100 August Martin students.

STAFFING: 1.2 Board of Education staff units. Also 25 York College tutors.

Benjamin Franklin and City College of New York

STARTED: September 1974.

FUNDING: $28,769.

LOCATION: Benjamin Franklin High School (Man).

EMPHASIS: Development of a college preparation project, based in part on remedial programs offered at the college. Emphasis on social studies, English, basic writing, and college study skills. Includes a lab in which trained tutors from the college work with students on reading, study skills, and writing.

TARGET: 25 11th graders, plus the entire 12th grade curriculum in the courses just listed.

STAFFING: The equivalent of 1.5 staff units from the Board of Education. Three CCNY faculty members help in the classroom, supervise the tutoring, and help plan the 12th year program at the high school.

Curtis and Staten Island Community College

STARTED: 1974.

FUNDING: $72,276: Board of Education, $39,676; Board of Higher Education, $32,600.

Educational Programs for Special Target Groups

LOCATION: Curtis High School (SI).

EMPHASIS: Training in reading, expository writing, and beginning work in social studies. Work within the school's new English skills center. It has three main activities: (1) the teaching of reading and writing to students in need of special assistance; (2) teacher training; and (3) development of effective teaching techniques and materials. 1975-76 was the second year of the center. Developed many productive relationships among college and high school staff. Have begun to have an impact in the regular classroom. Team teaching and open classroom approaches used.

TARGET: 270 students have been diagnosed in the center; 150 have been served directly, 9th-12th grade students.

STAFFING: 1 full-time 2 part-time faculty from the college. 1 Board of Education staff unit. 5 teachers regularly volunteer prep periods in addition.

Herbert Lehman with Lehman College

STARTED: 1975.

FUNDING: $39,786: Board of Education, $28,854; Board of Higher Education, $10,932.

LOCATION: Herbert H. Lehman High School (Bx).

EMPHASIS: Remediation in reading, expository writing, math, and social studies. To lessen the gap between requirements for high school graduation and skills necessary to succeed in college.

TARGET: 60 in English, 11th graders. 24 in math classes, another 100-150 in tutoring.

STAFFING: 4 college and 4 high school faculty work part time on this.

John Jay and Brooklyn College

STARTED: 1974.

FUNDING: $44,965: Board of Education, $27,052; Board of Higher Education, $17,913.

LOCATION: John Jay High School (Bkn) and a neighborhood resource center in the Red Hook area.

EMPHASIS: To improve attendance, truancy patterns, and school performance of 9th graders who are low achievers. Upgrades basic skills in math, reading, and writing. Provides tutorial and vocational counselling.

TARGET: Low achieving 9th graders, with regular truancy patterns.

STAFFING: Brooklyn College psychologist, guidance interns and student teachers. Mini-school coordinators and teachers from the school 2.0 staff units from the Board of Education.

Julia Richman and Hunter College

STARTED: 1974.

FUNDING: $46,518; Board of Education, $28,855; Board of Higher Education, $17,663.

LOCATION: Julia Richman High School (Man).

EMPHASIS: Development in basic skills in expository writing, math, and science for 11th and 12th graders who are far below grade level but have a definite interest in attending college. Goal is to improve students' skills so that they will not need remediation at Hunter and will qualify for placement into mainstream classes.

TARGET: 70-80 low achieving 11th and 12th graders, interested in attending college.

STAFFING: 2.2 staff units from the Board of Education. 5 high school faculty work on the program. 4 faculty and 5 social work interns from Hunter.

Port Richmond and Staten Island Community College

STARTED: September 1974.

FUNDING: $72,276: Board of Education, $39,676; Board of Higher Education, $32,600.

LOCATION: Port Richmond High School (SI).

EMPHASIS: Remediation in reading and math. Individualized instruction through the use of many student teachers and other college students. Develops a network of personalized supportive services.

TARGET: 91 9th graders, two or more years behind in reading and math.

STAFFING: 1 faculty person from both the high school and college, plus student teachers (4 full time) and other college students.

Seward Park and Hunter College

STARTED: 1974.

Educational Programs for Special Target Groups

FUNDING: $55,699: Board of Education, $45,087, Board of Higher Education, $10,612.

LOCATION: Seward Park High School (Man).

EMPHASIS: Curriculum in high school subject areas geared toward communication, e.g., reading, expository writing. Communication workshops in media analysis. Off-site internship in senior year, with "hands-on" experience in communications in area of specialization. Direct admission of graduates to Hunter College Communications Department.

TARGET: 92 students, selected by interest, rather than by performance. 10th and 11th graders.

STAFFING: Several faculty from high school and college work part time. 3.0 staff units of the Board of Education, with college staff and student teachers.

Springfield Gardens and York College

STARTED: 1974.

FUNDING: $97,460: Board of Education, $38,324; Board of Higher Education, $59,136.

LOCATION: Springfield Gardens High School (Q).

EMPHASIS: Intensive instructional programs and remediation in math for students who may apply to CUNY. Both high school faculty and staff of the college work through undergraduate tutors. Math lab.

TARGET: 450 students in 11th and 12th grades who need remediation.

STAFFING: 8-15 York undergraduates work as tutors, under the supervision of 1 high school teacher and 1 York faculty person. The latter selects the tutors and helps coordinate the math program. 2.25 staff units from the Board of Education.

Susan E. Wagner and Staten Island Community College

STARTED: 1975.

FUNDING: $5,410.

LOCATION: Susan E. Wagner High School (SI).

EMPHASIS: Raising math and reading levels.

TARGET: 187 students reached in math, 75 in reading. 9th-12th graders.

STAFFING: 2 faculty each from the college and high school. 0.6 staff units of the Board of Education.

Thomas Jefferson and Brooklyn College

STARTED: 1974.

FUNDING: $74,269: Board of Education, $45,087; Board of Higher Education, $31,182.

LOCATION: Thomas Jefferson High School (Bkn).

EMPHASIS: Remediation in reading, writing, and arithmetic skills. Mathematics tutorial center.

TARGET: Students with deficiencies in these basic skills.

STAFFING: 3.0 staff units of the Board of Education. College staff from Brooklyn College serve directly with Jefferson faculty.

Walton and Morris with Lehman College

STARTED: 1975.

FUNDING: Same as Lehman High School.

LOCATION: At the schools (Bx).

Wingate and Brooklyn College

STARTED: 1974.

FUNDING: $45,026: Board of Education, $36,070; Board of Higher Education, $8,956.

LOCATION: Wingate High School (Bkn).

EMPHASIS: To design and test a two-year course in math to replace the existing pre-algebra course, aimed to prepare "slower students" to take algebra. The Scott-Foresman "Activities and Application in Mathematics" used to improve modules developed by Brooklyn College and Wingate instructors. Now considering modification of the existing algebra-geometry sequence.

TARGET: Slower students in math.

STAFFING: 2.0 staff units from the Board of Education. Two faculty members from Brooklyn College and the staff of the Mathematics Department of Wingate.

High School Division-Cuny Research

An offshoot of the college preparatory skills program is the High School Division-CUNY research project in reading and expository writing.

Educational Programs for Special Target Groups

STARTED: Fall 1976.

FUNDING: $46,018, all from the Board of Higher Education.

LOCATION: Over 20 classrooms throughout the public schools, citywide, and once a week at the City University Graduate Center.

EMPHASIS: Developing curriculum and teaching strategies in reading and expository writing to meet the needs of high school juniors and seniors and college freshmen with problems in English.

TARGET: As above.

STAFFING: High school teachers and CUNY staff.

Community College-High School Articulation Career-Oriented Programs

There are seven articulation programs dealing with careers, funded at roughly $40,000, and involving 4 community colleges. Each school usually emphasizes a particular career specialty. One individual high school and three pairs are involved. There is also one alternative campus school.

Central Commercial and Louis D. Brandeis with Borough of Manhattan Community College

STARTED: Central Commercial in 1974, Brandeis in 1975.

FUNDING: $17,409: Board of Education, $5,861; Board of Higher Education, $11,548.

LOCATION: Both high schools (Man).

EMPHASIS: To develop a 3-year articulated data processing instructional program.

TARGET: All students in those schools.

STAFFING: Each high school has .2 Board of Education staff units.

High School Redirection and Staten Island Community College

STARTED: 1975.

FUNDING: $5,518: Board of Education, $1,803; Board of Higher Education, $3,715.

LOCATION: High School Redirection (SI)

118 Inventory of Educational Improvement Efforts

EMPHASIS: To provide college level courses to highly motivated, college-bound high school students attending High School Redirection.

TARGET: As above.

STAFFING: .2 Board of Education staff units.

Middle College High School (see also pages 18-19)

PROGRAM: Designed as an alternative high school to provide the secondary school student with intensive help in basic skills and a comprehensive introduction to career education while attending classes physically situated within a community college.

Prospect Heights and James Madison with New York City Community College

STARTED: January 1975.

FUNDING: $2,253, all of it by the Board of Education.

LOCATION: In both schools.

EMPHASIS: To raise the educational and career aspirations of high school seniors by enrolling them in an articulated college marketing program to be taught by high school personnel in the high school.

TARGET: High school seniors.

STAFFING: .2 Board of Education staffing units at Prospect Heights and .05 at Madison.

Theodore Roosevelt and George Washington with Bronx Community College

STARTED: January 1975.

FUNDING: $13,510: Board of Education, $9,018, Board of Higher Education, $4,492.

LOCATION: In both schools.

EMPHASIS: To raise the educational and career aspirations of disadvantaged high school seniors by enrolling them in an articulated high school/college marketing program.

TARGET: Disadvantaged high school seniors.

STAFFING: Each high school has .5 Board of Education staff units.

Educational Programs for Special Target Groups

Guidance and Counseling Services for College-Bound Students

Computer Assisted Guidance Project (CAG)

STARTED: February 1974.

FUNDING: $319,750. Board of Education, $206,250; Citibank, $113,500.

LOCATION: In five high schools: Brandeis (Man), Lehman (Bx), Midwood (Bkn), Francis Lewis (Q), and Port Richmond (SI).

EMPHASIS: The project provides current and specific information about colleges, scholarships, and careers. It is a commercially packaged, computerized program developed by Timeshare, Inc., an affiliate of Houghton Mifflin, which has four data banks: 4-year colleges, 2-year colleges, occupations, and scholarship aid. Students use a terminal that provides them with information concerning careers and occupations, the educational requirements of each, the educational or vocational institutions offering these requirements and the institutions' characteristics, and scholarships available for pursuing education. The benefits of the program include: the ability to store large amounts of easily retrievable data, thus relieving guidance counsellors of time-consuming research; allowing students to be free of the bias of some guidance counsellors; giving students an awareness and orientation to computer usage; and allowing academic teachers in high schools to use career information as a means to instill interest in a particular subject matter.

TARGET POPULATION: All college-bound students in those five high schools. Roughly 10,000 used it.

AUSPICES: High School Division of the Board of Education, in collaboration with Citibank, which provided 35% of the funding, and the Center for Advanced Study in Education of the Graduate School and University Center of the City University of New York. Also, the Institute of Research and Development in Occupational Education of CUNY.

CHANGES: Has moved through pilot phase in the five schools to being evaluated and now being considered for continuation and expansion to other schools.

High School-College Continuum

LOCATION: Walton (Bx), F. D. Roosevelt (Bkn), and Charles Evans Hughes (Man).

EMPHASIS: Effecting a meaningful articulation between high schools and post-secondary institutions by providing intensive guidance in career development for 11th grade students. Works in conjunction with Bronx Community College, New York City Community College, and the Brooklyn and Vorhees Centers (private trade schools). Provides for "hands on" experiences, sharing of facilities, and utilization of resource people and facilities. Provides in-depth information on career programs, stressing technological fields among the options in post-secondary schooling. Also assists students in assessing their interests, abilities, aspirations, and values in making realistic career choices.

TARGET: 11th grade students in the three high schools.

STAFFING: A coordinator, plus a counsellor and paraprofessional at each of the pilot schools; released time to counsellors at the participating colleges.

AUSPICES: Bureau of Educational and Vocational Guidance.

The Handicapped

A special target group for whom services have expanded considerably in recent years, mainly because of citizen advocacy and litigation, is the handicapped. The New York City school system has always had many bureaus for various categories of students labelled as handicapped (there are now 6), but the programs have never been adequate enough to meet the need. This has resulted in the development of more than 25 alternative, contracted out, private schools, functioning outside the Board of Education, though largely funded by it under state law. These schools have an association, Oasis, that watches closely over relevant legislation and Board of Education rulings, as it attempts to maintain their funding.

One indication of the political strength of constituencies concerned with increasing and improving educational services for the handicapped is the way in which they influenced the reorganization of school headquarters in 1973, which will be described in a later section. Originally that reorganization consolidated high schools and special education programs in one headquarters unit, but the pressure from groups representing the handicapped for their own division was so strong, as was that from the high schools, that each was made into a separate and autonomous unit.

A major event in this regard was State Education Commissioner Nyquist's landmark decision of November 1973, in the Riley Reid case, a class action suit against the New York City Board of Education for not providing appropriate educational services for this target group. As a result of his own separate investigation that uncovered serious deficiencies in services, Nyquist ruled that the class appeal was properly brought in this matter, and he ordered the Board of Education to correct those deficiencies, citing State Education Law 4404, which requires that all handicapped students be provided with adequate educational services.

Many citizen advocacy groups, including Queens Lay Advocate, maintain that the Board of Education's programs are inadequate both in quality and in level of services. School officials claim that they are doing all they can to increase the amount of money available for special education programs, as well as their quality. A chancellor's task force on special education that includes representatives from citizen advocacy groups, in addition to school administrators, is now exploring some of the critical policy questions in this field.

Many of the administrative problems in special education have been well-reviewed in a recent study by the Deputy Chancellor's office. It highlights the following critical developments: from 1970-75, the target population served by the Division of Special Education (the handicapped) increased from 27,865 to 39,553, a growth of 50%, and at a time when the high schools and community school districts (elementary and junior highs) lost population. Along with that growth in number of students came a corresponding one in the special education budget from $110 million in 1970-71 to $241 million in 1975-76, exluding federal funding. This budgetary as well as enrollment increase was, of course, accelerated by the Riley Reid decision, as well as by the development of more sophisticated diagnostic techniques and an additional state aid apportionment, first available in 1974-75. The city obtained just under $42 million then and received an increase up to an estimated $57,256,142 in 1975-76. Federal funding has also increased, from $12,839,382 in 1974-75 to $18,017,022 for 1975-76. It is clear, then, that programs for the handicapped are an increasingly important part of the educational services in the city.

A major controversy about these services that is likely to go on for some time is the extent to which they should be delivered within the Board of Education or outside. There are an estimated 5,000 students in the contracted-out schools that are served by Oasis, their association, and their funding comes mainly from the state and the Board of Education budget. That money pays for the entire tuition of these students, but there is some question regarding the Board of Education's willingness to keep funding these programs at a time when the school system as a whole, even if not the Division of Special Education, is experiencing such severe budget cuts. There is litigation on the issue at the present time, as advocates for the private schools experience increasing difficulty in maintaining the level of funding they had received before from the Board of Education. They see that development as part of a slow process of the Board's gradually absorbing all programs for the handicapped under its own jurisdiction.

Our inventory considers two broad categories of innovative and/or supplemental programs for the handicapped: (1) those that are run by the Board of Education and result from federal funding; and (2) those that are run outside, in the sub-contracted alternative schools. The federally funded programs are, in turn, divided by type of funding source.

Federally Funded Programs

Title I, Special Services and Special Schools

Total amount of funding for 1975-76 was $7,799,789.

Educational Programs for Special Target Groups

Program for Multiply-Handicapped pupils

FUNDING: $359,239.

LOCATION: 6 elementary schools, 2 intermediate schools: P.S. 33 (Man); 76, 160(Bx); 52 (Bkn); 201 (Q); and 3 (SI) and I.S. 144 (Bx) and 237 (Q).

EMPHASIS: Provides individualized and additional small group instruction to improve students' skills in reading and math. Multi-media and multi-modality techniques and materials used.

TARGET: 300 Title I eligible, multiply-handicapped students, ages 5-21. Students are non-graded and have a reading and mathematics range of pre-K-3.

STAFFING: 65. 35 teachers, 20 paraprofessionals, 4 family assistants, 2 senior typists, 1 coordinator, 1 psychologist, 1 social worker, 1 guidance counsellor.

Bridge to School Program

FUNDING: $158,157.

LOCATION: P.S. 108, 198, Babies Hospital, 626 West 165 Street, and Harlem Hospital, 530 Lenox Avenue (Man); P.S. 23, 49, 92, 110, and 160 (Bx); P.S. 298, 397, and Carey Gardens Day Care Center, 2964 West 23 Street (Bkn); P.S. 18 (SI).

EMPHASIS: Supplements an early childhood readiness program for teaching disabled children who need individualized attention to develop reading and math skills. Taught individually and in groups of two and three. Combination of teacher-made and commercial materials. Classes are ungraded.

TARGET: 150 Title I eligible learning disabled children, ages 5-7, located in four boroughs, exluding Queens.

STAFFING: 10. 7 teachers, 1 coordinator, 1 teacher-coordinator, and 1 part-time school secretary.

Division of Special Education and Pupil Personnel Services (DSEPPS), Supplementary Reading Program for Handicapped children

FUNDING: $1,803,106.

LOCATION: 57 schools: P.S. 9, 11, 17, 33, 40, 46, 68, 79, 101, 106, 108, 126, 135, 137, 171, 171, CMHC (Man); 4, 24, 51, 63, 92, 140, 145, 148, 160, 184, 155 (Bx); 11, 3, 43, 56, 63, 144, 147, 117, 178, 180, 184, 192, 226, 270, 287, 327, 328, 335, 396 (Bkn); 3, 112, 118, 134, 160, 183, 187, 188, 209 (Q); 18, 61 (SI).

EMPHASIS: To improve the reading ability of Title I eligible pupils who require intensive instructional help in reading; and to install and maintain a reading instructional program across bureau lines in certain DSEPPS unit sites.

TARGET: 2,325 Title I eligible handicapped pupils, ages 5-16.

STAFFING: 82. 64 teachers of special education, 4 educational assistants, 3 assistant coordinators, 5 school secretaries, 3 guidance counsellors, 1 coordinator, 1 senior typist, 1 supervisory clerk.

Mainstreaming—Supportive Educational Services for the Learning Disabled

FUNDING: $328,531.

LOCATION: P.S. 115, 192 (Man); 18, 48, 60, 64, 93, 154 (Bx); 21, 90, 188, 219 (Bkn); 116 (q).

EMPHASIS: Supplements regular tax levied classroom instruction for neurologically impaired pupils. Individualized and small group instruction in reading and math provided by Title I teachers, one per school. Services 4 hours a week.

TARGET: 360 neurologically impaired students in those schools, approximately 30 per school.

STAFFING: 12 teachers.

Transitional Classses Program

FUNDING: $322,244.

LOCATION: P.S. 146 (Man): 14, 99, and I.S. 155 (Bx); P. S. 236 Hegeman Diagnostic Reception Center, 740 Hegeman Avenue, and Atlantic Diagnostic Reception Center, 316-318 Atlantic Avenue (Bkn); P. S. 26 and 71 (Q).

EMPHASIS: Supplementary remedial service in reading and mathematics. A minimum of 30-45 minute daily period of individual and small group instruction given by Title I staff. Guidance counsellors provide supportive services. Staff training.

TARGET: 310 Title I emotionally handicapped students.

STAFFING: 17. 8 teachers, 3 guidance counsellors, 2 educational associates, 1 teacher trainer, 1 supervisor of alternative programs, 1 acting supervisor, 1 attendance teacher, 1 senior stenographer.

Educational Programs for Special Target Groups

Improving Instruction of Socially Maladjusted and Emotionally Disturbed Children in Special Schools

FUNDING: $2,276,846.

LOCATION: P.S. 8, 58, 82, 91, 106, 162, 169, 205, 226, (Man); 12, 185, 186, (Bx); 36, 85, 141, 368, 369, 370, 371, (Bkn); 4, 9, 23, 75, 224 (Q).

EMPHASIS: Remedial math and reading. Intensive small group and individualized instruction in 24 day schools, psychiatric hospitals, and residential and day treatment centers. Varied approaches to instruction ranging from reading resource centers in the day schools to in-class small group and individual instruction in the treatment centers. Staff training and articulation of the program with the existing tax levy program. Also follow-up services.

TARGET: Approximately 2,000 reading retarded, socially maladjusted, and emotionally disturbed children.

STAFFING: 136. 88 paraprofessionals, 24 teachers, 13 teacher trainers, 5 secretaries, 5 guidance counsellors, 1 coordinator.

Individualized Instruction for Physically Handicapped and Mentally Retarded Children in Special Schools

FUNDING: $569,250.

LOCATION: 3 occupational training centers in 21 schools; 4 hospital schools ("400" schools); The School for the Deaf (J-47); The School for Language and Hearing Impaired (P-158).

EMPHASIS: Intensive remedial program in reading and math. Wide range of ability and age grouping. Small group and individualized instruction. Bilingual remedial services at the School for Language and Hearing Impaired.

TARGET: 500 physically handicapped and mentally retarded students.

STAFFING: 48. 40 paraprofessionals, 6 teachers, 1 coordinator, and 1 secretary.

Program for Institutionalized Children, Educational Services for Pupils In Child Caring Institutions for the Neglected and Delinquent

FUNDING: $1,047,543.

LOCATION: 137 public and private child caring agencies in the city.

EMPHASIS: Compensatory and supplementary educational services to children resident in public and private child caring institutions. To improve abilities in reading and/or mathematics. All instruction in facilities provided by the institution or in the on-premises school. Program developed by Board of Education personnel.

TARGET: Roughly 2,062 students, ranging from kindergarten to the 12th grade, in close cooperation with the institutions.

STAFFING: 320. 239 part-time teachers, 11 full-time teachers, 33 part-time paraprofessionals, 18 part-time supervisors, 2 full-time supervisors, 15 part-time clerical positions, 2 full-time clerical positions.

Corrective Reading, Corrective Mathematics, and Bilingual Instruction of Pregnant School Age Girls

FUNDING: $934,873.

LOCATION: Center for Continued Education P-911, P-912, (Man); Teen Aid High School, P-931, Community School for Comprehensive Education, P-932, (Bkn), Martha Neilson School, P-921, (Bx); Ida B. Wells School, P-941 (Q).

EMPHASIS: Individualized and small group instruction in corrective reading and math. Guidance counsellor and social worker in each school provide supportive services. Also bilingual instruction in reading and math to non-English-speaking pregnant girls.

TARGET: 1,200 secondary school age Title I eligible girls who are pregnant and retarded in reading and/or mathematics.

STAFFING: 124, 64 teachers, 20 paraprofessionals, 12 teacher aides, 6 guidance counsellors, 5 social workers, 5 assistant principals in charge, 1 project director, 1 administrative associate, 1 teacher in charge, 1 school psychologist.

ESEA TITLE III, Section 306

Center for Multiple Handicapped Children

FUNDING: $45,951.

LOCATION: Center for Multiple Handicapped Children, 105 East 106th Street, New York, NY 10029; Center for Multiple Handicapped Children, P.S. 187, 61-25 Marathon Parkway, Little Neck, NY 11362.

EMPHASIS: Supplements an existing program now functioning at the Center for Multiple Handicapped Children in Manhattan. Provides a plan

Educational Programs for Special Target Groups 127

of action for that Center, serving as a national demonstration site. Makes available educational innovations in curriculum and clinical evaluative instruments. Provides training and technical assistance to other agencies and cities to replicate the Center's programs. Disseminates information for replication purposes.

TARGET: 200 students, ages 6-21, with multiple handicaps, who will be transported from parts of Brooklyn, Queens, and The Bronx to the Queens Center.

STAFFING: No additional personnel other than the Center's own staff.

Modification of Children's Oral Language

FUNDING: $60,738.

LOCATION: P.S. 4, 40, 47, 76, 83, 87, 158, I.M. 82, Julia Richmond Annex, and New York School of Printing (Man); P.S. 8, 49, 110, I.M. 160, 180, Bronx Habilitation Unit, and 65 Annex (Bx); 31, 108, 144, 147, 154, 197, 272, 275, 279, 291, J.H.S. 278 (Bkn); P.S. 22, 71, 88, 120, 150, 163, 164, 191, 203, I.S. 237, J.H.S. 158, (Q); P.S. 18 (SI).

EMPHASIS: This is a staff training program for teachers and supervisors working with various categories of handicapped. Provides training in Monterey Learning Systems, programmed language instruction materials, criterion referenced tests, 3-5 day refresher training for tax levy staff in the Bureaus for Speech Improvement and for the Hearing Handicapped.

TARGET: 44 teachers and 6 supervisors who provide therapy for 320 handicapped, brain injured, learning disabled, hard of hearing, and mentally retarded children who also have significant language deficits.

STAFFING: Consultants from CUNY and Monterey Learning Systems.

ESEA Title VI-B, Educational Services for Unserved Handicapped Children

The total amount of funding is $3,240,000

Individualized Instructional Program for Emotionally Disturbed Children Unable to Particpate in Formal Education Programs

FUNDING: $31,000.

LOCATION: P.S. 106, Bellevue Psychiatric Hospital, 30th Street at 1st Avenue, New York, NY 10016.

EMPHASIS: Provides educational and supportive clinical services to emotionally handicapped children who are unable to attend community schools. These children require a specialized and individualized educational program with supportive psychiatric and social services to prepare them for re-entry into the normal stream. Emphasizes perceptual and cognitive skills, attitudes, behavioral patterns, and skills necessary for future success in the mainstream. Articulation with community schools and communication with parents.

TARGET: Emotionally handicapped children, ages 5-18.

STAFFING: 5. 2 teachers, 2 educational assistants, 1 guidance counsellor.

Itinerant Instruction in Mobility for Blind School Students

FUNDING: $13,771.

LOCATION: J.H.S. 104 (Man); I.S. 145, Taft High School (Bx); I.S. 88, Erasmus High School (Bkn); Grover Cleveland High School (Q).

EMPHASIS: Teaches blind and visually impaired students how to move about more independently in their daily lives. Students receive individual mobility instruction two hours a week in procedures that will improve their independent travel skills and eventually will lead to their use of public bus and subway.

TARGET: 16 blind and visually impaired students who are attending the above-listed schools.

STAFF: 2 teachers.

New Directions in Teaching Reading to Seriously Disturbed Adolescents Who Were Unserved

FUNDING: $46,372.

LOCATION: P.S. 106, Bellevue Psychiatric Hospital, 30th Street at First Avenue, New York, NY 10016

EMPHASIS: Remediation in reading for adolescents who were previously unserved because of their severe socially unacceptable behavior. Uses a modality of media, drama, and motion education to involve youngsters with severe reading and emotional problems in the process of communication. Through a total involvement approach youngsters re-integrated into a school setting. Clinical services provided by the hospital.

STAFFING: 2-1/2. 1 teacher of reading and media; 1 educational assistant; and 1/2 teacher of motion education.

Educational Programs for Special Target Groups

New York Associate Center

FUNDING: $224,349.

LOCATION: 400 First Avenue, 7th floor, New York, NY 10010 (Man); Truman High School (Bx); P.S. 154 (Q); Staten Island Occupational Training Center, Prospect and Harvard Avenues, Staten Island, NY 10301.

EMPHASIS: To improve the education of handicapped children between the ages of 3 and 21 by training professionals, parents, and students through workshops, in-service courses, conferences, publications, and the free loan of multi-media instructional materials and equipment. Conducts an on-the-job training program for students from the occupational training centers.

TARGET: More than 10,000 persons in public, private, and parochial schools.

STAFFING: 26. 12 teacher trainers, 8 paraprofessionals, 2 senior typists, 1 project director, 1 library coordinator, 1 media coordinator, 1 administrative associate.

Outreach Program for Disadvantaged Mentally Retarded Children

FUNDING: $35,112.

LOCATION: P.S. 40, Room 400; all CRMD (Children with Retarded Mental Development) classes in Districts 1 and 2, some in Districts 3 and 4; crisis consultation in Districts 5 and 6 (Man).

EMPHASIS: Helps disadvantaged mentally retarded students and members of their family better utilize community health, recreation, and social services by making appointments, escorting children and parents to the service agencies, and doing follow up. Also offers counselling services and assistance in difficult home situations. After school recreation programs and parent-teacher workshops organized by the administrative staff. Meets many outstanding and unmet needs of this special population.

TARGET: 400-500 disadvantaged retarded children in elementary and junior high schools in Manhattan, their parents, and siblings.

STAFFING: 19. 15 paraprofessionals, 2 teachers, 1 social worker, 1 senior stenographer.

Parent Outreach Program and Staff Development

FUNDING: $19,375.

LOCATION: J.H.S. 47, School for the Deaf, East Annex (Man).

EMPHASIS: Provides training to the professional school staff and families of deaf students in the language learning process and in the use of sign language. Twice a week after-school training sessions for the professional staff, and weekly training sessions for the families.

TARGET: 40 professional staff members and the families of approximately 200 deaf students enrolled in the East Annex of the School for the Deaf.

STAFFING: 9. 2 instructors in manual communication, 2 paraprofessionals, 1 part-time teacher, 1 part-time coordinator, 1 part-time school secretary, 1 research consultant, 1 instructor in language curriculum development.

Pre-Kindergarten Program for Hospitalized Handicapped Children

FUNDING: $70,615.

LOCATION: St. Mary's Hospital, 216th Street and 29th Avenue, Bayside, NY 11360; King's County Hospital "E" Bldg., 515 Clarkson Avenue, Brooklyn, NY 11203.

EMPHASIS: To prepare hospitalized handicapped children of pre-school age for entrance into a regular program for the physically handicapped at Board of Education hospital schools. Development of intellectual skills; exploration of appreciation and attitudes; experiences in social interaction; and organized play activities to improve existing motor skills and to develop new ones. When pupils reach 5 years of age, they are admitted to the kindergarten class maintained by the Board of Education in these hospital schools.

TARGET: 20 children.

STAFFING: 5. 2 teachers, 2 educational assistants, 1 school secretary.

Pre-School Home Training and Community Orientation Program for Children with Delayed Development

FUNDING: $119,000.

LOCATION: Bronx, Queens, and Brooklyn.

EMPHASIS: Family worker and a project social worker visit the home. Involve the mother in the educational process so that she can incorporate the role of the trainer in her everyday activities and provide the child with individualized cognitive needs in preparation for school. Parent workshops; individual counselling for mothers and children; facilitate contact with appropriate clinics and hospitals; educational program and curriculum demonstrations in classroom setting; visitations to classes for parents; and regular trips with project staff for parents and children. Relies heavily on Piaget's and Skinner's theories.

TARGET: Children with delayed development.

STAFFING: 8. 4 family assistants, 1 teacher, 1 school social worker, 1 guidance counsellor, 1 senior stenographer.

Pre-School Program for Emotionally Disturbed, Perceptually Handicapped and Language Impaired Children

FUNDING: $82,726.

LOCATION: P.S. 106, Bellevue Psychiatric Hospital, 30th Street at 1st Avenue, New York, NY 10016.

EMPHASIS: Provides early diagnosis, intervention, and remediation for severely disturbed pre-school children who have language and perceptual impairments. Carefully structured activities, developed in a therapeutic supportive milieu, to help promote social and physical development.

TARGET: 40 youngsters, aged 2-1/2 to 5 years.

STAFFING: 5. 2 classroom teachers, 1 language development specialist, 1 specialist in perceptual development and motor education, and 1 educational assistant.

Pre-School Readiness Program for Handicapped Children

FUNDING: $93,830.

LOCATION: P.S. 198- Medical Affiliation: Dept. of Child Psychiatry, Mount Sinai Medical Center; P.S. 183- Medical affiliation: Dept. of Pediatric Neurology, New York Hospital, Cornell University Medical Center (Man).

EMPHASIS: Provides model early intervention settings for pre-school handicapped children. Emphasizes social, emotional, cognitive, language, and perceptual motor development; also arranges for necessary clinical testing through the affiliated hospitals. Involves the parents of the children in the process.

TARGET: 40 handicapped pre-school children, ages 3-4.9, with deficits in language, cognitive, social, emotional, and perceptual motor development.

STAFFING: 6. 2 teachers, 2 educational assistants, 1 school secretary, and 1 coordinator.

Special Education of the Handicapped

FUNDING: $3,240,000.

STARTED: 1975.

LOCATION: Various institutions for the handicapped, such as Willowbrook, and regular public schools.

EMPHASIS: Basic educational services. Remediation in reading, math. Children with severe handicaps attend regular schools for a full day, the first time such children are attending regular schools.

TARGET: Approximately 7,000-9,000 severely emotionally handicapped children, some living in institutions such as Willowbrook.

STAFFING: Special teachers, nurses, doctors, and therapists.

Teacher Training and Program Development in Motor Education for the Mentally Retarded and Other Handicapped Individuals

FUNDING: $105,247.

LOCATION: P.S. 19, 76, 84, 79, 115, 154, 171, 199, and Multiple Handicapped Center (Man); P.S. 4, 32, 65, 71, 89, 110, (Bx); 84, 91, 105, 110, 199, 225, 244, 251, 327, 396, and Brooklyn School for Special Children (private agency) (Bkn); P.S. 19, 63, 90, 97, 133, 138, 144, 163, 201, 206, and Queens Development Center (Q); P.S. 13, 16, 19 (SI).

EMPHASIS: Trains classroom teachers of the handicapped in motor education techniques; teaches parents motor education techniques so they can assist their children at home; develops curriculum and testing techniques. Provides the handicapped child with the opportunity to participate in motor experiences that will improve and develop perceptual and sensory motor proficiency and improve communications skills.

TARGET: Classroom teachers of the handicapped, both mentally retarded and other handicapped.

STAFFING: 17. 11 resource specialists, 2 master teachers, 1 teacher coordinator, 1 curriculum developer, 1 physical therapist, 1 senior typist.

Young Adult Training and Living Center Through Simulated Work Experience and Development of Habilitation Skills

FUNDING: $403,396.

LOCATION: 3 centers; one each in the Bronx, Brooklyn, and Staten Island.

Educational Programs for Special Target Groups

EMPHASIS: Provides basic educational services for severely retarded young adults. Each trainee placed in an orientation class for evaluation and observation and then placed into the following workshop areas: home economics; sheltered workshop where learn skills and behaviors necessary to work productively and independently; physical education; functional academics for survival—telling time, money usage, acquisition of a signature; long term-orientation with speech therapy, weekly trips and socials, special lunch program, sex education and family living skills, and travel training. The goal is community placement for all program participants.

TARGET: Severely retarded young adults, ages 15-21.

STAFFING: 41. 14 special education teachers, 14 educational assistants, 3 family assistants, and others, including school social worker, school psychologist, 2 speech teachers, 1 resource teacher, 1 senior stenographer, 1 supervisor.

Title VII, Bilingual Programs for the Handicapped

The total funding for these programs is $563,480.

Bilingual Program for Children in BCRMD Classes

FUNDING: $232,860.

LOCATION: P.S. 171 (Man), P.S. 42 (Bx); P.S. 10(Bkn); P.S. 150 (Q).

EMPHASIS: Provides bilingual services for Spanish-speaking children in classes for the mentally retarded. Resource room used. One group that is most limited in English-speaking ability in one bilingual instruction group. Another group less limited in English take part in most of the regular activities of their classes, including ESL instruction. Itinerant teachers in bilingual speech and school and community relations.

STAFFING: 15. 4 bilingual resource teachers, 4 bilingual classroom paraprofessionals, 1 teacher trainer, 1 curriculum specialist, 1 bilingual speech teacher, 1 bilingual teacher in school and community relations, 1 project secretary, 1 school aide.

TARGET: 100 Spanish-speaking children in classes for the mentally retarded.

Bilingual Program for Physically Handicapped Students

FUNDING: $330,620.

LOCATION: District 1: P.S. 97, 134, 188; District 4: J.H.S. 13, P.S. 155, 146; District 7: P.S. 40, 51, 65, 37, I.S. 38, 155, 184; District 12: P.S. 23, 61, 102, 129, 150, 234, I.S. 158, J.H.S. 133; District 13: P.S. 11, 270, 307; District 14: P.S. 16, 17; J.H.S. 126; District 15: P.S. 131, 321; I.S. 88, 293;

EMPHASIS: Designed to benefit non-English-speaking students who are in classes for the physically handicapped. Intended to improve their ability to communicate effectively in Spanish and in English. Provides bilingual supportive services. Intends to create a positive self-image and pride in their ethnic background. Provides orientation and assistance for the classroom teachers and involves non-English-speaking parents and community members in the education of the handicapped.

TARGET: Non-English-speaking handicapped students in the above schools.

STAFFING: 16. 7 teachers, 3 teacher trainers, 3 paraprofessionals, 1 guidance counsellor, 1 teacher coordinator, a senior clerk.

VEA-4B Umbrella for Secondary Handicapped Students

Total amount of funding is $957,765.

City Wide Integration of Handicapped Students In Vocational Training

FUNDING: $197,000.

LOCATION: High schools throughout the city.

EMPHASIS: Vocational training program of integrated services, varying with each facility, depending on space, skilled personnel, and appropriate trade training areas. Part-time after-school shop programs to provide trade training to academic students. Skills training in typing, printing, plumbing, jewelry, dental mechanics, optical mechanics, and office machine repair. Also special driver education program for severely physically handicapped students at three high schools.

TARGET: Handicapped high school students throughout the city.

STAFFING: 1 coordinator, part-time shop teachers, teacher aides, and 1 school secretary.

Continuing Vocational Training for Mentally Retarded Adults

FUNDING: $27,000.

LOCATION: Marcia S. Gewirtz, Bureau for Children with Retarded Mental Development (BCRMD), 65 Court Street, Brooklyn, NY 11201.

EMPHASIS: Provides adult vocational training to clients in obtaining saleable job skills in specified areas and to working clients to upgrade present skills. Child care services provided for clients who would otherwise be unable to attend. Clients served 3 nights a week for 2 hours a session. Services include outside referrals.

TARGET: 200 handicapped adults.

STAFFING: 10. 5 teachers, 2 paraprofessionals, a guidance counsellor, 1 clerk typist, 1 teacher-in-charge.

Cosmetology and Hair Styling for Handicapped Institutionalized Children

FUNDING: $25,000.

LOCATION: P.S. 25 (SI).

EMPHASIS: Provides occupational skills training to 20 institutionalized high school students. Receives support and follow up services through the institution. Provides training in all aspects of cosmetology and hair styling. Utilizes instructional supplies and equipment representative of industry.

TARGET: 20 institutionalized high school students.

STAFFING: 2. 1 principal, 1 teacher.

Division of Special Education and Pupil Personnel Services (DSEPPS), Center for the Development of Special Vocational Education Programs for the Handicapped

FUNDING: $141,000.

LOCATION: High schools throughout the city.

EMPHASIS: Serves all handicapped secondary students and adults needing special vocational education and job placement. Designed to expand the means by which comprehensive special vocational services may be made available to the handicapped. Involvement with business, industry, private agencies, and parent groups. Also provides assistance to existing programs.

TARGET: Handicapped high school students throughout the city.

STAFFING: 2. 1 coordinator, 1 supervisory stenographer.

Distributive Education, Office, and Clerical Skills Training Program for Brain Injured Adolescents

FUNDING: $66,000.

LOCATION: P.S. 751 (Man).

EMPHASIS: Provides brain injured adolescents with occupational training for entry level positions in distributive, clerical, and office occupations. Provides intensive training in office machine operation, duplicating machine operation, typewriting, filing, and distribute sales. Utilizes instructional supplies and equipment representative of actual employment situations.

TARGET: 144 brain injured adolescents.

STAFFING: 6. 3 teachers, 2 educational assistants, 1 supervisor/assistant principal.

Food Preparation Skills for Severely Disturbed Adolescents

FUNDING: $33,765.

LOCATION: P.S. 106, Bellevue Psychiatric Hospital, 30th Street and First Avenue, New York, NY 10016.

EMPHASIS: Designed to provide entry level skills training in food selection, preparation, inventory, packaging, serving, mathematical, and sales skills. Also focuses on the social and behavioral skills required to obtain and hold a job. Practical skill experience in food preparation and management an integral part of the program. Supportive clinical and counselling services provided by Bellevue Psychiatric Hospital; employment opportunities developed by the job developer.

TARGET: 50 emotionally disturbed adolescents.

STAFFING: 2. Principal coordinator and 1 teacher.

Health Occupational Training Program for Brain Injured Students

FUNDING: $44,000.

LOCATION: Francis Lewis High School (Q).

EMPHASIS: Provides entry level skills training in health careers. Receives support services through four Queens hospitals and tries to provide balanced services in career orientation, personal adjustment, skills training, and placement.

TARGET: 75 neurologically impaired and physically handicapped students.

STAFFING: 5 teachers.

Landscape Gardening and Nursery Management for Handicapped Students

FUNDING: $26,000.

LOCATION: P.S. 25 (SI).

EMPHASIS: Provides occupational skills training in plant science, ornamental horticulture, and floriculture with emphasis on nursery and field work. Utilizes representative supplies and equipment and also receives supportive and follow up services from the institution.

TARGET: Handicapped students in the above institution.

STAFFING: 2. 1 principal/coordinator, 1 teacher.

Occupational Skills Training Program for Multiple Handicapped Students

FUNDING: $36,000.

LOCATION: Center for Multiple Handicapped Children, 105 East 106th Street, New York, NY 10029; Center for Multiple Handicapped Children P.S. 187, 61-25 Marathon Parkway, Little Neck, NY 11362.

EMPHASIS: Uses an individualized prescriptive approach to introduce elements of therapy into vocational skills training. Occupational training in production skills, mail room operations, and distributive business and clerical skills. Clinical staff (social workers, guidance counsellors, and psychologists) provide liaison and follow up with job placement agencies and sheltered workshops.

TARGET: 80 students, ages 15-21.

STAFFING: 3. 1 director/supervisor, 1 teacher, 1 educational assistant.

Office and Distributive Education for Severely Disturbed Adolescents

FUNDING: $59,000.

LOCATION: P.S. 106, Bellevue Psychiatric Hospital, 30th Street and First Avenue, New York, NY 10016.

Office Practice Skills Development for Neglected and Dependent Students

FUNDING: $25,000.

LOCATION: P.S. 25 (SI).

EMPHASIS: Provides entry level skills training in typing, bookkeeping, business machines operation, sales, inventory, and clerking. A job developer and teachers provide training in work habits and attitudes. Support services through Bellevue Hospital.

TARGET: 50 emotionally disturbed adolescents.

STAFF: 1 principal-coordinator, 2 teachers, 1 part-time school secretary.

Placement and Referral Center for Handicapped Adults

FUNDING: $157,000.

LOCATION: Bruce Wood, 131 Livingston Street, Room 623, Brooklyn, NY 11201.

EMPHASIS: Vocational counselling, job placement, and vocational orientation. Also provides referral to rehabilitation agencies, training programs, and special schools. A main goal is to establish a central registry of handicapped students who leave school, to maintain regular follow up and placement services. Has a large program with the Youth Service Agency and the Human Resources Administration employment program, providing strong liaison with city personnel and the Mayor's Office for the Handicapped.

TARGET: 1,000 handicapped young adults.

STAFFING: 6. 2 teachers, 2 job developers, 1 educational associate, and 1 coordinator.

Vocational Assessment and Occupational Training for Institutionalized Adolescents

FUNDING: $49,000.

LOCATION: Lt. Joseph P. Kennedy, Jr. Home, 1770 Stillwell Avenue, The Bronx, NY 10469.

EMPHASIS: Provides vocational assessment and skill training in clerical practice, business machine operation, and distributive sales. Also facilitates job placement. Program receives support services through the agency and tries to provide well balanced career orientation, skills training, personal adjustment, and placement service.

TARGET: 140 emotionally disturbed adolescents.

STAFFING: 3. 1 coordinator (agency person), 1¼ teachers, 1 clerk typist.

Vocational Evaluation and Job Placement Program for Hearing Handicapped Adults

FUNDING: $72,000.

LOCATION: Job Placement Program, 421 East 88th Street, New York, NY 10028.

EMPHASIS: Provides training and job placement in industry for young adults. Uses a case work approach in providing job placement, training referrals, career development, job development, and support and follow up services.

TARGET: 100 trained and untrained young adults, unemployed and out of school individuals, and students in schools and programs under the aegis of the Bureau for Hearing Handicapped Children.

STAFFING: 4. 1 supervisor, 1 coordinator/teacher/job developer, 2 job developers.

National Highway Traffic Safety Act

Total amount of funding is $216,717.

Driver Education for Physically Handicapped Students in the Division of Special Education

FUNDING: $39,957.

LOCATION: Charles Evans Hughes High School (Man); Roosevelt High School (Bx).

EMPHASIS: In-car and classroom instruction, tailored to the special needs of the disabled. Specially equipped cars with dual controls and other devices to help compensate for individual disabilities.

TARGET: Physically handicapped students.

STAFFING: 1 teacher.

Driver Education for Young Adults in Special High Schools and Institutions for the Socially Maladjusted in District 75

FUNDING: $176,760.

LOCATION: A mobile unit traveling to schools all over the city.

EMPHASIS: Driver education for socially maladjusted adolescents and young adults with a history of poor scholastic and personal achievement. Opportunity to obtain a driver's education certificate and an employable skill.

TARGET: Socially maladjusted adolescents.

STAFFING: 9. 6 teachers, 1 teacher-in-charge, 1 driver, 1 school secretary.

Federal Health and Nutrition Act, State Food on the Table Act,

DSEPPS Breakfast Program

FUNDING: $323,500.

LOCATION: Elementary and junior high schools and special schools for the handicapped throughout the city.

EMPHASIS: Daily breakfasts, free and at reduced prices.

TARGET: 4,000 students in special education schools and bureau classes (for the handicapped) in regular schools.

STAFFING: 2. 1 coordinator, 1/2 secretary.

AUSPICES: Division of Special Education and Pupil Personnel Services (SEPPS).

Title III Mini-Grants

There were 5, totalling $14,517. They included programs for the handicapped in functional living skills, educational remediation for emotionally disturbed adolescents, parents skills training, training in ornamental horticulture, and the use of a lending library to increase parental involvement in the remediation of children's handicaps.

Contracted-Out, Alternative Schools

There are 25 contracted-out schools:

Educational Programs for Special Target Groups

Manhattan

The Adams School
248 East 31st Street
New York, NY 10018

Kaliski School
127 West 79th Street
New York, NY 10024

Archdioceses of N.Y.
Special Education Program
1011 First Ave., 18 Floor
New York, NY 10022

Lorge School
380 Second Avenue
New York, NY 10010

Avard Learning Center
15 West 65th Street
New York, NY 10023

New York University Reading
Institute
725 Broadway
New York, NY

Churchill School
22 East 95th Street
New York, NY 10028

Reece School
180 East 93rd Street
New York, NY 10029

Henry Street School
40 Montgomery Street
New York, NY 10002

Stephen Gaynor School
22 West 74th Street
New York, NY 10023

United Cerebral Palsy
122 East 23rd St.
New York, NY 10023

Brooklyn

Archway School
274 Garfield Place
Brooklyn, NY 11215

Harlyn School
60 West End Avenue
Brooklyn, NY 11235

Buckingham School
23 Buckingham Road
Brooklyn, NY 11226

Hebrew Institute for the Deaf
2025 67th Street
Brooklyn, NY 11214

Rugby School
196 New York Ave.
Brooklyn, NY 11216

Queens

Alternative Solutions for
Exceptional Children
39-28 41st Avenue
Long Island City, NY 11101

Life Skills Schools
93-30 Queens Blvd.
Rego Park, NY 11374

Inventory of Educational Improvement Efforts

Buckingham School
183-02 Union Turnpike
Flushing, NY 11366

Martin De Porres Schools
29-28 41st Avenue, Room 508
Long Island City, NY 11101

Horizon School
71-64 168th Street
Flushing, NY 11365

Herbert G. Birch School
188-15 McGlaughlin Ave.
Holliswood, NY 11423

Linden School
195-21 Hillside Avenue
Hollis, NY 11423

Lowell School
43-00 171 St.
Flushing, NY 11358

Some of these schools responded to our inquiry. The following information was gleaned from those responses:

Adams School

EMPHASIS: Creates a therapeutic milieu in which every child learns at his own level. Basic academic training. Senior high school career center with work-study, on the job training. Small classes.

TARGET: 64 students, ages 7-14 with average or above IQ but with learning disabilities related to neurological impairment or emotional problems.

Archway School

STARTED: 1968.

EMPHASIS: School for neurologically impaired students with emotional problems. Emphasis on speech therapy and perceptual work on elementary level. Work-study program on high school level. Returns some students to mainstream schools; prepares others for the General Equivalency Diploma; introduces older students into a realistic work environment through a work study program. Individualized instruction and many supportive personnel, e.g., psychologist, guidance counsellor, reading and learning disability specialists, and speech and art therapists.

TARGET: 100 students, K-12.

STAFFING: 12.

Buckingham School

STARTED: 1968.

Educational Programs for Special Target Groups

EMPHASIS: Mainly an academic program for children with emotional problems and learning disabilities. Goal is to return as many students to mainstream education as quickly as possible. Many return after a year or two.

TARGET: 5-15 year-olds.

Churchill School

STARTED: 1972.

EMPHASIS: Program for children with learning disabilities. Special effort to get students back into mainstream public schools in 2 to 3 years. Teach basic academic skills in an open, yet structured environment. Encourage group interaction, parent participation, easy access to teachers, physical activity, and nutritional guidance.

TARGET: 76 students, ages 5-13, non-graded.

STAFFING: 17: 10 teachers, psychologist, sensory motor therapist, director of research, and other administrative staff.

Harlyn School

TARGET: 190 children, emotionally disturbed and neurologically impaired.

Henry Street School

STARTED: 1972.

EMPHASIS: Helps students with severe learning problems. Academic and vocational training. Small classes. Much individual counselling. Career education program in the high school. Students also attend other mainstream and alternative schools to receive instruction not offered in the Henry Street School. Intensive college and post-secondary counselling program. Many supportive services.

TARGET: 100 students, ages 12-21, from low income families and with learning, social, and emotional problems.

STAFFING: 20.

Lorge School

STARTED: 1961.

EMPHASIS: Provides an academic program for children with learning disabilities (emotional, organic, or neurological) who are not mentally retarded. Offers full academic and pre-vocational program in a therapeutic environment. Structured for the student who finds it difficult to achieve through traditional educational methods. Art, shop, and physical education, in addition to academic program. Remedial reading. Lower, middle, and upper schools. Special pre-vocational program includes electrical repair, food trades, woodworking, beauty culture, and office skills.

TARGET: 120 middle- and upper-school students, 80 in lower school. Ungraded classes. 8 students in each class.

Rugby School

STARTED: 1951.

EMPHASIS: Provides three major areas of assistance: (1) an intensive academic program; (2) individualized counselling program; and (3) the maintenance of a structured environment. Social and recreational activities combined with academic work. Pre-vocational workshops for students who have reached a plateau academically.

TARGET: 150 students, ages 5-17, who have had difficulty making social and academic adjustments at home and school. These children may be retarded, have perceptual problems, emotional disturbance, brain injury, or seizure disorders. Mainly lower IQ students.

Chapter 2

Inventory of General Purpose Educational Programs

The innovative programs reviewed thus far have been geared, by and large, to special target groups—the handicapped, the poor, pre-schoolers, dropouts, those with drug problems, and so on. There are many other efforts at improvement, however, that are of a more general nature. While they may also reach some special groups, they constitute attempts to develop new programs that are not pinpointed to the same degree to such groups. Programs relating to basic skills in reading and math and those dealing with the arts and environmental education are the kind that are included here. They are generated by units within the school system that deal with curriculum and instruction.

A key strategy of the Board of Education in this regard was Chancellor Scribner's 1970 decision to set up a mechanism for locating, supporting, institutionalizing, and diffusing innovative educational programs. It was called the *Learning Cooperative* and was set up inside the system, but considered not quite of it. It was concerned exclusively with innovation but had no authority, existing only in an advisory capacity vis-a-vis schools and districts. It provided, however, an important point of contact (linkage) between the schools and outside funding and resource agencies such as foundations, universities, and business.

One of the main things the Learning Cooperative did

was to establish a network of what were called "Beacon Light" schools, all of which met the criteria established for what constituted "innovative" and "successful" schools. The Cooperative provided increased outside resources for these schools, linked them to one another, became an advocate for many promising programs there and elsewhere in the system, and was the system's internal catalyst and advocate for educational innovation, particularly in elementary and junior high schools. Several of the contributing foundations and other private sector sources expressed disappointment at what they regarded as the limited results or impact of all this activity; but we will leave for another report the complex interpretations related to results. Few educational reform strategies have had significant impacts, and this may have been no exception.

The Learning Cooperative became part of something bigger in 1973, when an administrative reorganization of school headquarters established a consolidated Division of Educational Planning and Support into which it was integrated. In addition to the Learning Cooperative, that Division included all the main curriculum bureaus and other central headquarters units responsible for particular educational programs, e.g., the Offices of Career Education and Bilingual Education. If one of the Learning Cooperative's problems in the past had been its "outsider" status—having no line authority over schools that it wanted to help innovate—that problem was compounded in the larger Division of Educational Planning and Support, where the same staff, advisory capacity in relation to schools and districts existed. Recently that Division has been reorganized once more, this time into two sets of centers—one for developing new educational programs and the other for assisting in their implementation.

The main programs to be reviewed here are encompassed in both centers, particularly the first, called the Center for Educational Development. They include: (1) the Beacon Light schools; (2) an arts-in-general education program and others, outside the school system in the arts, that collaborate with the Learning Cooperative but are important enough in their own right to merit separate consideration; (3) miscellaneous programs including a collaborative planning project with the New York Urban Coalition, an individually guided instruction (IGI) program, and one on environmental education. We will also include (4) Title III programs, whose funds are earmarked exclusively for innovations.

Beacon Light Schools

This designation constitutes more of a general strategy than a program. It involves selecting out those schools in the system that meet the types of criteria mentioned below and attempting to generate a "critical mass" of such schools that may begin to develop and diffuse innovative programs throughout the system. These schools thus constitute a Beacon Light School network, each member of which must be nominated either by the community superintendent or, if it is a high school, by the Executive Director of the High School Division. The criteria include, among others: (a) a diversity of programs and considerable choice among them for students; (b) extensive drawing on outside resources for staff and student development; (c) an open and participative school decision process, involving students and parents as well as educators; and (d) a staff who are open to new ideas and see themselves as learners, not just as authorities and experts. Many of these schools have an arts program, and many have been designated by headquarters as optional, unzoned schools, the latter description going to those model schools that may have space for students outside the immediate area or district.

STARTED: 1971, shortly after the Learning Cooperative got underway.

FUNDING: Tax levy, plus outside funds through the Learning Cooperative.

LOCATION: Now constitutes a network of 90 schools in 31 districts: 58 elementary schools, 25 junior high or intermediate schools, 5 mainstream high schools, and 2 alternative high schools.

148   Inventory of Educational Improvement Efforts

EMPHASIS: To support innovative educational programs in designated schools and help institutionalize and diffuse them throughout the system. This involves creating linkages to various funding and educational support agencies, including school headquarters.

TARGET: Students, staff, and parents in these schools, and eventually to many more schools and their constituencies.

INFORMATION: Various materials prepared by the Learning Cooperative, including *The Beacon Light Notebook,* compiled and edited by Donna Brorby, 1972-74 Urban Fellow, July 1974; and a list of Beacon Light Network Schools, November 25, 1975.

Arts-in-General Education

STARTED: September, 1975.

FUNDING: Much outside, private support: John D. Rockefeller, 3rd Fund, $50,000; ESAA Special Arts Grant, $30,000; Exxon, $9,000; New York Foundation for the Arts, $84,000; National Endowment for the Arts, $16,000; Central Midwestern Regional Educational Laboratory, $40,000, and many others.

LOCATION: In 13 districts and 32 schools: District 1–P.S. 19 and J.H.S. 56; District 2–P.S. 41, 198. J.H.S. 104, 167, Clinton program; District 3–P.S. 75, I.S. 44; District 4–P.S. 96, 108, 50 (East Harlem Performing Arts), 121; District 6–P.S. 98, 187, 189, J.H.S. 52; District 8–P.S. 152, J.H.S. 125; District 10–P.S. 9, 115; District 12–P.S. 61; District 21–J.H.S. 239; District 22–P.S. 152, 312; District 25–J.H.S. 218; District 28–P.S. 48; District 31–J.H.S. 2. Also in LaGuardia High School of Music and Art, J. F. Kennedy High School, High School of Fashion Industries, High School of Art and Design, and Erasmus High School.

EMPHASIS: To integrate the arts into all learning in the school. Involves having artists in residence, students visiting art and cultural centers. Funds not used for salaries but mainly for consultants, documentation, evaluation, and the like.

TARGET: Students in those schools.

STAFFING: None, except program director and artists in the schools.

INFORMATION: Reports by the Project Manager, Carol Fineberg. Also, her article, "New York City: An Urban Arts in Education Program," *Principal,* Vol. 55, Number 3, January/February 1976.

G.A.M.E., Inc. (Growth Through Art and Museum Experience, Inc.)

STARTED: 1972.

FUNDING: Support from many city, state, federal, and private funding agencies. These agencies include: the Board of Education through District 3 and the Learning Cooperative, New York State Council on the Arts, National Endowment, Rockefeller Brothers Fund ($76,500), New York Community Trust, Edward Noble Foundation, Helena Rubinstein, Museum Collaborative, and others.

LOCATION: 260 West 86th Street., New York, NY 10024; District 3 - P.S. 9, 75, 84, and 166; also in museums.

EMPHASIS: This is a community-based art education program, organized in collaboration with 4 public schools in District 3. It trains children and teachers in basic art activities as they relate to the acquisition of primary skills in the elementary grades, including reading, writing, and arithmetic. Work with children and teachers in weaving, book making, horticultural, natural science, clay, filmmaking, photography, and woodworking at its community resource center. Classroom teacher liaison person works within the schools extending these projects, and museum instructors relate students to exhibits and collections. An after-school art and craft program for children and adults. Also, special park and community events.

TARGET: Students and teachers in these schools and adults in the community.

INFORMATION: From the program.

Miscellaneous Programs

In addition to the 3 programs described below, other projects under the jurisdiction of the Learning Cooperative, now the Center for School Development, include: Open Education Advisory Program, Follow Through, Principals As Leaders, and Early Childhood Integration Centers, all described elsewhere in the inventory.

Environmental Education

STARTED: 1974.

FUNDING: Through the Learning Cooperative.

LOCATION: At the Gateway National Park's Environmental Study Center, Floyd Bennett Field, Brooklyn; the New York Aquarium, Coney Island; South Street Seaport, Manhattan; and other locations around the city.

EMPHASIS: Exploring the city's marine environment; experiences in camping and outdoor recreation; training in the use of community resources. Special teacher training workshops and meetings.

TARGET: Those students and teachers interested in environmental activity.

INFORMATION: Center for School Development.

Individually Guided Instruction

STARTED: A few years ago.

FUNDING: National Institute of Education money.

LOCATION: 7 schools in Districts 2, 9, and 15.

EMPHASIS: This program was adopted as part of New York State's Redesign Program. Meetings are held among schools, training is provided for the teachers, and general liaison with the state is carried out.

New York Urban Coalition Program

STARTED: 1975.

FUNDING: $60,485 from the Urban Coalition.

LOCATION: 6 to 8 schools in Districts 27 and 32. Recently another 6 to 8 schools in Districts 19 and 30 added.

EMPHASIS: Four demonstration modules, each consisting of a junior high school and its feeder schools have been formed. Through cooperative efforts of the Urban Coalition, the Center for School Development, and the community school districts involved, management plans are being developed to improve the teaching learning process, and to focus existing resources on the problems of the schools. Citywide, district-wide, and school-community meetings are held continuously to insure that everyone involved can participate fully in the process.

Title III Programs

There are three categories of Title III programs, all of them funded under the Elementary and Secondary Education Act and earmarked exclusively for innovations. They are mini-grants, of which there are 108 throughout the system and extend to non-public schools as well, none of them

General Innovative Educational Programs 151

exceeding $3,000; Section 306 grants through New York State; and federally funded Title III.

Mini-Grants

FUNDING: $284,000 for 1975-76.

LOCATION: In schools in all 32 Community School Districts, in high schools, and programs for the handicapped, and in non-public schools.

EMPHASIS: Stimulate creative solutions to educational problems. Support the field testing of what look like promising ideas.

AUSPICES: State Education Department.

Section 306 (State)

FUNDING: $367,928.

Title III (Federal)

FUNDING: $393,674.

District 3

STARTED: 1975.

FUNDING: $82,567.

LOCATION: P.S. 165

EMPHASIS: Bilingual program. Bilingual teacher classroom lessons are video-taped; lessons further developed after regular school hours by classroom teachers under the guidance of consultants with expertise in bilingual education.

STAFFING: 23. 17 bilingual teachers, 4 consultants, 1 project director, and 1 senior stenographer.

District 7

STARTED: 1975.

FUNDING: $65,000.

LOCATION: I.S. 139 (Bx); St. Jeromes Parochial School.

TARGET: 70 8th grade students.

EMPHASIS: To foster greater student understanding of government. Students investigate local neighborhood problems and seek solutions compatible with democratic processes. Through such problem-solving experiences, they learn more about government.

STAFFING: 7. Also consultants.

District 18

STARTED: 1975.

FUNDING: $109,560.

EMPHASIS: Identifies neglected and abused children. Diagnosis and referral made to the Bureau of Child Welfare and Juvenile Family Court. Parents attend organized workshops. Children referred to remediation and re-entry classes. Stress placed on positive social and emotional development in the children.

District 21

STARTED: 1975.

LOCATION: Mark Twain School for the Gifted and Talented

EMPHASIS: An exemplary junior high school created for gifted and talented students. Desegregated student population. Title III funds used to develop innovative, interdisciplinary curricula based on student interests as well as Board of Education courses of study. Consultants and representatives of major ethnic groups in the community serve as visiting faculty.

TARGET: 560 7th graders identified as gifted and talented.

STAFFING: 1 teacher, 2 school secretaries, curriculum consultants.

District 23, Education for Survival

STARTED: 1975.

FUNDING: $75,000.

LOCATION: J.H.S. 271 (Bkn).

EMPHASIS: A program designed to enhance student achievement by enriching the curriculum with experiences relevant to the students. Parental involvement increased by conducting workshops for parents at which prominent business leaders from the community will speak.

TARGET: 411 students. 360 from J.H.S. 271 and 81 from Our Lady of Loretto.

STAFFING: 4.

District 31, Development of Math Activity Prescriptions for Classroom Teachers

STARTED: 1974.

FUNDING: $79,560.

EMPHASIS: Math prescriptions were developed and field tested in 1974-75. Emphasis for 1975-76 on disseminating the program by providing teacher training to the adopters of it. Mailings, displays, conferences, press releases.

TARGET: Math teachers.

STAFFING: 3. 2 teacher trainers and 1 clerk.

Multi-Sensory Approach to Bilingual Pre-Algebra

STARTED: 1975.

FUNDING: $18,723.

LOCATION: George Washington High School (Man).

EMPHASIS: Developing workbooks for Spanish-speaking students to prepare for elementary algebra.

TARGET: Roughly 150 students in 5 bilingual classes.

STAFFING: 4.

Chapter **3**

Inventory of Administrative and Staffing Inovations

Teacher Training

There has been increasing interest over the past decade in improving the training of teachers for service in inner city schools. This relates directly to the changed racial and ethnic composition of those schools and to the need for reaching new minority students. But it extends well beyond that to some basic questions regarding the importance of more field-based training and more performance-based assessments of teaching. Several efforts have been made over this period to improve pre- and in-service training for teachers, some of them supported by federally funded programs. Most of those programs are encompassed by the Education Professions Development Act of 1976 and include: (1) Teacher Corps, to attract and train qualified teachers for service in poverty area schools and to involve colleges and universities as well as community organizations in this process; (2) Triple T, a program no longer in existence, which also involved new approaches to teacher training involving college, public school, and community people as co-participants; (3) Urban-Rural School Development Program, with a very similar focus; and (4) Career Opportunities, providing paraprofessionals with higher education and teaching prospects. Private sector teacher centers are also described.

The common themes that run through all these programs are the importance of establishing closer linkages between colleges, inner-city schools, and parent and community organizations and of improving the skills of teachers in relating to minority students. Roughly $15 million of federal money has come into New York City since 1967 for teacher training under these programs.

In addition, several teacher centers have been established in New York City in recent years, most of them funded by the private sector, e.g., foundations and corporations, and run under private auspices. Several started with an explicitly open education philosophy and were largely offshoots from programs developed in this mode by Dr. Lillian Weber of CCNY, a leading figure in the open education movement. Over time, however, each center has tended to take on its own particular style, and many have become neutral with respect to open vs. more traditional and structured classroom approaches. Their staffs have taken the view that classroom effectiveness is possible in any of several modes.

The main emphasis in these teacher centers is to improve the capacity of teachers for effective problem-solving in the classroom; to enrich their repertoires of new curriculum and instructional materials that have been developed nationally; but, at the same time, to de-emphasize pre-packaged products or techniques for any given classroom situation. Much of the emphasis now is on in-service rather than pre-service training, mainly because the schools are not hiring many new teachers. There is often a strong emphasis as well on experiential learning approaches that involve working with teachers in actual school situations, rather than expounding on techniques and principles in the abstract.

Another more recent development has been to help teachers by working with the school as a totality, recognizing that for teachers to be effective they need much backup and support from all other participants in the school, particularly the principal and supervisory staff. This approach involves convening the principal, students, parents, community groups, and even higher level administrators, e.g., the community superintendent. Such an emphasis on school-based planning to include all the main constituencies has become the main focus of several recent programs (see chapter 5).

We will review first the federally funded programs, providing rough summary data, where possible, on those no longer in existence, but concentrating mainly on those in operation in 1975-76. Then we will describe the various private teacher centers.

Teacher Corps

Established by Congress in 1965, the Teacher Corps is a nationwide effort to provide children from low income families better educational opportunities and to improve the quality of teacher education programs for both inexperienced teacher-interns and certified teachers. It offers school districts in low income areas, their communities, and nearby universities the chance to work together, plan, and operate innovative programs for better training and utilization of teachers. It is specifically designed to (1) attract to low-income areas and train inexperienced teacher interns; (2) attract community volunteers to serve as part-time tutors or full-time instructional assistants; (3) attract and train educational personnel to provide relevant remedial educational training for juvenile delinquents, youthful offenders, and adult criminal offenders; and (4) support demonstration projects for retraining experienced teachers and teacher aides.

There have been several waves of Teacher Corps programs in New York City, each involving various colleges working in collaboration with local schools and districts. Since 1970, roughly $4 million has come into the city for Teacher Corps programs that have been concentrated in Districts 1, 3, 4, 5, and 6 in Manhattan and 10 and 12 in the Bronx. Fordham has been perhaps the most active university in these programs, through its School of Education, with

Administrative and Staffing Innovations 157

Bank Street College of Education and City College of New York also having an extensive involvement. Since 1973, there has also been an important Bilingual Teacher Corps program that trains prospective bilingual teachers under the joint auspices of the Office of Bilingual Education at school headquarters and City College of New York. That program alone has had close to $800,000 in funding and has operated in Districts 1, 4, 6, and 12.

The Teacher Corps programs for the 1975-76 school year include: (1) Bank Street School of Education, working with P.S. 179 in District 3; (b) Teachers College, Columbia University, working with P.S. 144, also in District 3; (c) Fordham University, School of Education, working with I.S. 137 in District 10 in the Bronx; and (d) Office of Bilingual Education, Teacher Corps, at school headquarters, working with CCNY and several schools in the districts mentioned above.

Bank Street College of Education

STARTED: 1973.

FUNDING: Roughly $350,000: $265,000 to Bank Street; the rest to the school.

LOCATION: P.S. 179 and Bank Street.

EMPHASIS: In-service training for teachers in the school; help school develop new educational programs; provide graduate course credits for teachers; development of school-based teams, with a master teacher as the leader; work with all school constituencies; develop within the school a capacity for its own renewal, with Bank Street and its Teacher Corps staff as a resource.

TARGET: Teachers within the school, though the entire school and its active constituencies are also the target.

STAFFING: 4 Bank Street staff, but many within the school as well.

AUSPICES: A consortium of Bank Street and the school, with the Teacher Corps director from Bank Street running it, in collaboration with a policy committee composed of all constituent groups.

CHANGES: Bank Street shifted from 3 schools to 1; from pre-service to in-service; also established more school- and community-based leadership;

understanding the cultures of the school and its various constituencies; and act more as a resource rather than as an expert and authority.

INFORMATION: Pamphlets from program.

Teachers College, Columbia University

STARTED: July 1974.

FUNDING: $200,000 (1975-76).

LOCATION: P.S. 144 in District 3, and Teachers College.

EMPHASIS: To provide a field-based, competency-based teacher education program for a group of 10 Teacher Corps internes; to promote community involvement in education; to develop new educational programs; and to retrain in-service teachers. Have worked with 90% of the school staff; improve teachers' management techniques for classroom.

TARGET: Experienced teachers within the school work intensively with 35 of them; also with students.

STAFFING: 5 full-time, 6 part-time. Teacher Corps director, graduate student assistant, TC instructor, community coordinator, 2 team leaders.

CHANGES: From pre-service to in-service. Had a program in the 9th cycle (1974) that focused on student internes working with the school and community organizations. Then, in 10th cycle, shifted to in-service training of experienced teachers.

Fordham University, School of Education

STARTED: Previous Teacher Corps grants in 1971 and 1973; later project started in July 1975 and funded through June 1977.

FUNDING: $222,205 to Fordham University; $123,905 to District 10.

LOCATION: In District 10 in the Bronx, mainly in the Angelo Patri School, reportedly one of the only open education intermediate schools in New York City, with a capacity of 1,800 children.

EMPHASIS: Provides a field-based pre- and in-service program for the training of teachers, paraprofessionals, teacher aides, interns and supervisors so they may more effectively respond to the special needs of the urban child; includes employment for some former Teacher Corps interns in the district alternative school; "learning managers" to assist in the training program; an emphasis on bilingual and multicultural programs; close collaboration between university faculty, teachers, teacher aides, and these "learning managers" from past Teacher Corps cycles. Individualized learning programs for students; the development of competency-based techniques for training and evaluating teachers; a strong open education format; and equally strong parent, community, and union involvement.

TARGET: Students, interns, in-service teachers, and Fordham University faculty.

STAFFING: 37 people, including Fordham staff, teachers, teacher aides and paraprofessionals; learning managers, an advisory council and school supervisors and administrators.

AUSPICES: Board of Education and Fordham.

CHANGES: Past Teacher Corps programs were in pre-service training. This one is for in-service training.

INFORMATION: From the program.

Office of Bilingual Education, CCNY

STARTED: 1973.

FUNDING: $179,000.

LOCATION: Office of Bilingual Education, Bilingual Teacher Corps, 66 Court Street, Brooklyn, NY 11201, and P.S. 192 (Man).

EMPHASIS: In-service training for all teachers in that school. Also pre-service training for Master's degree candidates in bilingual education at CCNY, School of Education. Community-oriented program, with high school equivalency programs for adults in Spanish and English. Educational programs for public school students involve team teaching, individualized, diagnostic services, small group tutoring, and courses for the school's multi-cultural population.

TARGET: All the teachers and students in that school and several Master's degree candidates at CCNY.

STAFFING: 4 at the Office of Bilingual Education; 2 at CCNY, with some others on split lines.

CHANGES: Used to be in four districts and train undergraduates. Now in one and just trains graduate students and teachers in that school.

INFORMATION: From the Bilingual Teacher Corps office.

Triple T (Training of Teacher Trainers)

This federally-funded program ran from 1969-1973 and constituted an attempt to transform the training both of teachers and of teacher trainers, e.g., professors of education. It was based on the following kinds of diagnosis of what was wrong: Liberal arts offerings in universities were divorced from teacher education courses in pre-service teacher training, reflecting a general professional estrangement of these two faculties and making it difficult to transfer what is learned in college to the classroom experience in public schools. In addition, college training has failed to prepare teachers to adapt their approaches to the culture, traditions, and personalities of inner-city students, particularly to individualize their approaches to instruction. Finally, university faculty—both in the liberal arts and schools of education—had failed to assume much responsibility for in-service training, and in both pre- and in-service training had evidenced too little familiarity with people and conditions in inner-city neighborhoods and schools.

The Triple T concept involved the restructuring of teacher education, based on the above analysis. Unlike similar past efforts that emphasized the attitudes and skills of teachers only, Triple T focused on enlisting the active partnership of liberal arts faculty, education faculty, parents, community persons, students, teachers, and public school and college administrators. All these participants were involved on a parity basis in developing new models of teacher education. The program thus involved the training of teacher trainers, hence the term Triple T. It essentially involved restructuring teacher education, based on this parity principle.

The program took different forms in different universities. One of the biggest efforts, again, was at Fordham, which had an extensive program with District 3 on the Upper West Side of Manhattan during this period, with an estimated $1 million in funding. But Hunter, CCNY, Brooklyn, Lehman, and Richmond Colleges had extensive programs as well, working at schools near their campuses. Though the funding ran out in 1973, the program did have some important spill-over effects. Several of the colleges have incorporated some of the components of Triple T into their teacher training, and the Fordham program was directly responsible for the opening of a learning center at P.S. 163 in District 3, in which Fordham still has some involvement.

Urban-Rural School Development, District 12

This national program involves the development of local school and community councils that create their own projects and are responsible for their implementation. They involve teacher training and various educational programs in the school. The local council has a team manager who is responsible for the day-to-day administration of projects and serves as liaison with the Office of Education, state and local administrators, and project contractors and subcontractors. The New York City-based program has been in District 12 in the Bronx. It has received $1,265,000 since the program began in 1971.

STARTED: 1971.

FUNDING: $220,000 in 1975-76.

LOCATION: 3 schools in District 12: C.S. 54 (K-6), C.S. 134 (K-6) and J.H.S. 136 (Bx).

EMPHASIS: To make teacher training responsive to the needs of the school, the staff, and the community; to develop decision making capabilities in school and community personnel; to assess the educational needs of the school and community; and to establish a sense of accountability within the school for key decisions and for its performance. Course work at Fordham, degree program.

TARGET: Staff and students within the three schools. 2,220 students in all.

STAFFING: 6 administrators, 6 teachers, 9 paraprofessionals, 18 parents, and students and community residents.

CHANGES: Decline in student body by over 1,000, due to fires that have decimated the area.

INFORMATION: From the program.

Career Opportunities Program

The main purpose of this program, which began in 1970 and brought in $10 million over the next five years, is to attract low income people to careers in schools serving a similar clientele, thereby improving education and developing jobs and careers. It was one of several paraprofessional programs in the New York City schools and existed in the three Model City districts of the South Bronx, Harlem-East Harlem, and central Brooklyn. The participants earned credits each year toward a Bachelor's Degree in education and were required to live and/or work in public schools in those communities. The program was directed by the city Office of Personnel, and each community had a council whose members advised it and screened applications.

STARTED: 1970.

FUNDING: $10 million, 1970-75.

LOCATION: Office of Personnel, 39 Park Row, New York, NY 10038

This is the central office. Also in the three Model Cities communities mentioned above.

EMPHASIS: As indicated above. Provided 30 credit hours of instruction a year, allowing participants to become qualified teachers in 4 years. The participating colleges included College of Mount St. Vincent, Fordham (both Bronx and Lincoln Center campuses), Lehman College, Bronx Community College, Marymount Manhattan College, University of Massachusetts, and Bank Street.

TARGET: 800 adults: 60% black, 35% Spanish (mainly Puerto Rican from East Harlem), and 5% white. 600 women. 227 Vietnam veterans. Veterans received tuition, stipends, and G.I. Bill benefits, and 35 were financially assisted in graduate studies leading to degrees at Bank Street.

INFORMATION: Office of Personnel. Also George R. Kaplan, *From Aide to Teacher: The Story of The Career Opportunities Program*, New Careers Training Laboratory, 1975.

Private Sector Teacher Centers

City College Advisory Service to Open Corridors and the Workshop Center for Open Education

Administrative and Staffing Innovations 163

A major new educational program, both in New York City and nationally, has been the development of open education, described in chapter 1 (see pages 84-7) and due largely to the leadership of Professor Lillian Weber, City College of New York. The first open corridor, as the approach was first called, started in 1967, and as it expanded, the need for support services for teachers did as well. In 1970, with the help of Ford Foundation funds, Weber set up the City College Advisory Service to Open Corridors to train advisors who would serve as guides, mentors, counsellors, and aides to open corridor teachers. By the spring of 1972, so many teachers, principals, and parents were involved that another kind of supportive service was needed. Teachers needed a place to continue their development. The special requirements for work in open education culminated in the creation of the Workshop Center in the fall of 1972, providing the kind of format that fit the re-training needs of teachers.

City College Advisory Service

STARTED: 1970.

FUNDING: Ford Foundation, National Institute of Education, Learning Cooperative of the Board of Education, CCNY, and community school districts. Around $1 million.

LOCATION: City College, Convent Avenue and 140th Street, 6 Shepard Hall, New York, NY 10031.

EMPHASIS: Provides support services for teachers who are working to make their classrooms more "open," by training and assigning advisors as counsellors, guides, mentors, and aides. Provides on-site assistance to more than 200 teachers, working alongside them in the classroom and meeting with them after school hours. The college itself provides a Master's program to support the further development of teachers who have reorganized their classrooms, including as well as Summer Institute for Open Education.

TARGET: Teachers and other staff involved in open education programs in New York City schools. Has reached up to 5,000 teachers and other participants in its programs.

STAFFING: 7 full-time, 2 part-time.

Community Resources Institute, Brooklyn College

STARTED: 1969.

FUNDING: Foundations, several federal agencies, Brooklyn College, School of Continuing Studies, Ford Foundation grant of $417,348 for early years, New World Foundation.

164   Inventory of Educational Improvement Efforts

LOCATION: Community Resources Institute, Brooklyn College, 96 Schermerhorn Street, Brooklyn, NY 11201.

EMPHASIS: Provides in-service training for teachers, including the development of curriculum and other educational program materials. Works with teachers, parents, paraprofessionals, and administrators in schools across the city, concentrating in Districts 7, 10, and 12 in the Bronx.

TARGET: Mainly teachers, but other school constituencies as well.

STAFFING: Varies between 3 and 10, depending on funding, needs of the program being served, and the ability of the various groups served to in turn serve others requesting assistance.

AUSPICES: Attached to Brooklyn College, downtown Brooklyn extension.

CHANGES: Puts more emphasis now on teachers' own assessments of their work and on their developing strategies to achieve self-defined goals. This contrasts with earlier emphasis on material or curriculum-oriented workshops.

INFORMATION: Materials available on various curricular topics, but none now describing the program.

Learning Center, P.S. 163, District 3

STARTED: 1973, as a direct result of Fordham's Triple T and Teacher Corps programs.

FUNDING: $107,770: 45% from District 3; 14.2% from HEW (Teacher Corps grant through Fordham); 12.2% by Fordham; and 4.6% by Morgan Guaranty ($5,000). Chase Manhattan Bank also gave $5,000.

EMPHASIS: After doing a survey of teachers in District 3 and of Fordham faculty to ascertain their needs, concerns, and interests, the Center's staff developed workshops for full-time and apprentice teachers, paraprofessionals, parents, and Fordham faculty. Workshops are generally after-school hours and led by professionals from teacher training institutions. Center staff are available during the day for individual consultation, impromptu or planned workshops, and demonstration of curriculum materials. Workshops in math and science; clinics on reading diagnoses and prescription. The Center has stimulated new ideas among the more conservative teachers.

LOCATION: P.S. 163

TARGET: More than 1,500 teachers and parents from all 23 schools in the district attended workshops or visited the Center during its first year.

STAFFING: 2 teachers.

INFORMATION: Brochures from the Learning Center.

Open Education Advisory Program

STARTED: 1973.

FUNDING: $325,000 from the Rockefeller Foundation over 3-year period, plus some city tax levy money.

LOCATION: In 24 schools in Districts 2, 3, 4, 6, 11, and 22.

EMPHASIS: Provides for the support of open education programs in the public schools. Advisory services provided by the leading developers of open education techniques from CCNY, Fordham, Queens College, and the Creative Teaching Workshop.

Workshop for Open Education

STARTED: 1972.

FUNDING: Close to $200,000 in 1975-76; from Rockefeller Brothers Fund ($45,000); National Institute of Education ($71,198); District 3 ($40,000); the Learning Cooperative ($18,000); City College ($11,500).

LOCATION: Same as City College Advisory Service above. Both support teachers in their schools. District 3—P.S. 75, 84, 87, 166, 163, 144, 145, 9; District 2—P.S. 3, 40, 41, 190, 158, 26.

EMPHASIS: Supports, through workshops, seminars, conferences, and consultations, the professional growth of school people who are making changes in the learning environments of elementary school students.

TARGET: 5,000 people a year.

STAFFING: 3 full-time; 2 part-time.

CHANGES: Outside funding has decreased for both programs, while school and district funding has increased. More emphasis on training teacher trainers in the open corridor schools and thereby institutionalize a self-sustaining process.

INFORMATION: Extensive materials available from the program.

Creative Teaching Workshop, Teachers' Program

STARTED: January 1969.

FUNDING: Total funding has been roughly $1 million. For most recent years: $143,700 (1973); $120,737 (1974); $161,195 (1975); and $199,724 (1976). Carnegie Corporation has given close to $400,000 overall; Exxon $90,000; $25,000 from Rockefeller Brothers Fund; $5,000 from Center for School Development through the Board of Education; Arca about $71,000; and other sources.

LOCATION: Office: 115 Spring Street, New York, NY 10012. Has worked in many schools and districts throughout the city. Particular concentration in District 22 (P.S. 152, 139, 197); District 17 (P.S. 397); District 19 (P.S. 243); and District 4 (P.S. 50, 206, 7). Also works with the Board of Education at the Center for School Development.

EMPHASIS: To help teachers, supervisors, and other school participants to become more effective problem solvers. Provides in-service training for teachers, largely on the school site itself, by helping to generate there a school-based planning process that involves all the main constituencies—principal, teachers, students, parents, and community organizations. Uses experience-based learning and management-by-objectives techniques. Does not provide any "products" or "expert" advice on education programs. Views the school and its participant constituencies as a totality and attempts to treat it in that perspective: (1) advisory work with teachers and principals; (2) a principals' leadership study workshop that meets weekly; and (3) in-service workshops at CTW offices and in schools.

TARGET: Teachers, principals, students, parents, and other involved participants in schools. Teachers and principals are the main targets.

STAFFING: From 5-12, depending on funding.

AUSPICES: Private, independent, though with many collaborative relations with individual schools, other teacher centers, other private sector organizations, and school headquarters. Participated, for example, in Open Education Advisory Commission, with Dr. Lillian Weber, Community Resources, Inc., and other teacher center directors.

CHANGES: Moved away from providing curriculum and instruction materials at the CTW headquarters where teachers could visit to on-site training in problem-solving. Also changed from working mainly with teachers to working with principals also and with the entire schools. Emphasize more and more developing local leadership and problem-solving capability.

INFORMATION: From program. Also being evaluated by Center for New Schools, Chicago.

Supervisor Training

Many educators and school critics have begun to focus in recent years on the principal as a key factor in determining the degree of "success" and "effectiveness" of schools. Comparisons are made, for example, of ghetto schools that achieve markedly different results in reading and other achievement test scores, even though they serve the same types of students. The conclusion is often reached that the principal made the difference—, his or her educational leadership (a capacity to recruit, motivate, retain, and develop teachers), their management and political skills, their commitment to improving academic performance and well-being of minority students, and the like. Consider the following:

> The principal is probably the most important actor in making the school work.—William W. Wayson, *The National Elementary Principal,* April 1972
>
> ... the leadership style, the educational know-how, and the supervisory organizations that principals and their assistants develop continue to be the most potent forces in determining school excellence.—J. Lloyd Trump, *Where Will They Find It?*, National Association of Secondary School Principals Monograph, 1972
>
> ... any proposal for change that intends to alter the quality of life in the school depends primarily on the principal.—Seymour B. Sarason, *The Culture of The School and The Problem of Change,* 1971

The judgements made about principals are often quite clinical, and there is no well-established body of theory and research that permits a more precise delineation of traits and behaviors associated with school effectiveness. Educational researchers are now just beginning to develop a methodology for exploring this question, involving "profiles" of effective and ineffective principals. Needless to say, such research constitutes a big threat to many educators who have to be continually reassured that the results will be used for training and development only and not in a punitive way.

Virtually all the federally funded programs under the Education Professions Development Act (EPDA) referred to in the previous section concentrated on teachers and omitted principals from much serious consideration. Now that there is more awareness of the critical role that principals play in the schools and of the tremendous need for better training, perhaps federal programs will be developed in the future that reflect that. In the meantime, the amount of money that has gone into principals' training is miniscule in comparison with the more than $15 million that New York City has received from the federal government over the years for teacher training. The programs that do exist, however, are important and deserve to be covered in an inventory such as this.

Several such programs have been developed in recent years, and they tend to converge around a few common themes, including: (1) *the need for principals to learn how to effectively delegate many administrative functions,* so that they can spend much more time on pedagogical matters (curriculum, instruction, teacher recruitment, support, and upgrading) as educational leaders; (2) the need for principals to become more effective at *planning and organizational development*—to be able to look at their schools and their outside relationships (community, district headquarters) as a totality, to diagnose problems, and move in a participative way with all its main constituencies toward better problem solving; and (3) *the need for more minority principals* who understand the culture and socio-economic circumstances of minority students, who relate well to them, and who may constitute important role models for many of them, as well as for the wider community.

We are including five such programs in this inventory, all except one of them run with strong private sector initiative and involvement, though in collaboration with the educators. The private sector is involved as a way of filling a gap resulting from the failure of school systems and the public sector to exercise much initiative in this area. As just mentioned, no federal programs dealing with the professional development of educators focused on this issue. And from the point of view at least of the business part of the private sector, joined in many cases by other private sector people (universities, research and development agencies, consultants), a big problem of the schools is "mismanagement."

The programs we review are: (1) the *principals as leaders project,* funded primarily by Chase Manhattan Bank and involving Bank Street and the Learning Cooperative as co-participants; (2) *the instructional administrators program at Fordham,* funded by the Ford Foundation, to train and upgrade minority supervisors; (3) the *Creative Teaching Workshop's recent work on principal leadership training,* resulting from the recognition that its earlier teacher training programs needed this additional component; (4) *the Economic Development Council's management studies of principals' leadership styles and preferences,* done for the Division of High Schools and aimed at improving administrative training and promotion practices in the high schools; and (5) *the Center for Educational Management's supervisory training programs within the Board of Education,* done with tax levy monies to improve the management skills of community superintendents, principals, and assistant principals.

Center For Educational Management

Supervisory Training Programs

This unit at school headquarters, which used to be called the Office of Educational Management Training, has been involved for many years in management training activities. One of its first efforts was training community school districts staffs in business management techniques during the first couple of years of decentralization. After the training was taken over by the Economic Development Council, an outside, non-profit business group, and by the Deputy Chancellor, the Office became involved in a series of management training programs for community superintendents, principals, and assistant principals. It became involved in teacher retraining as well, particularly as related to mid-career teachers and those involved in special education programs. The line between management and education is sometimes hard to draw, and this Office, located in the Division of Educational Planning and Support, tended to approach training from the perspective of how it could enhance the education programs in schools and districts, not just from a business management and efficiency perspective. It has recently been involved in three programs: (1) the training of supervisors in performance planning, in the context of the Chancellor's edict that a system of measuring supervisors' effectiveness and accountability be devised; (2) executive development institutes for community superintendents and elementary and junior high school principals; and (3) a voluntary after-school professional development program for mid-career staff to upgrade themselves and for staff involved in special education programs.

Executive Development Institutes

STARTED: 1972.

FUNDING: City tax levy and some Ford Foundation funding.

LOCATION: In the districts. Met 3-4 times a year.

EMPHASIS: Management training sessions in which superintendents planned the agenda and the implementation was done by the Office. The sessions covered critical issues facing the districts and schools and how they might be handled. Outside speakers were sometimes called in as expert consultants.

TARGET: All 32 community superintendents, plus 64 elementary and junior high school principals, two per district, both selected by the superintendent. Very well attended and constituted one of the only times during the year when the supervisors came together to discuss educational matters.

INFORMATION: Materials on the institutes available at the Office.

Instructional Administrators Program

STARTED: February 1969. Continued for 3 years through early 1972.

Administrative and Staffing Innovations 171

FUNDING: $161,000 from the Ford Foundation and the Board of Education, the latter through the granting of sabbaticals to the participants.

LOCATION: Fordham University at Lincoln Center, School of Education, Columbus Avenue and West 60th Street, New York, NY One semester of classroom studies at Fordham; and one semester in a field-based internship in schools and various community agencies.

EMPHASIS: Giving minority educators a year of graduate study, subsidized by the Ford Foundation—with a concentration on administration, supervision, and urban studies—to help them become more credentialed and facilitate their subsequent promotion to higher level supervisory and administrative positions in the New York City school system.

TARGET: 60 minority educators, almost all of them licensed teachers and assistant principals in the New York City schools. 20 each year for 3 years.

STAFFING: 4 full-time Fordham faculty.

CHANGES: Moved over time to a more balanced academic and field-based training, with one semester for each.

INFORMATION: A final report prepared by Fordham.

Performance Planning

STARTED: 1973. No longer in effect as of June, 1976. Started to implement Chancellor's edict as mentioned above.

FUNDING: City tax levy.

LOCATION: Workshops in 22 districts and at school headquarters.

EMPHASIS: To develop a performance planning system that clarifies the dimensions of responsibility of supervisors in the New York City schools; specifies goals, objectives, and strategies in this context; and appraises supervisors' performance. It was a program of supervisory training through workshops on performance planning. Used such techniques as management by objectives (MBO). The supervisors' professional association, the Council of Supervisory Associations, regarded the entire strategy as a threat, being particularly concerned about the rating aspect of it in which performance would be measured, and it eventually had to be disbanded. The Chancellor rescinded his earlier edict for the development of such a system.

TARGET: All supervisors in the New York City schools. All were reached.

172   Inventory of Educational Improvement Efforts

STAFFING: 1 person full-time for 6 months; 4 others part-time in workshops, on supervisory days.

INFORMATION: Two monographs that had been prepared for the workshops: *Guide To Performance Planning,* September 1974, and *Performance Planning in Action,* September 1975. The latter included a planning kit, an overview of performance planning systems across the nation (48 school systems involved with it were identified and the main ones described), and a review of all the concerns the supervisors had expressed with regard to what the systems involved and how they would be used, attempting to reassure them.

Pupils with Special Educational Needs

STARTED: 1975.

FUNDING: Tax levy.

LOCATION: At headquarters and the districts.

EMPHASIS: Workshops in which program coordinators and other staff led discussions on problems in teaching in special education programs and how they may best be handled.

Voluntary After-School Professional Development Program

STARTED: 1970, but program on helping mid-career teachers and supervisors develop strategies for upgrading themselves is quite recent.

FUNDING: Tax levy.

LOCATION: Headquarters and the districts.

EMPHASIS: Workshops in which discussions were conducted around problems of this mid-career group and what they might do to solve them.

Other Programs

Creative Teaching Workshop, Principals' Program

STARTED: 1975.

FUNDING: $30,000 for one year from Exxon.

LOCATION: 115 Spring Street, New York, NY, and in a special laboratory school, P.S. 152, District 22, Brooklyn, where the Workshop has been informally assisting the school and principal for 3 years.

EMPHASIS: To develop principals' effectiveness as educational leaders and change-agents within the school, through workshops and discussion groups aimed at providing principals with the opportunity to explore their own learning and to inquire into ways to facilitate their roles as educational leaders.

TARGET: 6 New York City principals.

STAFFING: A few Workshop staff, plus outside consultants.

INFORMATION: CTW reports. (See also pages 165-6.)

Economic Development Council's High School Principal Studies

STARTED: April 1973.

FUNDING: The equivalent of roughly 2½ on-loan executives for one year, about $65,000.

LOCATION: Field studies (interview and observation) in 30 high schools (6 from Manhattan, 6 from The Bronx, 6 from Queens, 10 from Brooklyn, and 2 from Richmond). Also meetings with top administrators in the Division of High Schools.

EMPHASIS: Based on 2 separate studies of how high school principals spend their time, e.g., on administrative vs. educational matters, and on what they see as their high priority problems. A training program is being developed whose purpose is to help present and future high school principals delegate many more of their administrative responsibilities, so that they may spend more time providing educational leadership. Explorations now ongoing are related to developing more explicit and codified recruitment criteria relative to this leadership style; and restructuring the role of the high school principal to encourage more delegation and provide more trained staff in administrative-support activities.

TARGET: New York City high school principals.

STAFFING: 4 business people on loan, each of whom worked for part of a year or part-time on it, plus whatever limited resources the Division of High Schools allocated to it.

CHANGES: Started as a consulting study. Initial recommendations were to restructure the high school principal's role to provide for an assistant principal or deputy with administrative expertise. This evolved into a training program for principals now in office, without structural changes. The training program is seen as a first step, with others to be decided later. Still at a very early stage.

INFORMATION: Two reports by the Economic Development Council, delivered to the Division of High Schools.

Educational Leadership Seminar

STARTED: 1974.

FUNDING: $45,000 from Exxon Corporation to the University of Virginia.

EMPHASIS: A 6-week summer seminar for teachers selected by their principals for their leadership potential. Designed to develop their understanding of leadership roles (principals, superintendents) in public education and to indicate the role of public education as an institution and its relation to the wider society. One of the only programs nationally that tries to motivate teachers toward such leadership roles rather than attempting specific training for principalships through formalized study.

TARGET: 3 elementary school teachers from District 13 in 1974; 7 from districts 4, 13, 21, and 22 in 1975; and 9 from the same districts in 1976.

AUSPICES: Curry Memorial School of Education, University of Virginia.

Elementary School Principal as an Educational Leader Project

STARTED: Spring 1972. Still in existence.

FUNDING: $260,000 from Chase Manhattan Bank, 1972-75. $25,000 in 1975-76 from the Learning Cooperative, which received the money in a grant from the Rockefeller Brothers Fund.

LOCATION: 12 elementary schools in the New York City metropolitan area, 8 within the city. They include: District 4–P.S. 112 (Man); District 11–P.S. 87, 112, District 12–Early Learning Centers #1 and #2, District 8–C.S. 232 (Bx); District 17–P.S. 138, District 23–P.S. 150, (Bkn).

EMPHASIS: Training principals to become more effective educational leaders in their own schools. This involved isolating the leadership functions necessary for school effectiveness and the competencies required in the enactment of each function. Four key competency areas that were identified and used in the training were: management and administration; developing a humanist climate; providing an in-service program for staff development; and developing a cooperative parent-community relationship.

TARGET: Principals in 12 elementary schools in the New York City metropolitan area, 8 from the city.

STAFFING: 10, many part-time, 6 from Bank Street; 2 from the Learning Cooperative; 2 from Chase Manhattan Bank.

AUSPICES: A joint, collaborative project, with Chase as the primary funding source; Bank Street, through its Dean, Gordon Klopf, as a main source for conceptualizing and designing the program, reviewing the relevant literature and educational practice elsewhere, and leading the training sessions; and the Learning Cooperative of the Board of Education.

INFORMATION: Many publications by Klopf and his colleagues at Bank Street, including: Gordon Klopf, *The Principal and Staff Development in The Elementary School,* 1974; and Judith Crooks Burnes, Klopf, Ethel Scheldon, and Sallie Blake, *Report of The Program for The Development of The Elementary School Principal as an Educational Leader,* 1975. Also *Princeps,* Occasional Paper 1, April 1973, and Occasional Paper 2, April 1974.

Management Modernization and Reform

School reformers, management consultants, educators, and business executives have shown increasing interest in recent years in improving the management of school systems. The application in the public sector of such techniques as cost-effectiveness analysis, management by objectives (MBO), program-planning-budgeting-systems (PPBS), management information systems, organization development, and executive training has spread to public education. The New York City school system is no exception to this trend, and it has experienced much management improvement activity since 1970, when decentralization first began.

Several organizations and individuals have been active in this area, and each is described separately in the inventory. They include: (1) the Economic Development Council, a private, non-profit corporation with a membership of over 200 large companies, that has provided extensive and free management consulting services to the Board of Education and community school districts; (2) the Deputy Chancellor, who has worked in collaboration with EDC as well as independently in developing new management procedures and an improved management analysis capability in the Board of Education; (3) several management consulting firms that have had contracts with the Board of Education, including Peat, Marwick, and Mitchell, McKinsey, Cresap, McCormick, and Paget, and Touche Ross; and (4) the Division of Business and Administration in the Board of Education. There is in addition (5) some important recent work in developing automated attendance information systems, both in Brandeis High School in Manhattan, through the initiative of the Economic Development Council and the Exxon Corporation and in many community school districts as a result of technical assistance efforts by the State Education Department. These five clusters of activities constitute close to an exhaustive list of the main management improvement efforts in the New York City school system.

Economic Development Council

A unique program, having national significance, is the management consulting services provided the Board of Education by the Economic Development Council. The Council has provided on-loan executives from its member corporations who have worked both with school headquarters and community school districts to help restructure their organizations and introduce new management procedures. The uniqueness of this program is that New York City-based corporations have donated these consulting services on a voluntary basis, at no cost to the Board of Education; the services have then been organized through a Council task force headed by a retired chief executive. The Council and this executive have then worked closely with board members and school administrators on implementing the recommendations of its various management studies; and this has taken place on a much larger scale than any previous efforts by similar business groups, either in New York City or elsewhere.

Administrative and Staffing Innovations 177

STARTED: Early 1971, on an invitation by Chancellor Harvey Scribner and the Board of Education.

FUNDING: Roughly 45 person-years of executive time, valued at $1.2 million, plus other services in kind, e.g., management training programs and corporate consulting assistance in the use of new technologies (computerized information systems), probably adding up to another $1 million since 1971.

TARGET: School headquarters, particularly its top policy-making and management structure, and its various business and administrative operations. Also the management of community school districts and of high schools.

LOCATION: At school headquarters, in the districts, at EDC, and at the offices of various EDC member corporations, e.g., IBM, McKinsey.

EMPHASIS: Modernizing the structure and management procedures of school headquarters, community school districts, and high schools in the context of decentralization. The main sets of activities include:

Headquarters Reorganization: Developing a new, more consolidated organizational structure at school headquarters, permitting more long-range planning, more delegation of authority from the Chancellor and central board, and eliminating some of the duplication and ambiguity of authority that had existed before. This was to make the system more responsive to citizen interests and new needs by helping it function more efficiently and relate more productively to the districts, e.g., in providing technical assistance, setting standards, monitoring district programs, and the like. The reorganization involved consolidating all business and administrative functions under a Deputy Chancellor and all educational or pedagogical ones under the Chancellor. It also involved freeing the central board and Chancellor from many administrative tasks, delineating more clearly than in the past lines of authority and various functions and responsibilities. EDC continues to assist the board in this reorganization and in assessing its impacts.

Individual Projects in Business and Other Headquarters Units: EDC has also worked on several projects dealing with particular business and headquarters functions, including: payroll, auditing, budget and fiscal operations, supplies, construction, school planning and research, teacher accountability, legal offices of the Chancellor and board, public relations, teacher absenteeism, management information systems, and the central board's functions. These projects have resulted in reports with recommendations that EDC continues to follow up on, in collaboration with school officials.

Community School District Management: EDC has worked with several community school districts, on invitation, to help them improve their management and general operations. They include District 24 (Queens), 7 (Bronx), 2 and 6 (Manhattan), and 17 and 32 (Brooklyn).

STAFFING: A task force of between 5 and 15 on-loan executives at any given time.

AUSPICES: EDC, a private, non-profit corporation, in collaboration with the Board of Education.

CHANGES: Three new directions in EDC's work, flowing out of this management work and its school-renewal efforts in high schools to be discussed in chapter 5: (1) The development of a Council for Education of New York City, in the planning stages since 1971, that would provide an organized, voluntary coordinating service for all private sector educational activities in the city. It would include business, labor, parent, and other community groups as well as the Board of Education and the City University of New York. (2) Assisting the Board of Education establish budget priorities and evaluate the reorganization and its general performance. (3) Informal explorations with many top city and state officials on the feasibility of establishing an entirely new top structure for the Board of Education and for selecting the central board and Chancellor, with the goal of establishing much closer relations with City Hall and much more accountability. These new directions result in part from EDC's assessment of the implementation and impact of its reorganization plan that fell, in its words, "far short of its ultimate aim" (*Proceedings of the Tenth Annual Meeting,* EDC, April 7, 1976, p. 25).

INFORMATION: From EDC, particularly its annual reports and many consulting study reports.

Deputy Chancellor

STARTED: November 1973, with the creation of this office under the headquarters reorganization, initiated by EDC.

FUNDING: All tax levy; $632,279 for Deputy Chancellor; $462,119 for Office of Budget Operations and Review; and $423,492 for the Project Management Unit.

LOCATION: At headquarters, in various headquarters units, and all districts. A system-wide activity.

EMPHASIS: To improve the policy and management analysis capability of the Board of Education, as well as the actual management of the entire system. The Deputy Chancellor has several units that do this. Two of them, Policy Development Unit and Project Management Unit, constitute its analytical arm. There is, in addition, a district business management team. The Office has issued many policy papers, e.g., on the allocation formula for the districts; on the state aid formula; on the UFT collective bargaining agreement of 1975 and its broader effects on the system; on seniority and layoffs; on systems planning in accounting and personnel; on strengthening business management in the division of special education and pupil personnel services; on the school lunch program; an audit manual; a standard business operations manual; and many others.

The office has tightened up procedures for headquarters monitoring of district expenditures and programs. It has also worked on changing civil service and personnel practices related to recruiting management analysts and now has a new education administrator series, similar to what had been recommended 25 years ago in the Strayer-Yavner report on the management of the New York City schools. Has worked to replace ex-pedagogues with trained administrators for headquarters administrative positions.

STAFFING: Roughly 40-50 staff in all, including 11 secretaries.

INFORMATION: From the Deputy Chancellor's Office.

Management Consulting Firms

Several consulting firms have worked with the Board of Education since decentralization to try to help improve its management. This includes fiscal, accounting, and other management control relations of headquarters and the districts, the management of each considered independently, and exploring ways in which headquarters could be completely reorganized to function more as a technical assistance agency and service center under decentralization.

The first three consulting firms the Board of Education brought in were Peat, Marwick and Mitchell, McKinsey, and Cresap, McCormick, and Paget; and there seemed to be a mutually compatible division of labor among them. McKinsey tended to concentrate on broad, strategic questions on how headquarters would be restructured under decentralization and what management functions the districts would take over. Peat, Marwick, and Mitchell emphasized much more nuts-and-bolts, day-to-day operating problems, e.g., developing financial and accounting systems for the districts and later for headquarters and straightening out the payroll. Cresap, McCormick, and Paget was hired exclusively to train community school board members, though it had done some fairly large-scale management and financial studies of headquarters in the 1950s.

Cresap, McCormick, and Paget

STARTED: 1969.

LOCATION: Community school districts and more centralized meetings in Manhattan and at school headquarters.

EMPHASIS: Training community school board members so that they might function better under decentralization.

INFORMATION: Training manuals and materials, prepared for the workshops.

McKinsey & Co., Inc., Management Consultants

STARTED: 1969. Ended by late 1970.

FUNDING: Roughly $100,000 in contracts.

LOCATION: Headquarters and District 14.

EMPHASIS: A series of strategic studies related to how to make decentralization work. Its main point was that the system should be redesigned with a "bottom up" strategy, building a management capability first in the community districts and boards and then, based on such an analysis of local problems and needs, work on headquarters. Prepared a major document for Chancellor Scribner when he arrived in 1970 on the "management requirements for successful decentralization." Also did several other studies: an analysis of alternative budget allocation formulas for the districts; revisions to the budgeting and budget modification processes; an assessment of management needs under decentralization in a sample

Administrative and Staffing Innovations 181

district in Brooklyn; assistance in decentralizing and strengthening such support services as procurement, data processing, school lunch, and pupil transportation; and an analysis of alternatives for retention of computer-assisted-instruction.

INFORMATION: Many reports from McKinsey.

Peat, Marwick, and Mitchell

STARTED: 1969, with decentralization.

FUNDING: An estimated $1 million in contracts over the period 1969 to 1975.

LOCATION: At school headquarters and the districts.

EMPHASIS: Began with a project to assist the board in the design and implementation of a community district financial accounting system. Since then it kept getting involved in additional proposals to expand its assistance in related fiscal activities. First, it expanded the scope of its services to include an analysis of the board's central financial organization, made recommendations for its improvement, and provided implementation assistance. Then it helped develop budgetary control mechanisms to prevent the kind of major operating deficit and district over-spending that took place in 1970-71. It also worked on helping develop more management control over payrolls, the management of reimbursable programs, and, more generally, on the organization and staffing of business and administrative functions.

Taken as a totality, its work involved 7 broad areas: (1) district accounting; (2) boardwide financial accounting systems; (3) payroll; (4) position and budget control; (5) audit; (6) reimbursable claims; and (7) financial organization and management development.

INFORMATION: Many major documents prepared by Peat, Marwick, and Mitchell staff, particularly in the period from November 1969-September 1973; and several progress reports written for board members and school administrators.

TOUCHE ROSS

STARTED: 1975.

FUNDING: $100,000 contract.

LOCATION: School headquarters.

182   Inventory of Educational Improvement Efforts

EMPHASIS: Helped the Division of Business and Administration with its planning process. Provided staff professionals and management assistance in that activity. Study of the Bureau of School Lunches.

Division of Business and Administration, Board of Education

STARTED: 1970.

EMPHASIS: Worked on some key management problems of the system, including: consolidating the payroll system; establishing tighter headquarters controls over district hiring (put in a pedagogical position control system) to prevent the over-hiring and over-spending of 1970-71; also worked on computerization and on developing a planning process.

FUNDING: City tax levy. Budget request was $76,753,289.

Automated Attendance Information Systems

Attendance and Cutting Information Project

STARTED: 1972.

FUNDING: Private sector. Exxon,

LOCATION: Louis D. Brandeis High School (Man).

EMPHASIS: A system to find out which students are cutting classes and who is absent. Each morning teacher submits report on who is in homeroom class and in subject classrooms. The information returned to teacher the same day. Timeliness of the information is known to students who are aware that their records are up-to-date on absences and cutting. After 5 days of either an absence or cutting, a post card is mailed home. Also, each dean receives a summary report of cutting and absences.

TARGET: Entire school.

STAFFING: 1 teacher full time, 1 school aide, 20 hours a week, for clerical help.

CHANGES: Since 1972, has expanded from part of the school to the entire school; from punch cards to computerization at a smaller cost.

INFORMATION: EDC prepared an evaluation of work done on the project for the first 3 years.

State Education Department, Office of Urban School Services

STARTED: 1971.

EMPHASIS: Introduced to all community school districts an exception reporting system for recording attendance, a system that had been used throughout the state but not in New York City. 28 districts have incorporated the system. Reporting attendance by exception, with a card kept on each student over 40-week period. Began with a 1971 task force of the State Education Department and the Board of Education. Done through the Bureau of Attendance at school headquarters.

Chapter 4

Inventory of Political Action, Advocacy, Consumer Rights Programs

Despite the relative calm in New York City's educational politics in recent years, in contrast to the many school wars of the 1960s over desegregation and community control, civic and educational interest groups still pursue a substantial amount of advocacy work and political protest. Furthermore, given some of the traumas of the 1975-76 school year—the UFT collective bargaining agreement and its aftermath, the fiscal cuts, staff layoffs, program cutbacks and terminations, numerous conflicts between community school boards and headquarters, the adequacy of particular programs that have been the subject of litigation and state rulings (e.g., bilingual, programs for the handicapped), the continued dissatisfaction of many citizen groups with the schools' performance, and the beginnings of more serious efforts by civic groups and legislators to explore the future of decentralization, the selection and composition of the central board, and its relations with City Hall—it seems likely that political conflict will continue and probably increase once more.

This section of the inventory reviews some of the activity related to political actions. Unlike the other sections, it is organized exclusively in terms of particular types of organizations, all of them private sector ones. They include: (1) citywide citizen advocacy groups; (2) coalitions of such citywide groups, usually formed around a single issue or related set of issues; (3) legal agencies and programs; (4) neighborhood, district, and more locally-based groups, which remain disparate as they have always been, reflecting as they do so many divergent interests; (5) some locally-based education programs that some of these groups have developed, in addition to their political advocacy efforts; and (6) media and consumer information activities.

What this section indicates, as alluded to briefly in the introduction, is that there remains in New York City an active, sophisticated, and important array of politically-oriented private agencies and citizen groups that are deeply involved in pressing the Board of Education to be more responsive to their interests. Though they rarely come together in any enduring coalitions—a reflection in part of their diversity and numbers—they remain a potent force.

Such organizations should, of course, be distinguished from other private sector ones that are more apolitical and whose main change-related activities involve collaborative programs with the Board of Education in which they provide oney, consultants, technical assistance, and other support services to school programs. The many corporations, foundations, and universities listed throughout this inventory attest to that other important private sector role; and in the final sections we will discuss the contributions of each toward change.

Citywide Citizen Advocacy Groups

Aspira of New York

STARTED: 1961.

FUNDING: Private, city, state, federal, and foundation grants.

LOCATION: Central headquarters: 296 Fifth Avenue, New York, NY 10001; and in Districts 1, 7, and 32.

EMPHASIS: Aspira has several programs aimed at improving the educational opportunities and services of Hispanic students. (1) It initiated a major class action suit against the Board of Education in 1971, Aspira, et al. v. Board of Education, et al., as part of its legal work, resulting in the consent decree of August 1974. The Board of Education agreed at that time to devise a system to identify and classify Spanish students and then provide them an educational program in their native language—training teachers in English and Spanish as part of this program. (2) It has a parent training institute to help parents assume more active roles in the education of their youngsters and to become more sophisticated evaluators of school programs. (3) It has a student motivation center to help high school students remain in schools and develop more positive self-image and improved school performance. (4) It has an Educational Opportunity Center that includes counselling for seniors in high school who want to go on to college as well as for college and graduate.

INFORMATION: Program descriptions and annual reports from Aspira.

Citizens Budget Commission

This is a good government organization concerned with management efficiency in local government. It has done many studies over the years of different agencies and programs and generally plays a research, monitoring, and lobbying role as an advocate for citizen interests. It did a study of school decentralization, funded by the Rockefeller Brothers Fund, entitled *The Role of Local Community School Districts in New York City's Expense Budget Processes,* June 1975. The study seemed to attract little attention and have little impact. It was an attempt to assess the effectiveness of the community school districts in the preparation and administration of the school system's expense budget. One of the main findings was that there was a lack of communication and cooperation between the central Board of Education and the community school districts in the expense budget process. Community districts were found to lack timely funding information and technical assistance from headquarters. Some districts submitted unrealistically high budget requests, thereby lessening their credibility as a participant in headquarters budget decisions. Finally, the central board was found to continue to impose rigid restrictions on community district budget administration. The report concludes with recommendations for increasing district participation in the budget process and for generally increasing its rationality. The Commission is located at 110 East 42nd Street, New York, NY 10017.

Citizens Committee for Children, Special Education Project

An organization of professional and lay experts in various fields of child care, seeking to initiate and improve services for children. It was founded in 1944 by Eleanor Roosevelt, Stanley M. Isaacs, and Adele R. Levy. It has been involved in one major project on special education, which is described here, and in two coalitions, the Educational Priorities Panel and Joint Action for Children, both described in the following section, "Coalitions of Citywide Groups." CCC's participation in the Educational Priorities Panel began in the early planning stages in the fall of 1975. Henry Saltzman, Executive Director of CCC, conceived the idea and arranged for the funding.

CCC has also received support from the Foundation for Child Development for monitoring a Medicaid program (see page 191).

STARTED: Late 1974.

FUNDING: $200,000 grant from the Herman Goldman Foundation.

LOCATION: Field work involving the monitoring of special education programs and classes in six random community school districts: P.S. 30/31, 10, and 123 in District 5 (Man); P.S. 140, 36, and J.H.S. 101 in District 8 (Bx); P.S. 230, 321, and J.H.S. 293 in District 15 (Bkn); P.S. 226, 225, and J.H.S. 303 in District 21 (Bkn); P.S. 144, 132, J.H.S. 263 in District 23 (Bkn); and P.S. 115, 162, and J.H.S. 158 in District 26 (Q).

PROGRAM: The project involves field monitoring and study of the organization of the Division of Special Education and Pupil Personnel Services at school headquarters as well as of funding, legislation, teacher training, and certification as related to special education. CCC is evaluating all aspects of the programs for the handicapped with a view toward making recommendations for changes in practice, administration, training, and relationships of schools to other provider agencies such as mental health, health, and private schools. Activities also include a Special Education Cabinet of responsible federal, state, and local officials concerned with the implementation of special education programs and an Issues Subcommittee of parent, provider and advocacy organizations to give the program a broader base of input and impact.

TARGET: Not a direct service project but attempts to affect all 42,000 handicapped students in the city and the teachers and support personnel in the programs as well.

STAFF: 2 and a fraction. A director with research, administrative, and management skills; an Associate Director with expertise in working with retarded and language impaired students; and a part-time research assistant.

CHANGES: Major changes in the programs for the handicapped relate to the passage of federal legislation, the city's fiscal crisis, Board of Education reorganizations, and various recertification changes of the Board.

INFORMATION: Proposal available, plus draft of all relevant state statutes.

Community Council of Greater New York

The Community Council of Greater New York is an information and research action center, created and supported by private and public social welfare agencies, to attend to the public interests of the citizens of New York in the health and welfare field. It is a voluntary association of individuals and organizations engaged in public education defined in its broadest sense. Its main education-related activities involve several studies of the schools that involve monitoring school effectiveness.

FUNDING: From the Foundation for Child Development.

LOCATION: Studies cover schools throughout the system.

EMPHASIS: The Council has conducted two main studies: one on school attendance, a second on breakfast and lunch programs in the New York City schools. Since the latter is a focus of considerable study and political activity in itself, it is covered in the next separate section. The attendance and absenteeism study was an attempt to determine the effects on children and on their families of children's absence from school for an extended period of time and to further determine the services and alternative education programs available to children out of school. Funded by the Foundation for Child Development, it resulted in a report, *Attendance in New York City's Public Schools,* June 1975.

That study concluded, based on visits to 51 schools, that "the breakdown they had observed in the attendance system is indicative of a major breakdown in the whole public school system" (p. 15). It also found: "1. that published attendance figures do not reflect the full numbers of children who are out of school; 2. that attendance procedures developed by schools do not deal with the underlying problems of children who are out of school; and 3. that many children who are out of school do not come into contact with attendance teachers and other school professionals who could help them return to school" (p. 2 of a proposal to follow up on the study, September, 1975). Finally, it found that the major question of what actually happens to children when they are out of school remains unanswered. This study was done under the auspicies of the Children's Services Monitoring Committee, composed of people from a wide variety of private and public agencies. Policy issues considered by the committee included the Board of Education's suspension procedures, particularly the kinds and effectiveness of services available for suspended and absent students; the location of agencies throughout the city that can provide help to out of school children; and the availability of alternative schools.

STAFFING: 1 project director, 1 graduate student, and several students through the Foundation for Child Development.

TARGET: Out-of-school students.

INFORMATION: The report mentioned above, plus other materials produced by the Children's Services Monitoring Committee. The *Report on School Attendance* will be officially published by the Foundation for Child Development as part of its *State of The Child* report.

Community Service Society, Committee on Education

This is a voluntarily supported, non-sectarian social agency committed to social change and services for poor and disadvantaged people of New York City. It does this through studies monitoring various programs and through lobbying. CSS's main activities that are relevant for this inventory are carried out by its Committee on Education, part of its Department of Public Affairs.

STARTED: January 1972.

FUNDING: All internally by Community Service Society.

LOCATION: The Committee, one of eight program committees within CSS's Department of Public Affairs, functions out of its own offices at the Society: 105 East 22nd Street, New York, NY 10010.

EMPHASIS: Focuses on those aspects of education that affect children who suffer the greatest disadvantages, e.g., the physically and emotionally handicapped, minority-group isolated, low income isolated, non-English-speaking students, and the educationally disadvantaged. This set of concerns extends the scope of the committee's attention to the governance and administration of the schools attended by such students and to opening educational opportunities and options for them from pre-school through college. The following subcommittees and programs reflect these concerns:

> Subcommittee on Legislation: Analyzes educational legislation in Albany and Washington as related to the Committee's priorities and concerns.
>
> Subcommittee on Pupil Personnel Services and Special Education: Determines the adequacy of existing programs as related to the needs and rights of handicapped students.
>
> Subcommittee on Alternative Schools and Alternative Approaches to Education, including Bilingual Education: Prepared two reports on bilingual education in New York City.
>
> Program on Education for Parenthood: Deals with sex education.
>
> Subcommittee on Graduate School Program: Supervises program that CSS runs.
>
> Board of Education Budget: A subcommittee was established in 1976 to deal with the Board of Education budget, examining budget requests and the educational part of the city's expense budget to determine priorities for educational spending. A member of the Educational Priorities Panel.

TARGET: Disadvantaged, poor, minority, and handicapped students.

STAFFING: 5. 1 staff associate, 2 full-time staff assistants, and 2 secretaries.

INFORMATION: Copies of reports issued in recent years. They include: *Report on Bilingual Education,* June 1974; *Report on Bilingual Pilot Schools in New York City,* August 1975; *Education Legislation in New York State,* November 1975; and *Detour to Education: The Transportation Troubles of Handicapped School Children,* June 1975.

Foundation for Child Development

Though obviously not a civic interest group in the sense that all the agencies already described are, the Foundation for Child Development plays an important child advocacy role by identifying projects concerned with the effects of various social forces on child care institutions. The Foundation itself was founded in 1900, but this present focus of improving institutions that affect the lives of children and their families is only a few years old.

STARTED: 1975 for this more child advocacy vein.

FUNDING: It gives grants to scholars and organizations concerned with children.

EMPHASIS: To support the development of sound knowledge as a basis for rational change toward enhancing the welfare of children. The projects most directly related to that are:

> Citizens Committee for Children: Monitoring The Early and Periodic Screening, Diagnosis, and Treatment Program of Medicaid. CCC has been monitoring the Medicaid program with particular attention to the provision of diagnosis and treatment where screening reveals a need for follow-up and a greater effort to reach families and children who are eligible but not yet enrolled in the program. $68,925.

> Community Council: Support and then publication of its monitoring studies of school attendance and school meals (see pages 190-1 and 200-1).

INFORMATION: Annual Report. Also, *State of The Child* by Trude Lash and Heidi Sigal.

Implementing the Community Schools Concept in New York City

This is a potentially significant project that has been in the planning stage since 1974 and has been included here, despite its not having yet been implemented, because it is so important. Essentially it involves the multi-use of school facilities, with particular emphasis on using vacated or underutilized facilities as focal points for community activities and programs of various kinds. Its importance relates to the fact that in a period of such fiscal crisis, with shrinking public and private funding for all community services, there is a tremendous need in New York City to recycle existing resources by finding ways to minimize overhead expenses, eliminate duplication of costs, and use public facilities in the most efficient manner possible. Planning work had been done by the Mayor's Task Force on Community Schools, co-chaired by Deputy Mayor Paul Gibson and Jerome Becker, Chairman of the New York City Youth Board. This involves people from several agencies and grew out of a Community Schools Conference of January 1975, sponsored by the Youth Board, Community Council of Greater New York and New York University School of Education.

STARTED: 1974.

FUNDING: $20,000 New York State Office of Parks and Recreation.

LOCATION: The Department of City Planning has been designated to administer and implement the project. City Planning Department Fund, Barbara Braden, Project Director, 2 Lafayette Street, New York, NY 10007.

EMPHASIS: To implement the multi-use of schools (community schools) concept in New York City by establishing a model community school program in each borough; and advocating the community school concept citywide through the dissemination of information, provision of technical assistance, and recommendations on how to eliminate institutional barriers.

An effort will be made to select target school districts representing diverse socio-economic populations with differing service requirements. Additional criteria will include evidence of strong commitment by the local school board and its community to the community school concept; availability of school space; and reasonable potential for matching service needs with resources. Each model program would involve school personnel in the program; serve, where possible, an identified community coextensive with the public school attendance area; concentrate a comprehensive program (health, recreational, educational, cultural) meeting local needs as identified in a public school building or other specific public facility; extend the range of activities offered by the public school and enlarge the target population reached by existing school program; establish a vehicle for continuing identification of community interests, needs, and concerns; continue to increase the scope and quality of the program; attempt to serve all age groups within the community, with priority given to those groups whose special needs (the aged, handicapped, unemployed youth) are inadequately met; and establish a community advisory council to plan and implement the program.

The assumed benefits for the city would be reduction of public and voluntary agency expenditures for leased space; improved space and time utilization of public school buildings that would, in turn, result in increased revenues to the Board of Education from fees collected for space use by other agencies; and prevent unnecessary school closings with their consequent deleterious effects on surrounding communities. Local communities would benefit by the creation of centers to stimulate community self-help efforts and enhance neighborhood involvement with the schools; provide more comprehensive service delivery for all age groups; provide an opportunity for more exchanges among programs and their diverse clienteles using the facilities; and have a potential for reducing juvenile delinquency and vandalism by having neighborhood youth served by and involved in local schools.

PARTICIPATING AGENCIES: Deputy Mayor, Youth Board, Board of Education, City Planning Commission, Community Council of Greater New York, Office of Neighborhood Services, Department of Real Estate, Parks and Recreation Administration, and other public and private agencies.

INFORMATION: Department of City Planning, Youth Board, or Deputy Mayor.

Interface

This is not a citizen advocacy group in the usual sense, but it is included here as an organization providing technical assistance to citizen groups wanting to improve the school system. It is in that sense an important new third party in school and other city agency matters.

STARTED: 1974.

FUNDING: Grant from the Ford Foundation and Rockefeller Brothers Fund and supported as well by its consulting fees.

LOCATION: 52 Vanderbilt Avenue, New York, NY 10017

EMPHASIS: It provides research and management assistance to city agencies and citizen groups concerned with improving service delivery in city government. It does so through its own staff and through university consultants. Specifically it does studies as well as helps to develop agency programs and projects. Its main work in education includes: helping to plan and initiate a learning center at a South Bronx intermediate school, in collaboration with the New York Urban Coalition; coordinating research on the Board of Education's budget process for the Educational Priorities Panel, a coalition of parent and civic organizations; and doing the same for the Public Education Association in the latter's program exploring the prospects of improving the cost effectiveness of the public schools by supporting successful alternative schools programs.

TARGET: When related to education, the management and performance of the New York City schools.

STAFFING: Roughly 5.

New York City School Volunteer Program

This is not a citizen advocate agency in the sense that all the other organizations listed above are, but it is a citywide program that provides an important service to the schools by supplementing school programs through the use of citizen volunteers.

STARTED: 1956.

FUNDING: Has a budget of about $600,000 close to half of which is furnished by the Board of Education and school boards of participating community school districts. Many foundations and corporations make financial contributions to the program, including the Edna McConnel Clark Foundation that made a substantial one-year grant in 1974 to recruit and train older adults as school volunteers.

LOCATION: 20 West 40th Street, New York, NY 10018. Many programs, including pre- and in-service training, take place at this central office location. The program also provided volunteers to 250 schools in 28 community school districts in 1974-75.

EMPHASIS: Involves the structured use of unpaid volunteers to assist teachers and students in the public schools. Functioned as a pilot project of the Public Education Association with a Ford Foundation grant until 1962, when it was adopted by the New York City Board of Education. Volunteers serve on all grade levels, assisting in both instructional and non-instructional areas. They work only in those schools that request their services and only with pupils referred to them by school professionals. They serve as a supplementary resource—never a replacement—for educators in the school.

> The School Volunteers offer three kinds of educational programs:
>
> Reading help program: Volunteers serve as tutors for students referred to them. Generally these students are reading from one to three years below grade level and are receiving no professional remedial assistance. The same volunteer helps each student twice a week, at the same hour.

Conversational English program: Volunteers teach non-English-speaking students enough oral English to enable them to function in their classrooms. The method is audio-visual-lingual, relying completely on direct association of objects and words. Meet twice a week for a 30-minute period.

Early childhood program: for kindergarten-second grade students. The volunteers serve in the classrooms as an "extra pair of hands" for the teacher and as an enriching experience for the children. They help with classroom routines and with all activities requiring more than one adult.

The program's central office operates two units: (1) Direct tutorial services unit that recruits, trains, and supervises volunteers who serve either as tutors or classroom assistance; and (2) school volunteer resource center that provides guidelines, consulting services, and supplemental recruitment for school principals who recruit and supervise their own tutorial and non-tutorial volunteers.

TARGET: Schools and students throughout the city.

STAFFING: Over 3,000 volunteers.

INFORMATION: Annual reports, brochures, and other descriptive materials. Also *School Volunteer News,* the program's publication.

Public Education Association

This is the organization that has done the most broad-based advocacy research (and lobbying) in New York City for educational reform. PEA is a good government, civic reform organization, founded in 1895, that has been an important force for educational innovation since 1969 and had been off and on throughout its history. It has pursued several strategies in recent years, all oriented toward institutional change and all reflecting its strong support for decentralization. They include: (1) research on critical policy questions, e.g., collective bargaining, budgeting, services for the handicapped, community school board elections, the powers of community school boards, the use of community agencies and resources for education, school management, and many others; (2) acting as a catalyst to bring together some of the most influential civic groups and business to press for reforms on these policy issues; (3) providing legal and research support for neighborhood and community-based groups; (4) pursuing a broad legal program directed at school reform that cuts across all these issues; and (5) pursuing some educational program interests related to the further development of alternative schools and educational experiences outside the confines of the traditional classroom.

STARTED: All this activity has been underway since 1969, with the arrival of PEA's new director, David Seeley.

FUNDING: $300,000.

LOCATION: Public Education Association, 20 West 40th Street, New York, NY 10018.

EMPHASIS: PEA staff see their program as involving four broad substantive areas:

> Priority Budgeting: Available funds are allocated to the most educationally productive expenditures. Research, analysis, and coalition building are PEA's main strategies for achieving this. Particular events of the 1975-76 year in which PEA has been involved and which are related to the goal are: rejection of the UFT (teachers) contract by the Emergency Financial Control Board; establishment of the Educational Priorities Panel, a coalition of civic groups to assess the Board of Education's budget process; analysis of the Stavisky Bill; public testimony on the bill and the budget process; and the development of counter budget priorities.
>
> Balanced Collective Bargaining: Local school boards and educational consumer interests are represented, and management's position in the collective bargaining process is strengthened so that it will not feel compelled to collaborate with labor in ways counter to consumer interests.
>
> School-Site Management: The school, its principal, and staff are made accountable for school performance.
>
> Community Education: An attempt to help make schools more cost effective and to provide more options and alternatives to meet the individual needs of students. This set of activities, which PEA is just beginning, focuses on the better use of community resources and on integrated planning between schools and other youth service agencies and community organizations.

PEA's legal work merits separate consideration. PEA has a legal unit with one part-time attorney (its director is also an attorney). It has been supported by the Rockefeller Brothers Fund for $150,000 since 1973, and it

Political Action, Advocacy, Consumer Programs 197

has worked mainly in personnel and finance. The key issues in its personnel work relate to staff selection and accountability—improving the validity of examination procedures by testing more than in the past for "job relevant" skills and using on-the-job evaluation procedures—and legally redefining the role of principals to make them part of management and thereby accountable for evaluating teacher and school performance. Since principals have become unionized, they have attempted to define their role as non-managerial, with potentially negative implications in terms of their exercise of educational leadership. PEA's work on finance relates to inequities in state funding. The legal unit has also worked recently on the Board of Education's budget allocations to community boards and to poverty area schools in the context of the decentralization law and other state education law and on the legal aspects of increasing the numbers and scope of alternative schools.

TARGET: The basic institution of the Board of Education—personnel, finance, budget practices, educational programs, and patterns of management and governance. Its targets are also various educational consumers with grievances against the school system or headquarters, e.g., community school boards, parents, students, and other client groups.

STAFFING: 10 staff

CHANGES: Increasing emphasis on institutional change, advocacy, and legal work.

INFORMATION: PEA's *Reports,* a monthly publication from the PEA Information Services, is the most comprehensive source in the city for a consumer-oriented analysis of key policy issues such as PEA deals with.

Puerto Rican Forum

STARTED: 1957.

FUNDING: Department of Labor and HEW before. Now from the state.

LOCATION: 296 5th Avenue, New York City, N.Y.

EMPHASIS: The focus is on adult education for those youth and adults 16 or over who have dropped out of school. The main programs include: a bilingual bicultural drug abuse program, in which Spanish and Puerto Rican culture are taught to drop outs who have drug problems; a job referral unit; and a clerical training program. The Forum has many activities, but these are the ones most closely related to youth and education.

STAFFING: About 5 full-time people.

CHANGES: Originally the focus was on helping middle class and professionally-oriented people. Now it has shifted to Puerto Ricans who have no skills. It has developed a more direct service to the community and poverty areas.

United Parents Association

This is the city-wide federation of local parent associations whose main function is to represent parent and citizen interests in relation to the schools, through technical assistance, research, lobbying, and related activity. It participates with organizations like PEA in various citywide coalitions and publishes booklets and newsletters that analyze key school programs and policy issues. It has more representation in middle class areas of the city, but it has a significant minority constituency as well.

STARTED: Over 50 years ago.

FUNDING: From member organizations. Also some outside foundation funding, e.g., Rockefeller Brothers Fund made a grant of $35,000 in 1973 for the establishment of Project Plea, a litigation arm of United Parents Associations, designed to train and inform parents about their legal rights and to obtain and review court cases, grievance actions, and rulings of the Commissioner of Education as these affect parents' rights. It followed up this grant with another of $50,000 in 1974 as further support of Project Plea.

LOCATION: 15 East 26th Street, New York, NY 10010. Also, local parent associations throughout the city.

EMPHASIS: Works in a lobbying and technical assistance capacity, informing parents about school-related matters, mostly pertaining to decentralization and community school boards. Also receives input from local parent associations as the basis for devising legislative strategies. Participated in the Educational Priorities Panel, analyzing the Board of Education's budget. Has a Parent Legal Education Division to handle parent and student grievances, provide access to attorneys, and does research on legal questions. Also disseminates various brochures, booklets, and reports.

STAFFING: 13 paid staff and many volunteers.

CHANGES: Plays more of a political advocacy role now, due to decentralization. Also has much more of an active legal program than previously.

Women's City Club of New York

STARTED: 1915. Its most recent education work since 1970 is reviewed.

Political Action, Advocacy, Consumer Programs

FUNDING: A voluntary, citizens' organization.

LOCATION: 6 West 48th Street, New York, NY 10036.

EMPHASIS: Its general emphasis has been to make New York a better managed and livable city, through effective civic action that involves research, monitoring of city programs, lobbying, and other forms of political action.

The following lists recent Women's City Club activities in education, through its Education Committee:

- 1970-71- Protested the use of public money to support non-public schools. Called for the abolition of the Board of Examiners.
- 1972-73- Made a detailed study of the financing of the state university system. Started a study of the open admissions program of the city colleges.
- 1973-74 Initiated a study of reading and screening in early childhood education.
- 1975- Completed its report on open admissions, *The Privileged Many*. The report constitutes an endorsement of open admissions and reaches many specific conclusions about why it has not worked better and what has to be done. It deals with required changes both in the high schools and colleges.
- 1976 Joined the Educational Priorities Panel, which analyzes the Board of Education's budget processes.

INFORMATION: Brochures. The 1975 open admissions report.

TARGET: Varies, depending on the particular study or project.

School Breakfast and Lunch Related (Food) Reforms

Ordinarily, one might not regard school food programs as an important focus of educational reform efforts, but they are critical in New York, involving many students and enormous amounts of federal money. Though it may not be widely known, there is a lot of citizen advocacy activity related to these programs. There is a Hunger Task Force at the Community Council of Greater New York, staffed by Ms. Kathy Goldman, who had been active before in pressing for district control of food programs and had helped District 1 run its decentralized programs in this area. There is also a New York City School Breakfast Committee and a School Food Coalition, both of which have been active in pressing the Board of Education to improve the quality of food it buys and to change contracts, if necessary, with various vendors. State Comptroller Arthur Levitt issued an audit of the 1973-74 meal program that was very critical of the Board of Education's administration, indicating that contracts had been breached by vendors. An audit by the city comptroller's office in 1976 and reports by the Educational Priorities Panel, Touche Ross, and the Deputy Chancellor have all been very critical of the Board of Education's food programs.

Children's Services Monitoring Committee

STARTED: 1975.

FUNDING: Community Council of Greater New York and Foundation for Child Development.

LOCATION: Community Council of Greater New York, 225 Park Avenue South, New York, NY 10003

EMPHASIS: Monitoring of breakfast and lunch programs in schools throughout the city. This has resulted in a report published by the Community Council of Greater New York, *Monitoring: Breakfast and Lunch Programs in New York City Schools,* March 1975. That report was later published as a chapter in *State of The Child.* Monitoring has also taken place in parochial schools.

TARGET: Children in public and parochial schools.

STAFFING: Volunteers and 1 professional staff person.

INFORMATION: The report mentioned above. Main findings from visits to school food programs and responses from school lunchroom workers were that: (1) quality of food served (by appearance and taste) was low; (2) the lunchroom atmosphere got low ratings in many schools in terms

Political Action, Advocacy, Consumer Programs

of overcrowding, limited or no choice of food, portions too small for the age and size of the child served, and lacking sufficient garbage cans; (3) differentiation was made between children who receive free lunches and those who pay or bring their own lunch, even though federal regulations clearly prohibit any such discrimination, which is reflected in separate waiting lines and tables and payment by tickets instead of money; (4) menu planning and distribution got low ratings, with little reported opportunity for parent or student suggestion, with students not knowing the menu in advance nor being consulted in menu planning. Workers reported that though they knew the foods children preferred, this information was not used.

These were all reported as recurrent problems, and the report recommended that citizens be educated on the technicalities of food programs and that community school districts assume more power in decisions on the type of food, its quality, and quantity. It recommends more decentralization of food programs so that students would more likely get the kinds of food (by ethnic tastes) that they would want to eat, that more students would be eating, and that many more schools would serve breakfasts than now do.

Community Council of Greater New York Hunger Task Force

STARTED: Fall 1975.

FUNDING: None. Various agencies working with the task force give staff time to the work as do many volunteers.

LOCATION: Community Council of Greater New York, 225 Park Avenue South, New York, NY 10003.

EMPHASIS: To maximize the use of federal dollars in New York City for good programs and to maximize the participation of eligible people in those programs. Its staff person estimates, along with its member agencies, that New York City should now be getting over $400 million more per year in federal money than it is getting for child nutrition and food stamp programs. They also estimate that the Board of Education's refusal to help districts with the breakfast program or introduce it into the high schools is a loss of at least $22 million every year, in addition to the many jobs and other economic impact for the city. The passage of the Child Nutrition Act late in 1975 guaranteed funds for many of these programs.

In 1975-76, The Hunger Task Force's Child Nutrition Committee had been funded to do a monitoring project on the summer meals programs. They bring over $50 million into the city in July and August, yet no city agency willingly took responsibility, and the program would not be feeding 750,000 youth daily if it were not for community groups who have taken on sponsorship.

There are three areas of emphasis: food stamps, food for the elderly, and child nutrition. Works to establish coalitions and working groups on specific issues relating to these three areas of hunger advocacy. Main aim is to increase participation in the programs. This involves a combination of information services to agencies, direct contact with recipients and potential recipients, and work with city, state, and federal agencies that affect the program.

TARGET: Those eligible for the three areas of programs.

STAFFING: Through the Program Services Department of the Community Council. No specific staff available. Various agencies working with the task force give staff time to the work as do many volunteers.

Hunger Task Force, Child Nutrition Committee

FUNDING: $15,000 from New York Foundation.

STARTED: In 1975 as part of the Hunger Task Force (see above). However, much of the work is simply continuing what many groups and individuals have been doing for many years regarding various aspects of child food programs.

LOCATION: Citywide.

EMPHASIS: On four main areas: WIC (special program to raise nutrition of pregnant women and infants); school breakfast and lunch; summer meals program; and day care. The goal is to become the center for information, coalitions, and advocacy action for these programs. This involves developing specific expertise in each area and having one committee person be well versed in that area of child feeding in New York City.

The New York City School Breakfast Committee, still another client advocacy group, has received $15,000 to continue its work and will be housed at Community Council and work closely with the Child Nutrition Committee. The latter has received funding both from the Fund for The City of New York and New York Community Trust ($35,000) for a special monitoring project on summer meals program.

TARGET: Children in New York City.

STAFFING: A staff person from Community Council, plus volunteers and staff time from participating agency members of the coalition.

Political Action, Advocacy, Consumer Programs

AUSPICES: Community Council of Greater New York.

CHANGES: Now beginning to seek and receive foundation funding for programs that will bring millions of dollars to people in New York City as well as create jobs and contribute generally to the city's economic development. Making more agencies and civic groups aware of the fact that much federal funding available to the city is not being utilized, due to the ineffectiveness, inefficiency, and attitudes of various city agencies.

Coalitions of Citywide Groups

Alliance For Children

The Alliance was formed to strengthen decentralization and become involved in the community school board elections in the spring of 1975 and the UFT strike and contract that fall. Its membership included various civic groups interested in electing community school board members sympathetic to parent and community interests.

STARTED: January 1975.

FUNDING: Supported through private contributions. Total resources always quite nominal.

LOCATION: Citywide as a political action organization.

EMPHASIS: Its initial goals included the election of community school board members who adhered to the Alliance platform that called for strengthening school decentralization and for greater parent involvement in the schools. After the election, it concerned itself with the teachers' union strike and called for a more effective role for the community school boards in the bargaining process.

TARGET: Community school boards, parents, and students. The consumers and clients of the schools.

STAFFING: Through May 1976, there was a full-time director and secretary. Since then, no paid staff, just volunteers.

Educational Priorities Panel

STARTED: 1976.

FUNDING: $37,000 Rockefeller Brothers Fund., $15,000 from Edward John Noble Foundation, $15,000 Robert Sterling Clark Foundation, $7,500

Taconic Foundation, $5,000 New York Foundation, $3,000 New York Urban Coalition.

LOCATION: At offices of its member organizations and its main consultant, Interface (see page 193).

EMPHASIS: An analysis of the Board of Education's proposed expense budget for 1976-77, to ascertain the extent to which the cuts forced on the system by the fiscal crisis and the priorities it establishes insure that as much money as possible goes to the classroom. The concern, then, is with the basic allocation of monies. It is also concerned with productivity at the school level. Working on the assumption that the budget is a political document, it attempts to represent the clients of the system (students, parents, and other educational consumers), as the unions and professional associations have represented the educators. Particular budget areas of intensive analysis include leasing arrangements for school buildings, the school lunch program, and the custodians' contract. It has also been concerned with legislation necessary to modify existing practices and arrangements, e.g., to allow the dual use of school buildings.

The main proposals of its first study, April 1976, called for a reallocation of funds from administrative lines to direct instructional services. Based on its analysis, the panel suggested that a total of between $30 and $35 million could be shifted from administrative to instructional lines in the budget.

This is a coalition of 16 major civic organizations, including: Alliance for Children, Aspira of New York, Citizens Committee for Children, The City Club of New York, City-Wide Confederation of High School Parents Associations, Community Council of Greater New York, Community Service Society, League of Women Voters, New York Urban Coalition, Parents Action Committee for Children, Public Education Association, Queensboro Federation of Parents Clubs, Queens Lay Advocate Service, Urban League, United Parents Associations, and Women's City Club of New York.

TARGET: The budget process in the NYC Board of Education.

INFORMATION: Summaries of the Panel's work available from Interface.

Joint Action for Children

STARTED: Began formally in early 1976, after much prior planning the previous year.

FUNDING: A grant of $37,000 from the Rockefeller Brothers Fund to permit the equivalent of a year's operations. It is likely to be stretched to longer than a year.

LOCATION: 205 East 42nd Street, Room 2000, New York, NY 10017.

EMPHASIS: This is a coalition of four city-wide organizations—Citizens Committee for Children, Day Care Council of New York, Public Education Association, and United Parents Association—formed to ensure high priorities for programs serving children. Unlike the Educational Priorities Panel that was formed with a very specific goal—to indicate through a budget analysis how money could be released from school headquarters to districts and schools—the specific goals of this coalition are in the process of being developed. The stated purpose is to work for New York City children by strengthening child advocacy through exchange of information, planning joint strategies in an attempt to create a new force to press for children's rights. Much of the activity in recent weeks and months has been for the 4 agencies to learn more about one another's operations and to learn to work together. One emerging goal has been to try to effect more service integration among the city's many fragmented youth service agencies so that the program and service cuts that have to be made will cause the least harm to children. Coordinated, inter-agency planning, then, is one goal. The de-institutionalization of children is another. The Foundation co-sponsored a conference in the fall of 1976 on today's family as a foundation for the future.

TARGET: The children of New York City. Also effecting better coordination and integration of the fragmented delivery system as a means of better meeting the needs of the children.

STAFFING: 1 professional, part-time.

INFORMATION: From the program.

Legal Agencies And Programs

There has been a substantial amount of litigation in recent years relating to student rights and to such education policy and program issues as: expanding educational services for such special target groups as the handicapped and non-English-speaking students; protecting the rights of suspended students to remain in school and of high school papers to publish without censorship; changing civil service licensing standards and personnel practices to increase the number of minority educators in the system and to limit their being fired in large numbers in a period of budget cuts; changing the decentralization law to give the community school boards more power (for the advocates of decentralization) or less (for its opponents); re-zoning for desegregation; requiring the city to allot a fixed portion of its expense budget to education (the Stavisky Bill); and making principals legally designated as management.

Much of the litigation is carried on by just a few agencies and individuals. The New York Civil Liberties Union was one of the first and most active with regard to student rights, and it helped train some of the lawyers and volunteers who later worked in other agencies. The Public Education Association, already mentioned, has done much legal work. Perhaps the most active group now is Williamsburg Legal Services, which is involved in a variety of areas. Also the Puerto Rican Education and Legal Defense Fund was deeply involved in the class action suit related to bilingual education, though its main activities are in other cities and on other problems in New York.

New York Civil Liberties Union

The NYCLU has been involved for many years in programs related to protecting student rights in the city schools. In addition, it has helped train attorneys and paraprofessional staff for similar work in other agencies. Its main large project on student rights will be described here. It was, in addition, the sponsoring organization for the high school journalism workshop that was concerned with censorship issues. Finally, it has responded to requests from students and their parents relating to disciplinary problems, suspension, and censorship.

STARTED: The student rights program began in 1971.

FUNDING: $50,000 a year for two years from the Field Foundation and New York Foundation. NYCLU supported the program for another year after that.

LOCATION: Run from the NYCLU central office, 84 Fifth Avenue, New York, NY 10003, serving students and parents city-wide.

EMPHASIS: Protecting the rights of students who were subject to "arbitrary" treatment by the schools, involving suspensions, discipline, and/or freedom of expression.

TARGET: As stated above.

STAFFING: 2 lawyers, one researcher writer.

INFORMATION: Several reports, books, and pamphlets, including *Student Rights Handbook* of which several hundred thousand copies were circulated; *Rights of Students* by Alan Levine, attorney on NYCLU staff (Avon paperback); *Captive Voices* (Schocken paperback), describing the NYCLU nationwide study of high school journalism, including cases from New York. The handbook covers such issues as suspensions, transfers, and other removals from school; distribution of literature, buttons, and armbands; flag salutes and other ceremonies; dress and hair; parents' right to their children's school records; and many others.

There is also a report on the first two years of the student rights project (1970-72). It summarizes Board of Education policy and practice on student rights issues. The project had three main goals: information—telling people that students had rights and what those rights were; providing a place to call when students are denied their rights, with the NYCLU and this project becoming that place; and enforcement strategies, including litigation and having the project play a watchdog role. Though the project ended in 1974, the NYCLU still receives calls from students and parents with grievances against school officials, and it continues to respond by providing information and representing them.

Williamsburg Legal Services

STARTED: 1968, under the aegis of the Office of Economic Opportunity.

FUNDING: About $550,000 per year, through Community Action for Legal Services, the umbrella agency in New York City with fiscal and management responsibility for the legal services program.

LOCATION: Mostly in the Williamsburg and Greenpoint communities in Brooklyn, but has an increasingly city-wide focus. Office at 260 Broadway, Brooklyn, NY

EMPHASIS: It is a neighborhood law office serving residents of the above mentioned communities who are unable to afford private counsel. Its staff attorneys and paraprofessionals provide representation in a broad spectrum of areas, including housing, employment, family law, consumer or other commercial matters, welfare, and other governmental benefits. The office has had substantial involvement with legal issues surrounding public education since the community control movement. Its major areas of concern in this regard include the following:

Students' Rights: Representation at disciplinary hearings, access to and protection of active records, classifications, and assignment to "special" programs. Representation in this area, on an individual basis, frequently undertaken in conjunction with lay advocate groups, particularly Queens Lay Advocate Service.

Special Education: Obtaining special services to meet the particular needs of handicapped students both within and outside the public schools.

Local School Governance: Rights of parent associations, development of fair community school board election practices, and dissemination of voter and candidate information in cooperation with the Board of Elections, Board of Education, and various civic groups, including the Public Education Association, League of Women Voters, and United Parents Associations.

Public School Staff Selection and Retention Procedures: Development of job-relevant and non-discriminatory selection and seniority procedures. Participated in class action suit, *Rubinos et al. v. Board of Examiners et al.* (74 CIV 2240 S.D.N.Y.), alleging job discrimination and challenging the current examination and licensing system as violating the right of minority teachers and of public school students and their parents to an integrated public school faculty. Also represents parents of brain-injured children by seeking to help replace experienced teachers of the handicapped with more senior regular teachers who were or are about to be laid off and recertified to teach special classes.

Curriculum Development: Bilingual and bicultural education in District 14 (Williamsburg) with a heavy concentration of Spanish students.

Educational Rights: Sued, along with other organizations, in an unsuccessful attempt to stop the shortening of the school day, and encouraged the successful development of new state regulations defining the length of the school day at pre-cut levels.

District, Neighborhood, and More Locally Based Groups

ASFEC, see page 213.

Coalition of Associations of Black and Puerto Rican Educators and Supervisors

This is a recently formed group that has developed in response to the layoffs or "excessing" of many minority staff from the New York City schools with the fiscal cuts. It has been pressing three main issues: (1) the lack of any affirmative action plan in New York City, which ranked 30th of the 32 major American cities in 1972-73 in minority representation on staff and 32nd in ratio of minority staff to minority students. The new layoffs reduced minority representation to only 7% since September 1975, most of them black; (2) the virtual extinction of the group of "NTE" teachers (National Teachers Examination) many of them minority teachers who had been employed under special state legislation since 1971 and two-thirds of whom were laid off in September 1975; and (3) the discriminatory impact of favoring regular substitutes over more recently appointed regular teachers in layoff decisions.

This coalition's main activities have been to enlist broad-based support from many civic organizations, in addition to professional associations of minority educators, testimony at public hearings, and lobbying in Albany for new legislation that would curb minority layoffs by changing seniority rules. Also lobbying for an affirmative action law.

The main non-minority organizations supporting the coalition include, among others, Public Education Association, United Parents Association, and Queensboro Federation of Parents' Clubs.

Information available from Luis Mercado, P.S. 75, Manhattan, one of the leaders of the Coalition.

Community Development Agency Education Programs

This is the agency within the Human Resources Administration (HRA) of the City of New York that was funded by OEO and is responsible for community action programs throughout the city. Its education programs had included parent training for advocacy programs representing educational consumer interests (parents, students) and some high school equivalency programs leading to a diploma for out-of-school youth and adults. The community action component has been scaled down considerably, as federal and city funding have dropped since the 1960s. No significant school-related activity actually results from this agency's operations now. The programs exist within 26 designated poverty areas of the city and include such things as mobilizing local residents to vote in community school board elections.

Community School Boards Association

This is the organization that represents the community school boards, acting as their spokesman in relation to the central board, the city, Albany, and other public bodies. The Association does not represent all districts or all local citizen interests, which is not surprising, given the city's size and the tremendous diversity of local areas (in terms of population composition and educational needs), but it does seem to represent a majority of districts and is the closest the community boards have come to developing a citywide lobbying group.

STARTED: With decentralization, 1971.

FUNDING: Through membership dues, $500 per year for each community board.

LOCATION: Functions citywide. Has no central office or headquarters. President is Mr. Phillip Kaplan, chairman of community school board in District 15, 360 Smith Street, Brooklyn, NY 11231.

EMPHASIS: Various political and legal activities related to serving the interests of community school boards. During 1975-76, they have included: lobbying to get the Stavisky Bill passed to obtain more money for the schools and hold off any further cuts; court suit against the Board of Education for its shortened school day, to restore the lost time—a suit that the association lost; represented the community school board in an advisory capacity at all collective bargaining sessions with the teachers union; met with Board of Education representatives at regular Consultative Council sessions of headquarters and community boards; and involvement in miscellaneous other activities pertaining to the functioning of the school system as it affects the districts.

TARGET: Key decisions made at school headquarters, at City Hall, and in Albany that impinge on schools and districts, particularly decisions on budget, staffing, educational programs, and district rights and powers.

STAFFING: Run by volunteers. Officers and borough representatives.

Political Action, Advocacy, Consumer Programs

Harlem Parents School-Community Neighborhood Center

STARTED: In 1969, as a direct outgrowth of the I.S. 201 complex demonstration school district; since absorbed into District 5 under the decentralization law of the same year.

LOCATION: Paul Robeson Community Center, 514 West 126th Street, New York, NY 10027. Also at Community Association of East Harlem Triangle, 2322 Third Avenue, New York, NY.

EMPHASIS: The program has several components:

> *Parent Advocacy:* Assisting parents to gain access to student records and other information relating to school performance.
>
> *Student Services* of an Educational Nature: Includes tutoring to individual students and on a small group basis, both at the Center and in the home, supplemented by cultural enrichment activities (visits to museums, plays, and art festivals) and scholarships to independent schools.
>
> *Political Action:* A recent effort to examine the feasibility of education vouchers as an alternative to existing methods of financing schools. This involved both political activity pressing for enabling legislation and parent education within the community to promote greater local awareness of educational alternatives to public schools. This group has succeeded in getting a bill filed in the New York State Senate calling for a Voucher Demonstration Project. The group has also conducted school strikes, holding children out of public schools in the district, to protest and dramatize the poor education going on there.

TARGET: 200 students in District 5 being served by the educational program and others in the district.

STAFFING: 20 tutors and certified teachers and administrative staff, plus volunteers.

People Against Racism in Education (Pare)

STARTED: Early 1973, following a national conference of People Against Racism in Education in Chicago. New York City chapter organized formally in June 1974.

FUNDING: $2,500 a year, primarily through membership dues, conferences, forums, fund raising parties, sale of literature.

LOCATION: Citywide.

EMPHASIS: To help teachers understand and work against racist practices in the schools through workshops, curriculum development programs, in-service training classes, and racism awareness teams; to cope citywide with the UFT's racist policies in relation, for example, to discriminatory layoffs; to alert and organize community leaders and school staffs to prevent the escalation of racial conflict and violence such as occurred in Boston when black and Latin students were transferred to white schools. Helped prevent the escalation of racial violence at New Utrecht High School in Bensonhurst, Brooklyn, in September and October 1975, over a desegregation plan.

TARGET: Educators, college students, and especially prospective teachers, parents, and community leaders.

STAFFING: All volunteers.

CHANGES: Focused more on particular issues and school problems, e.g., discriminatory layoffs of minority educators and the Bensonhurst controversy over desegregation.

INFORMATION: From Charles Isaacs, 216 Park Place, Brooklyn; or Annie Stein, 400 Central Park West, New York, NY.

Queens Lay Advocate Service

This agency plays the same kind of strong advocacy role for students and parents in the Astoria-Long Island City area of Queens that United Bronx Parents does in the South Bronx, except that it concentrates most heavily on a single target group, the handicapped. Most of its clients are also minority students from proverty backgrounds. It, too, started out with some OEO funding and doing direct case advocacy for suspended students and other students whose rights were not being served by the schools. It moved on later to running its own educational programs as well as extending its case advocacy approach into a much broader issue advocacy one, e.g., it has reviewed and suggested changes in many Board of Education policies as related to student rights and programs for the handicapped.

STARTED: Spring 1970.

FUNDING: Close to $800,000 for all its activities. Much of it is now city tax levy monies for the alternative schools and group home that it runs. Historically it has received grants from Rockefeller Brothers Fund

($20,000), Norman Foundation ($7,500), Fund for The City of New York; New York Foundation, the Mayor's Criminal Justice Coordinating Council, and others.

LOCATION: Queens Lay Advocate Service, 29-28 41st Avenue, Room 508, Long Island City, NY 11101; Martin de Porres Center, 4-25 Astoria Boulevard, Astoria, NY; Martin de Porres School for Exceptional Children, 4-05 Astoria Boulevard, Long Island City, NY.

EMPHASIS: A consortium of child advocacy organizations that combines three sets of activities: direct case advocacy, representing individual students and their families; direct provider services, consisting of two contracted-out schools for the handicapped that it runs, a group home, and an affiliation with a special high school program; and broad issue advocacy, in which it has done major studies, participated actively on key task forces and commissions reviewing Board of Education policies with reference to the handicapped, high school drop outs, and suspended students.

Thus, it runs schools and a group home for the handicapped, suspended students, and drop outs; it provides legal representation for these students and others in this category, most of them minority students; and it is increasingly involved in policy-making by serving on the Chancellor's Task Force for Socially Maladjusted and Disturbed Children, on Governor Carey's Education Task force, on the Citizens' Committee for Children's Task Force to monitor programs for the handicapped, on Coalitions for the Education of the Handicapped, on the Children's Committee of the Queens Federation of Mental Health Agency, and on the Chancellor's Advisory Committee on Special Education. It has done a major study on drop outs and another large, frequently-cited study of the system for the education of emotionally handicapped children in New York City, *Lost Children,* funded by the John Hay Whitney Foundation.

It deals not just with schools but with all agencies involved in providing services for youth, including the courts, mental health, day care, and others.

TARGET: The handicapped, drop outs, suspended students, poor, minority students, and, more generally, students and parents in need of assistance because of problems with schools and other youth-serving agencies.

STAFFING: 54 people, including 1 attorney, 4 advocate caseworkers, 1 full-time volunteer at central office, and others.

AUSPICES: A private, non-profit consortium of three student advocacy organizations: Alternative Solutions for Exceptional Children (ASFEC), OEO-funded Education Action Center in Long Island City, and the Queens

Lay Advocate Service. ASFEC is a non-profit corporation, formed to improve services to poor socially and emotionally handicapped children. It has set up coordinated networks of services in targeted communities, the first being in the Long Island City-Astoria area in close cooperation with the Martin de Porres Community Service Center, the Steinway Mental Health Committee, and the Queens County Mental Health Society. The Education Action Center, a delegate agency of Qualicap Community Corporation, an OEO-funded community action agency, has provided direct services to individuals and families in the same area who have had problems with the schools. It monitors federal and state funding, to make sure that the funds reach the intended target populations. Finally, Queens Lay Advocate Service, formed in 1970 in cooperation with the New York Civil Liberties Union, trains paralegal volunteers to help parents and students with grievances to help assure fair treatment by the schools and responsive education.

In September 1973, the three agencies opened a central office to pool their resources and they were legally merged in the fall of 1976, to perform the following kinds of functions: (1) a central ombudsman with city-wide responsibility for protecting student rights, particularly poor emotionally and socially handicapped students; (2) a consultation unit to train people for advocacy work in different communities throughout the city; (3) an educational-rehabilitation service unit to help communities establish a network of services for this target population of students, such as ASFEC had been doing; and (4) a legal advocacy and research component to study laws affecting students and act as a legal consultant to the central and community offices.

CHANGES: (1) From the use of volunteers (parents) to professionally trained people (lawyers, educators); (2) from individual case advocacy to broader issue advocacy, policy studies, and the actual delivery of services in alternative facilities; (3) from a local, OEO-funded community action focus to participation on city and state task forces, commissions, and coalitions to shape educational policy for the handicapped; and (4) has become a more organized and focused advocacy unit.

INFORMATION: Many reports and their regular publication, *The Advocate.*

Teachers Action Caucus of the UFT

STARTED: 1968, during the teachers strike, as a group that opposed the closing of schools. It was made up of teachers, other school workers, and parents who felt that the strike over decentralization was not a contractual issue and that the UFT leadership was bent on dividing the staff from each other and from the black and Hispanic communities. The original name for the group was Teachers for Community Control. The name was changed the following year to reflect the goal of working as a caucus within the union, to turn its leadership around.

FUNDING: Completely from dues and contributions from members. Special contributions are asked from members for particular activities, e.g., ads, travel to conventions, and caucus meetings in other cities.

LOCATION: This is a city-wide caucus. Often reach individual schools through the mass media and even through the union newspaper. Have also had success in reaching people through demonstrations, speeches at local school board meetings, and Board of Education hearings. Judge themselves to be strongest in Districts 1, 3, 17, 23, 31, and the high schools. Office at 1133 Broadway, New York, NY 10010.

EMPHASIS: Attempting to save the public school system by joining with parents for smaller class size, full school programs, more interesting ones, full breakfast and lunch programs, after-school programs, continued free transportation, bilingual education, black history programs. Have fought to eliminate the Board of Examiners and to increase the number and percentage of black and hispanic staff. Have also pressed hard for more rights within the schools of unionized paraprofessionals, particularly grievance rights and salaries.

TARGET: All members of the teachers union, including teachers, school secretaries, paraprofessionals, guidance counsellors, and special education teachers, including unemployed UFT members. Have a membership of more than 200 and claim to reach more than 10,000 teachers and paraprofessionals.

STAFFING: All volunteers from among employed, unemployed, and even some retired teachers, some paraprofessionals, guidance counsellors. No full-time staff.

CHANGES: The main goals are the same: increased union democracy; quality education; and community control—the issue that started the caucus. As the short-term issues and forces have changed, the caucus has changed its priorities to reflect that. Recent issues relate to the fiscal cuts, e.g., the firing of so many thousands of teachers and other staff and the resulting deterioration of local school conditions.

INFORMATION: The TAC *Newsletter*.

United Bronx Parents

This was one of the most active community action and advocacy programs in education in New York City in the 1960s, funded heavily by OEO and some private sector sources, including the New York Urban Coalition. It has continued its advocacy efforts in the 1970s, but it has shifted to many educational programs as well. It has been widely referred to by federal agencies and educational research agencies as an important exemplary program.

STARTED: 1964.

FUNDING: Federal, state, and city; public and private. Present funding from the Agency for Child Development, the Human Resources Administration, and Addiction Services Agency in the city as well as from Albany.

LOCATION: 810 East 152nd Street, Bronx, NY 10455

EMPHASIS: Parent training for effective monitoring and evaluation of the public schools; continuing to play a citizen advocate role there. It also has many educational programs, including English as a Second Language for adults and drop outs; high school equivalency classes in Spanish; a day care center for children ages 3-6; family day care in the home; after school programs for 1st and 2nd graders; drug prevention; recreation; college referral for youth; and summer lunch and breakfast programs.

TARGET: Students and parents in the South Bronx.

STAFFING: Over 125 people in all these programs.

CHANGES: While still maintaining its advocacy efforts, it has shifted with the changes in federal funding to a wide variety of programs for different client (age) groups in the area.

Locally Based Programs

There are some locally based advocacy groups that are involved mainly in educational programs, which is their form of advocacy. While organizations like Queens Lay Advocacy Services and Harlem Parents Union do some of that, it is not their sole function as it is for the organizations listed here. Two of them, it will be noted, are in District 3 in Manhattan's Upper West Side, one of the most politically active of all the community school districts. Both are the only programs of their kind in the entire city.

Political Action, Advocacy, Consumer Programs

Joint Schools Committee College Entry Program

STARTED: 1961 in Manhattanville, West Harlem, when several local parents associations, very disturbed by the poor quality of their children's education, decided to work together to solve problems common to all.

FUNDING: 1960-69, volunteer, small contributions; 1969-71, Community Education Center and state funding; 1971, Exxon; 1971 on, Ford Foundation; 1972-73, Riverside Church, Episcopal Diocese, Deerfield Foundation, Joint Foundation, College Entrance Examination Board, New York Urban Coalition; 1973-74, ESAA federal grant; 1974 on, Episcopal Diocese, Riverside Church, College Entrance Examination Board, individual contributions.

LOCATION: Joint Schools Committee, 514 West 126th Street, New York, NY 10027.

EMPHASIS: The main emphasis has been to facilitate the educational achievement of minority group students. This has included: (1) Educational remediation and counseling, primarily to high school students, many of them already drop outs when received by the Committee. All these students required and received financial aid. It has provided these services to over 7,000 minority group youth, 90% of whom have finished high school and gone on to college or are still in high school. More than 60% are now attending college. (2) Developing new educational programs, including the elimination of social studies textbooks found to be racially and historically incorrect and their replacement with others. Also sponsored a successful reading program staffed by volunteers. (3) Worked for reduced minority group isolation by joining with parents throughout the city, particularly in West Harlem for desegregated open high schools. Achievements include access to such high schools for 9th graders of segregated J.H.S. 43 in West Harlem and the Board of Education's use of rented space as a way of opening school sites in white or integrated areas. (4) Set up an ombudsman advisory and advocacy service for poor minority students and their parents who felt the Board of Education had treated them unjustly, e.g., as related to lack of guidance services, follow up instruction, suspensions, and drop outs. Has represented students in schools where they were tracked or labelled as handicapped or as problems and helped get transfers to other schools or changes in the student's situation in the existing school. Has appeared at numerous suspension hearings, representing individual students. (5) Assistance in solving non-academic problems, e.g., housing, employment, day-care, health, for those wanting to continue education. (6) Cultural workshops—writing, art, photography, sewing—to instill confidence in minority youth and increase their motivation to achieve.

TARGET: Minority youth, particularly in the West Harlem area.

STAFFING: Paid staff members and volunteers.

CHANGES: Has become more citywide in terms of students served and has many more programs and services on a bigger scale.

Experimental and Bilingual Institute, Inc.

STARTED: Fall 1971, through the sponsorship of the local anti-poverty Massive Economic Neighborhood Development (MEND). Since 1973, it has become independent and has secured its own funds, due to cutbacks in the poverty program. The Institute has developed an extensive remedial educational program for East Harlem youth, most of them Hispanic, to better prepare them for college.

FUNDING: No data on present funding. Had obtained a substantial amount of public and private funding in the past, including $477,000 from the Model Cities Administration for basic operations; $643,000 from the U.S. Office of Education's Fund for the Improvement of Post-Secondary Education; $72,000, together with Hunter College, under a New York State Title I, Higher Education grant; $12,000 from the city's Manpower and Career Development Agency for a summer field work program; $5,000 from Chemical Bank and Consolidated Edison for the development and implementation of a fine arts program; $5,000 from the New York Urban Coalition toward the development of its library; $1,000 from the First National City Bank for a math and language skills laboratory; and others.

LOCATION: Experimental and Bilingual Institute, Inc., 177 East 104th Street, New York, NY 10029.

EMPHASIS: The Institute is an East Harlem based adult education college-feeder program established to insure a well trained resource of Puerto Rican, Hispanic, and black American professionals in the human service area. It is committed to (1) insure higher education opportunities for motivated adult high school graduates for whom language, poor academic preparation and guidance, as well as a lack of self-confidence would otherwise be barriers; (2) motivate students to pursue professional careers in areas of critical need to their community's development; and (3) instill in students a sense of social commitment and accountability to their community.

Particular programs include remediation in math and English, directed at developing pre-college proficiency; college level courses in math, English, Spanish, social sciences, natural and life sciences, and fine arts;

intensive tutoring on group and individual level, including use of the Institute's language lab; science equipment; audio-visual equipment and aids, and a mini-bookstore; a wide variety of supportive student services, e.g., counselling and guidance in the development of academic skills, including planning one's study schedule, use of the library and laboratories, and communicating with tutors and other faculty. It has a library and a broad community service program, through its advisory board, which encourages general community use of its facilities and educational programs.

TARGET: Adult high school graduates in East Harlem, primarily Hispanic. Has served roughly 300 a year.

STAFFING: 28: administrative and educational.

INFORMATION: Prospectus, bulletin, and other descriptive materials from the Institute.

Learning Disabilities Committee and Program, Parents' Association, P.S. 75 (Man)

STARTED: The first program began within the school in the spring of 1974 and lasted for two months; the present program began in April 1975.

FUNDING: The Committee's expenses came initially from parent donations. All work done on a volunteer basis by the 31 families who were members. The program was funded also from accrued tax-levy money ($3,000), Title I funds ($5,400), parents association donations ($590), and contributions from First National City Bank ($360) and Banco de Ponce ($50). Much larger grants in 1976, including New York Community Trust ($30,000), Frank E. Clark Fund of Manufacturers Hanover Trust ($10,000), Chase Manhattan Bank ($2,500) Ettinger Foundation ($1,800).

LOCATION: P.S. 75.

EMPHASIS: Provides training and support services for classroom teachers to serve children with learning disabilities in regular classrooms. Specifically, it has provided teachers with masters-level student teachers who are part-time learning disability specialist consultants and supportive personnel. 100 children have been reached in regular classrooms, and most have shown improvement in skill level and attitude.

TARGET: P.S. 75 elementary school students with learning disabilities. Could be done anywhere.

STAFFING: Masters-level student teachers working with regular classroom teachers. The need, however, to reach students with learning disabilities in that school is much greater.

CHANGES: Trying to expand, particularly to reach the school's Spanish dominant population, and now seeking more private and public funding. Regard the program a model for others in inner city schools.

INFORMATION: From Margaret Whelan, 270 Riverside Drive, New York, NY 10025, chairman of the Learning Disabilities Committee.

Pre-School Association of the West Side, Inc. (PAWS), Bank Street College of Education

This is a grassroots effort to cope with a problem not addressed by government agencies dealing with child care. In 1969, there was no neighborhood center for the exchange of information and support across lines of funding and sponsorship for early childhood programs, e.g., nursery schools, day care centers, and Head Start centers. This organization, PAWS, grew out of a recognition of that problem by many child care program representatives who were concerned with improving communication among existing programs and improving and expanding services for children on the West Side of Manhattan.

STARTED: 1969.

FUNDING: $38,929 for 1975-76. Roughly $33,000 from foundations; $1,400 from membership dues; $944 from individuals; $562 from corporations; and other sources.

LOCATION: Bank Street College of Education, 610 West 112th Street, New York, NY 10025.

EMPHASIS: Functions as a clearing house for parents seeking child care and for schools and centers that have openings for children. Informs parents of child care options they may not know exist. Assists agencies to adjust to changing conditions and demand in the neighborhood.

> Parents: Counselling done by phone, mail, and drop-in visits. Provides a directory of all West Side early childhood programs that it published in 1974 and updates annually. That directory is available throughout the community in various agencies, libraries, schools, and centers. Also reaches parents who may not know of PAWS services by frequent publication of child care information in a local, free newspaper.
>
> Schools and Centers: Provides technical assistance to child care agencies on matters of facilities, staff, incorporation, license and tax exemption, maintaining enrollment, budgeting, and finding resources for the classroom and for families.

Also an important liaison between local programs and citywide agencies. PAWS coordinator now the chairperson to the citywide day care community's advocate organization, the Ad Hoc Coalition to Save the Children.

Monthly PAWS Newsletter: Includes information on local programs, changes in legislation affecting them, job openings, and a calendar of conferences, workshops, and benefits.

Part of a national network of child care agencies: Hosted representatives of 11 other child care information and referral organizations from cities throughout the country in May 1975. This network has begun helping other communities begin their own information and referral organizations.

Funding help: Has helped stimulate several funding innovations in child care programs, including: (1) new, limited purchase of service agreements between the city and various child care agencies that integrate children eligible for publicly funded day care with those who pay full fees; (2) has had 20 VISTA volunteers work in day care and Head Start programs on the West Side, with their salaries paid by the federal government; they work in classrooms with children and one has been assigned as PAWS staff; (3) found in 1973 that some of the state appropriation for meals served to day care and Head Start children was being returned unspent, while centers were buying food with general day care funds. Through circulating this information to local centers and questioning the city's day care-Head Start funding office, PAWS helped ensure that such state funds for food were better utilized.

TARGET: Pre-school children and agencies serving them on Manhattan's West Side, generally defined as the area from West 59th to West 125th Streets, Central Park to Riverside Park. The uniqueness of the organization is this local geographic focus and its comprehensiveness regarding the variety of types of programs for children.

STAFFING: 3. Paid coordinators, 2 VISTA volunteers.

Information and Media Programs

A critical element in educational change efforts is developing a knowledgeable and sophisticated body of consumers who know what their rights are, how well the schools are performing and meeting consumer needs, and how to gain access to agency decision-makers to make them respond better. The one program that deals extensively with these questions is *City School News,* created by a consortium of corporations, foundations, civic leaders, and social agencies to generate information on a regular basis to the citizens of New York on the state of the schools. Information is disseminated mainly by radio, through public service broadcasting, but perhaps supplemented by other media as well. The other group of information-producing efforts in this vein is all the key studies prepared by civic groups and commissions, along with their newsletters, on the public schools.

City School News, Inc.

STARTED: Extensive planning began in 1973, but the project became operational in September 1976, when radio programs began. Three organizations got together in 1973—the Rockefeller Brothers Fund, Exxon Corporation, and the Fund for The City of New York—to investigate what kinds of information about New York City schools are available to parents. They formed a committee whose report indicated that the quality and quantity of information were quite limited and biased in terms of the "hidden agenda and persuasions of the sending group." Even parent and community leaders were often uninformed about what was going on outside their immediate school or district. Documenting the need, they proposed the establishment of a non-profit educational corporation to disseminate information about the schools through radio public service programming.

FUNDING: $50,000 Rockefeller Brothers, $25,000 Exxon, $15,000 New York Foundation, and $5,000 Chase Manhattan Bank.

LOCATION: City School News, Inc., 405 Park Avenue, New York, NY.

EMPHASIS: To provide parents and interested community members with the information necessary to allow them to monitor the schools effectively; to provide the kind of in-depth analysis of issues that is presently lacking in the media; to create, through coverage of otherwise closed decision-making, pressures to open up proceedings to consultation with all affected parties; and to improve the quality of reporting on education by the other media in the city, both by providing a new source of information on important issues and by challenging existing existing news sources to give more attention to this field.

TARGET: Public education consumers in New York City: parents, employers, students, and other interested citizens.

STAFFING: 5: director, assistant director, 2 journalists, and a secretary-receptionist.

Selected Studies and Reports

Attendance in New York City's Public Schools. Community Council of Greater New York, June 1975.

Breakfast and Lunch Programs in New York City Schools. Community Council of Greater New York, March 1975.

Detour to Education: The Transportation Troubles of Handicapped School Children, prepared for the Committee on Education by Florence Flast. Community Service Society, June 1975.

Education Legislation in New York State, prepared by Eleanor Stier. Community Service Society, November 1975.

Lost Children, A Descriptive Study of The System for the Education of Emotionally Handicapped Children in the City of New York, by William J. Jesinkey and Jane R. Stern. Alternative Solutions for Exceptional Children, Inc., 1974.

The Role of Local Community School Districts in New York City's Expense Budget Processes. Citizens Budget Commission, June 1975.

Report on Bilingual Education, prepared for the Committee on Education by Lois S. Steinberg. Community Service Society, June 1974.

Report on Bilingual Pilot Schools in New York City, prepared for the Committee on Education by Esther Johnson. Community Service Society, August 1975.

School Decentralization in New York City, prepared for the State Charter Revision Commission for New York City by Diana R. Gordon and Dr. Jacob Landers. June 1974.

Many management and policy analyses by the Deputy Chancellor's office, including *Strengthening Business Management in The Division of Special Education and Pupil Personnel Services.*

Newsletters

The following civic organizations issue regular newsletters and reports:

Citizens Committee for Children — Numerous reports and press releases on various school-related matters.

Economic Development Council — *Renewal,* newsletter, plus numerous reports, descriptions, and evaluations.

New York Urban Coalition — *Options-in-Learning,* monthly magazine reporting on strategies and experimental programs.

Public Education Association — PEA Reports. Contains extensive policy analyses of major school issues, including budgets, collective bargaining, school programs of all kinds, particularly for special target groups, licensing procedures for teachers and supervisors, financing, and other matters. Also quite technical. Has a strong consumer advocacy position that tends to be very critical of Board of Education practices.

Queensboro Federation of Parent Clubs — Monthly newsletter.

Queens Lay Advocate Service — The Advocate. Reports in a definitive fashion on Board of Education policies and practices related to student rights, with strong emphasis on the rights of various categories of handicapped students, dropouts, and suspended students.

United Bronx Parents — Periodic papers and analyses of school issues.

United Federation of Teachers — The New York Teacher. This is the union's forum to support candidates for public office and to wage campaigns around particular issues. UFT President Albert Shanker also writes a weekly column in the *New York Sunday Times* giving the union's positions on local school issues.

United Parent Associations — School Parent, and *United Parents Associations Newsletter.* Contains a lot of material relating to legislation, budget hearings, new school programs, and various school issues. Often very technical.

Chapter 5

Inventory of Participative, School- and District-Based Planning

The limited impact that various educational reform strategies had on the schools during the 1950s and 60s period were a great disappointment for citizen groups and educators. Compensatory education programs, desegregation, decentralization, pilot projects, alternative schools, open education, and new management techniques had all been pursued as reform activities that it was hoped might begin to effectively "turn around" the public schools. In fact, they did not, and there has been much soul-searching trying to figure out why. One explanation is that they had neither the resources (money), nor the political support to be effectively implemented, and there is probably much merit in that view. Another, however, that deserves serious consideration, is that too little attention was paid to the actual *process* of producing change in all these improvement efforts. This refers, in particular, to how the "outsiders" usually involved in such efforts, e.g., state and federal agencies, foundations, universities, corporations, and research and development firms, might best gain entry into the schools, what kind of helping relationship they should establish, to what degree they should attempt to impose a new model on the schools or let one emerge from a participative, school-based planning process, and what role they should play at implementation.

A landmark publication in this vein, urging a much more participative approach by educational change agents and reformers, is Seymour Sarason's *The Culture of The School and The Problem of Change* (Allyn and Bacon, 1971). Sarason, a professor of anthropology at Yale who has spent many years in improvement efforts with schools, spells out with many examples the components of what he regards as a productive participation strategy. He urges reformers not to come in with a critical and elitist approach, assuming that they, as experts, know more than the educators about what is wrong and how to correct it. A recent trend in line with Sarason's thinking has been the increasing application of organizational development techniques that have previously been applied more in business and industry than to public schools. An extensive literature now exists in this field, one of the most recent examples of which is Richard A. Schmuck and Matthew Miles (eds.), *Organization Development in Schools* (National Press Books, 1971).

As a close reading of this literature soon indicates, however, there are no established principles on how to proceed more effectively with change efforts, notwithstanding the compelling arguments that OD advocates make for the participative strategy. OD (organizational development) is a developing discipline with many sophisticated critics, some of them its own theoreticians, who question what they regard as the political naivete of most of their colleagues' underlying assumptions, e.g., that through persistent attempts at improved communication among all the key participants, one can move toward the effective implementation of change efforts in institutions. Indeed, even within OD itself, there are some practitioners arguing for more explicitly political strategies—e.g., coalition building and power confrontation approaches—as critical elements in the change process. We will review these issues in greater depth in the concluding section of the report.

Despite the ambiguities in this complex field, and partly to shed more light on them, both the National Institute of Education, through its school-based renewal grants, and the Office of Education have been funding various OD programs around the country. Two of the most significant of such programs now exist in New York City and are reviewed in

Participative, School, and District Planning

this chapter. One is the Economic Development Council's efforts at organizational renewal in 16 high schools, which began in 1968 and has been developing and expanding ever since. The other is the New York Urban Coalition's school and district-based planning programs, which now exist in several sites throughout the city and follow much the same format as EDC's. Each organization works in a close, collabroative way with school headquarters, community school districts, and individual schools; and each represents the successful mobilization of business resources for school change programs. NIE has funded both as important pilot projects and has contracted to have their experiences documented for use elsewhere.

Economic Development Council, School Renewal Program

The Economic Development Council, a non-profit, private corporation with a membership of over 200 mostly large corporations, has had a program of technical assistance and renewal in New York City high schools since 1969. It started with partnerships with 2 high schools, added 2 more the following year, 4 more in 1974, and now has 16. Over time, the model or approach changed and got progressively refined, relying less and less on outside business support and generating more impetus for renewal activity from within the system. It has been funded since 1974 by NIE and is regarded as an important demonstration program that has national significance in terms of developing strategies for business-school partnerships and self-renewal and OD efforts in inner-city high schools.

STARTED: 1969 after about a year of preliminary study and planning.

FUNDING: $5,100,000 since 1968. That includes Board of Education, EDC, foundation, and government funding, with EDC having played the lead or main role in securing the latter two. The EDC contribution has been roughly 61 person-years of executives-on-loan at a cost of $1.5 million; another $2 million from the Board of Education, mainly in compensation of teachers and administrators in the target schools; $240,000 from NIE; $150,000 from the Rockefeller Foundation; $105,000 from the Rockefeller Brothers Fund; $35,000 from the J.M. Foundation; $25,000 from the Robert Sterling Clark Foundation; and others.

LOCATION: In 16 high schools, with administrative support and technical assistance from the Access Office in the Division of High Schools, the Center for Educational Management (both at school headquarters), EDC headquarters, and Policy Studies in Education, a research and development agency that has provided extensive direction and consulting assistance to the schools. Economic Development Council, Inc., 260 Madison Avenue, New York, NY 10016; Policy Studies in Education, 52 Vanderbilt Avenue, New York, NY 10019.

The high schools are as follows: Benjamin Franklin, Charles Evans Hughes, George Washington, Julia Richman, Louis D. Brandeis (Man); James Monroe, Morris, Theodore Roosevelt, Walton (Bx); Bay Ridge, Bushwick, Eastern District, Franklin K. Lane (Bkn): Andrew Jackson, Thomas Jefferson, William Cullen Bryant (Q).

EMPHASIS: to stimulate a continuous, systematic, problem-solving process of change within schools, designed to more effectively meet the needs of students and staff. This is done through the application of behavioral science concepts and techniques, in particular utilizing participative methods wherever feasible with the help of both internal and external consultant facilitators. The objective is to provide an environment within which the desire for improvement can be supported and the creativity of teachers and students can be released.

The main emphasis, then, is on stimulating such a process within the schools. This has led to the generation of many new programs, including remedial English and math, career education, ESL, drug and absenteeism programs, intramural sports, in-service training for teachers, and others.

STAFFING: 5 from-EDC; assistance from school headquarters; and 2.8 staff units in each of the 16 renewal schools.

TARGET: 24 high schools, their planning and problem-solving process and educational programs. 8 of the 24 were added in late 1976. Ultimately, the target is all high schools in the city.

CHANGES: The project moved steadily away from extensive participation by on-loan executives recruited by EDC and more toward the Board of Education itself, creating the release time and staff units to direct the renewal process and generate new programs in each of the high schools. There has also been more and more experimentation with different types of planning councils or mechanisms within the schools, to see which ones work well under what conditions.

INFORMATION: Extensive reports, program descriptions, and internal evaluations from EDC and Police Studies in Education. Also the project's newsletter, *Renewal,* the first issue of which appeared March 1976.

New York Urban Coalition District- and School-Based Planning

The New York Urban Coalition was formed, as were so many other branches of the National Urban Coalition, in 1967, in response to the ghetto riots. Composed of business, labor, and minority leaders, it supported both activist strategies (e.g., its support and lobbying for community control) and the development of educational programs within the school system itself. By 1970, it had formed a new education program unit that pursued almost exclusively the second strategy of working collaboratively with educators. Its main programmatic emphasis was mini-schools, but by 1974, it had expanded its program to include a wide variety of district and school-based planning projects.

STARTED: 1970 with mini-schools, since 1974 the present strategy.

FUNDING: $640,025; $407,098 of Coalition funds and $232,927 from outside sources, including ESAA grants, NIE funds, and foundations.

LOCATION: New York Urban Coalition, 1270 Avenue of the Americas, New York, NY 10036. The local partnerships and planning programs have been in Districts 5, 7, 8, and 12; the Access Office in the Division of High Schools in relation to Coalition work in 10 mini-high schools; and the Learning Coop (now called the Center for School Development) for work on 8 Beacon Light schools.

EMPHASIS: To be a catalyst for positive change in the public schools by pursuing a broad range of intervention strategies, each of which is explored, critiqued, and modified as necessary, with the information generated from the programs then publicly and regularly shared with all interested agencies and citizen groups. The main present strategy, underway since July 1974, is school- and district-based planning or development teams, composed of all the main constituencies in the schools listed above. In addition to all the partnerships, mini-schools, Beacon Light schools, the Coalition publishes an important monthly magazine, *Options-in-Learning,* that reviews many intervention strategies and experimental programs it has been able to identify. It also has a volunteers project, an education program advisory committee of representatives of many agencies, in-service training programs for school personnel, and a very active fund raising program to generate more support for the interventions it has helped get underway.

TARGET: Districts, schools, and students throughout the public school system, through the development and spread of successful intervention strategies or institutional renewal models. 26 schools at present.

STAFFING: 19.

CHANGES: Moved from paying limited atttention to a participative planning process before 1974 to a strong emphasis on it after that. Now working with the Center for School Development to further expand on Coalition-initiated programs in the various schools and districts.

INFORMATION: Various program summaries from the Coalition as well as issues of *Options-in-Learning*.

Brief Summary:

District 5: 1974-76; I.S. 201; $8,000 a year from Coalition; 1 part-time facilitation person; 1,000 students.

District 7: 1974-76; I.S. 162; 1,000 students.

District 8: 1975-77; 3 I.S. 52, J.H.S. 125, I.S. 152; $8,000 a year from Coalition; part-time facilitating stafff in each school; 2,500 students.

District 12: 1975-77; C.S. 129, I.S. 134, C.S. 158; $150,000 in ESAA funds; 2,500 students.

Learning Cooperative Board of Education; 8 Beacon Light schools; $20,000 Fels Foundation.

Access Office Board of Education; 10 mini-high schools; $8,000 Urban Coalition funds.

Chapter 6

Main Trends in Educational Improvement Efforts

The reader has by now probably been so overwhelmed by the number and scope of the educational improvement efforts described and so immersed in detail as to be quite uncertain about the main trends and what all this activity adds up to. Yet it is important to have some over-all summary that suggests where school reform activity in New York is going—to indicate gaps as well as areas of duplication, overlap, and conflict. Such a summary may further indicate, even if only indirectly, what seems to work and what doesn't, by delineating those change efforts that have been abandoned, those that have continued at the same level of resources, and those that have become more prevalent. Such information may, in turn, suggest guidelines for agencies interested in intervening more effectively in the future.

This chapter presents such an analysis of trends, followed by a concluding one that reviews the main change strategies that have been pursued thus far in New York City. We end with suggestions about the kinds of strategies and combinations thereof that may be effective in the future.

Relevant Background

Before considering the trends, however, the reader needs some context against which they may be interpreted. Several general points are relevant. One is that despite all the change activity reported here, many of the schools' key client groups (e.g., parents, students, and employers) still find public education in New York considerably less than satisfactory. Admittedly, conceptualizing and measuring performance in such a public sector agency is extremely complex. Definitions are as varied as the interests of the many involved participants, and a public school system is not like a business corporation where agreed upon "bottom line" results can readily be used. The school system serves far too many interests for that—providing jobs, tenure, consulting and other contracts, and a training experience for future political leaders (e.g., by serving on community school boards, on the central board, or as civic group activists) as well as educational programs.

Just viewing the schools from the latter perspective, there have clearly been no dramatic breakthroughs as measured by reading and math scores, dropout, absenteeism, and suspension rates, and types of diplomas of high school graduates. Relevant information is still limited, but what we have does not indicate much, if any, improvement. A recent study of drop outs from New York City high schools by the Queens Lay Advocacy Service, for example, indicates a steady increase from 34% of all entering 9th graders who failed to graduate four years later in 1965-66 to 49.7% for the 1974-75 graduating class. Since one may reasonably assume that dropout rates are probably correlated with such other measures as reading and math scores, the picture is fairly grim.

Interpretations of these trends, however, are very complex, and whether the fault lies primarily with the system itself, with the conditions of poverty and segregation that affect its many minority students, with the general decline of the city, particularly its recent fiscal decline, or some combination is very difficult to discern in any precise way. New York's failures do not differ in this regard from those of other inner cities that face the same socio-economic problems, but that doesn't diminish at all the urgency of finding reform strategies that will reverse the decline. Indeed, the city's future economic viability depends on it, since one major reason for the middle class and business exodus that has so diminished the tax base has been an increasing lack of confidence in the public schools.

Though not facing the political turmoil of the 1960s that culminated in the community control controversy from which many participants have still not completely recovered, the New York City school system thus remains in very serious trouble. It faces, at a minimum, the following financial and institutional problems:

> Unprecedented fiscal cuts that made the 1975-76 school year one of the most traumatic in history, with promises for more of the same in the immediate future.
>
> Continued uncertainty and problems with decentralization, due largely to an ambiguous law that fails to spell out in enough detail the respective powers of headquarters and the districts and gives inadequate powers to the latter.
>
> A headquarters bureaucracy that, though improved in its structure, its managment, and in particular divisions, has not yet become the kind of effective service center and technical assistance agency required under decentralization and remains at best in an armed truce relationship with the districts.
>
> The districts themselves still in drastic need of improved management with important efforts just getting underway in that direction.
>
> There remains a limited cadre of talented and experienced managers within the system, particularly at the top, due to archaic civil service procedures.
>
> The system consequently remains insider-dominated and highly particularistic, with top appointments and program decisions based on loyalties and traditions going back many years.
>
> Finally, it is enmeshed in an intergovernmental network of legal and financial relations that constitute severe constraints on effective management. They include (a) its fiscal de-

pendence on the city, thereby limiting the school board and Chancellor's authority on important budget, staffing, and program decisions; (b) a general fragmentation of authority between school headquarters and city hall; and (c) a consequent limit on the extent of political accountability since it is difficult to pinpoint who is ultimately responsible for major school decisions.

In brief, the New York City school system has many institutional problems and shortcomings that prevent it from effectively delivering educational services regardless of its level of resources. The schools now face very serious budget cuts, but they don't have the institutional capability to deliver services effectively, even when given adequate funding. This poses a serious dilemna for reformers. If they argue against providing the schools with more funds, they are seen as anti-education and as aligned with conservatives concerned more with efficiency than with the city's youth and minorities. On the other hand, to support increased budgets without at the same time requiring major changes in the entire structure and operations of the system is to help spread inefficiency.

And yet there is a more positive side that is important to acknowledge in working out an effective reform strategy: (1) there remain in the New York City school system many talented and committed educators, running some good programs; (2) some of the same kind of talent, commitment to change, and involvement in various educational improvement activities exists within the private sector; and finally; (3) there are enough promising programs around, despite the many problems, that it is essential to take stock of them and support those that seem effective. Indeed, were these talented people and programs given the appropriate level of support and the right setting, there might well be some prospect of significantly improving public education in New York City. The failure to do so over the past couple of decades indicates that it isn't easy, but the stakes are so high and the talented people and good programs are in

Main Trends in Educational Improvement Efforts 235

enough abundance as to indicate that it is well worth the effort. The question is what should be done, how, and with whom. This inventory provides information that is helpful in at least beginning to answer those questions.

Principal Recent Trends

With this as background, we turn now to a summary of the main trends.

Alternative Schools

There has been a marked expansion of alternative school programs, both inside and outside the school system. The alternative high schools, the auxiliary services for high schools program, the mini-schools, the programs for the talented, the magnet schools, the contracted-out schools for the handicapped, and the open education programs are all examples. While most of the alternative schools were at one time outside the system, with their philosophy popularized mainly through the writings of the "romantic school critics" (Kozol, Kohl, Hentoff, Holt, Postman, Gross, and Dennison) whom some educators had dismissed as soft-headed and utopian, many of the concepts have now become incorporated into the regular school system. To be sure, it was not always done that smoothly, and serious questions can and should be raised as to whether these programs become diluted as they are absorbed into the existing school system.

Many educators are ambivalent about alternative schools. They like the schools' availability as dumping grounds for "problem students," but they don't want the staff to have the same academic credentials, and they feel quite threatened if the schools claim better results with these students, particularly if they are achieved at less cost than in mainstream schools. Several alternative high schools have made such claims and at least one, Auxiliary Services for High Schools, has some data to back them up.

There are some benefits, however, from having these schools in the system. The main one is that they do receive supportive services from such headquarters offices as the Division of High Schools, Career Education, Bilingual Education, and the Center for School Development. The Access Office within the Division of High Schools, for example, was set up primarily to oversee and support these programs, and it has been a source of help.

What is most needed now is much more information on the relative cost-effectiveness of these schools and much more political support to allow them to continue at some minimal level of support. We need to know which ones work and which don't, which components of their programs are more or less effective, and whether being inside or outside the system has more positive effects as related to the schools' performance and how.

Systems Approach

A second and related trend is the increased emphasis in many specialized programs on more comprehensive approaches to change. This is commonly referred to in academic and business circles as a systems approach, recognizing that any single problem is a result of many interacting causes. Thus, drug prevention programs are often linked up with various other services, e.g., job counselling, vocational and career programs, health services, basic skills development (reading and math), a bilingual component, staff development, and the use of alternative or mini-schools. The same could be said for programs that start out with a different emphasis. All are tending toward a more totalistic approach to school and student problems, based on the assumption that many aspects of the student, the school, and their environments must be changed for any significant improvements to take place. Faddism is quite rampant in educational reform efforts, and it is certainly possible for unthinking applications of this approach to result in programs that have the "new look" without a lot of substance. But the concept as such is a good one if applied thoughtfully.

A classic example, with mixed results, is the Haaren High School mini-school program. It involves a complete organizational and curriculum restructuring of the school, a major staff development component, an attempt to bring in more educational services, and more career-oriented programs. This totalistic approach is particularly warranted in a period of declining funds, when it seems worthwhile to have fewer and more comprehensive reform programs rather than proliferating so many specialized ones. Again, there is a great need for policy-relevant information on how these programs have fared, along with a political action strategy to generate the necessary support for those that seem most effective.

Cultural Pluralism

A third development that is particularly important in New York and other inner cities is educators' greater acceptance of the cultural pluralism of students as the basis for school programs. The establishment within the Board of Education of an Office of Bilingual Education and the active involvement of that office in staff development and in helping schools develop their own programs all reflect this emphasis. Much of it was a result of outside pressure, for example, the Aspira decision, but the system has nevertheless moved toward trying to reach minority students in the context of their own cultural heritage and experience.

It wasn't that long ago that school critics correctly

pointed to the white middle class (and sometimes even rural) bias of school programs and textbooks ("Dick and Jane readers") and to the schools' tendency to impose an alien culture on minority students rather than accepting as legitimate these students' ethnic traditions. This is not to abandon the notion that all students should be taught in the context of a common culture that will be central to their adult experience, but rather to acknowledge, accept, and work within the ethnic diversity that students represent.

Curriculum Innovations

Without going into great detail, we should also note the range of curriculum innovations that have characterized the period since 1970. Reflecting national trends career education programs have become more prominent in the New York City schools. Under the leadership of the Office of Career Education, many initiatives were taken in securing federal funds and using them for pilot programs that later were incorporated into regular tax levy funding. Bilingual programs, as just discussed, have been another new development, and the Office of Bilingual Education has played a similarly creative role in helping to support new programs in its field.

The other new curriculum developments, already reviewed, have been in: early childhood education; in the arts, with private sector money, the artists-in-residence, and agencies like the Teachers and Writers Collaborative involved in the schools; in open education, mainly through Dr. Lillian Weber; in alternative schools; in mini-schools; in environmental education; in individualized instruction; and in remedial reading and math programs, some of which try to deal with the social problems of students as factors affecting their proficiency in basic skills. The Beacon Light schools were one attempt to consolidate many of the above-listed programs and give them support.

Organizational Development

Viewing recent educational improvement efforts from the perspective of the types of change strategies adopted, there are two fairly pronounced trends. One is the increased emphasis on organizational development techniques as a way of bringing about change in schools by involving outside change agents in collaborative relations with the educators. The other is a clear shift in political action efforts from the broadside attacks on the school system in the 1960s for its failure to educate children to much more focused, more programmatic, and more research-based consumer advocacy efforts that are thereby much more effective in forcing the system to respond to citizen demands.

We regard the organizational development approach so important that we have devoted chapter 5 of the inventory to it, even though only two programs are included there. This strategy essentially involves a convening of all the main constituencies in the school, under the direction of a skilled group leader, to discuss its main problems, set priorities, develop programs, and help facilitate their implementation. The common use of such concepts as "participative planning", "school and district-based planning", and "local needs assessment" all reflects this strategy.

While the Economic Development Council's high school self-renewal program and the New York Urban Coalition's many school and district programs are the only examples of this strategy listed in that chapter of the inventory, it has in fact become a standard part of the repertoire of many others. Many teacher and supervisory training programs feature it, as well as those initiating management improvements, and the general philosophy is now wide-spread. As indicated, however, OD (organization development) is a field with a very limited knowledge base. It has yet to establish any validated principles of how to proceed with change, and it might well become one more fad that, uncritically applied, brings about little lasting change and more shattered expectations. This is not to deny the potential value of OD techniques but rather to indicate that getting institutions to change is much more complicated than standard OD techniques imply. As critics of OD have noted, the more bureaucratic and "political" an organization is, the more difficult it is to change it by the usual OD approaches.

Taking a more positive view, however, a recent development that flows directly from this OD philosophy has been the increased emphasis on new collaborative partnerships or linkages between the schools and outside private sector agencies, particularly universities and business. The many teacher training programs like Triple T and the Teacher Corps, the high school-college articulation programs, and the programs of EDC, the New York Urban Coalition, and of corporations working on their own are all examples. Much of the impetus for these collaborative relations came from the outside private agencies and from federal grant requirements. But it must also be said that the school system seems more open to such arrangements than in the past and had the same funds and private sector interest been available 10-15 years ago, the programs might not have begun or been as effective.

The shift in the community action efforts of civic groups has also been quite significant. Since the 1960s, with the demise of OEO, there has been a significant decline in political protest activity, but there is still considerable consumer advocacy work, though in new directions. Instead of taking on the system in its entirety and condemning it for its failures, there have developed much more rationalized advocacy efforts that are thereby much more effective in forcing the system to respond to citizen demands. The work of organizations like the Queens Lay Advocacy Service, PEA, Citizens Committee for Children, New York Civil Liberties Union, Aspira, Williamsburg Legal Aid, the Educational Priorities Panel, and the others listed in chapter 4 indicates the wide range of such activities. They include: monitoring and evaluating key school programs, effective lobbying and public testimony based on research studies, litigation, serving on key commissions and other policy-making bodies in an attempt to change school practices, representing individual clients (students, parents) with grievances against the schools, and even running programs to provide services that the school system has not made available. They constitute a more rational citizen advocacy effort than had existed in the past. There have always been private agencies doing "citizen watchdog" monitoring-type studies and lobbying, but there are now many more of them, and the quality of their research is often quite high.

Management Modernization

Another important trend is the beginnings of attempts at management modernization at almost all levels within the system. All of the projects reviewed—EDC, the Deputy Chancellor, the management consulting firms, the separate work on attendance, on management information systems, and on rationalizing headquarters and district management might well improve the capacity of the system to deliver services more cost effectively. Part of the failure of past reforms to have the impact their advocates had hoped for was the poor management and delivery system of the schools. Good educational programs, more money, and even talented staff would not have much impact if the system was unable to organize itself to use them well, particularly in the classroom.

Programs For The Handicapped and Non-English Speaking

We placed a lot of emphasis in the inventory on the development of programs for special target groups, and two deserve special mention—the handicapped and non-English-speaking. In each instance, a major court ruling forced the Board of Education to provide more services and give the group much higher priority than would otherwise have been the case. Special education programs have literally mushroomed since 1970, not yet meeting the tremendous need that exists but being far more extensive than ever before. The budget has increased accordingly during that time, and 26 alternative, contracted-out schools have been established as well, represented by their own association. Furthermore, one of the most effective consumer advocacy groups in the city, Queens Lay Advocate Service, now serves this special target group. Indeed, there is probably more organized and effective consumer advocacy for special education than for any other type of public school program.

Bilingual programs have had the same kind of exponential growth since 1970, in response to the same kinds of outside pressures. This target group, the non-English-speaking, is much bigger than the handicapped—close to 150,000, as contrasted to 40-50,000. At the same time, it faces much more severe political obstacles to having its programs accepted. The teachers union, for example, sees bilingual programs as a threat to teaching positions, since they require special licenses and language proficiency. In addition, bilingual programs rest more on state and federal funding than on city tax levy monies, and there is much less certainty about the long-term stability of such funding.

Inside and Outside Participants

Finally, we would like to emphasize a few other key trends: (1) the emergence of some key new inside and outside participants; (2) the new and more varied roles that both are playing, particularly the outsiders; and (3) the trend toward consolidation of private sector interventions, as these outside agencies seek to reach more of a critical mass through joining together into consortia and coalitions. This

Main Trends in Educational Improvement Efforts 243

latter development offers perhaps the most hope of any, since a big problem in the past had been the absence of enough concentrated power and pressure from the outside to make the system respond with needed changes.

One of the most prominent of the new participants is business. Its involvement has picked up considerably since 1970. Though its level of participation is still not very high relative to the need or to business's obvious economic stakes in the schools' performance, it is greater than ever before with some prospects now for even more involvement. The New York Urban Coalition, for example, had a budget of over $600,000 for its education programs in 1975-76, by far the biggest part of its total activity in the city. The Economic Development Council has had an even bigger program, being involved in 16 high schools and in continued management assistance efforts at school headquarters and in the districts.

This present inventory was funded by a consortium of four big corporations, each one of which has been involved in public education and other social programs for many years. They include, as noted in the preface, Exxon, Citibank, Morgan Guaranty Trust, and AT&T. Reviewing briefly some of their activities: Citibank has made a major commitment of time and money to a computerized guidance program in five high schools; Exxon has been deeply involved in supporting many projects, including teacher centers, arts and cultural programs, the City School News information service program, and the Puerto Rican Education and Legal Defense Fund; Chase has supported an important principal leadership program and a teacher center; Morgan Guaranty Trust has given several hundred thousand dollars to Lower East Side Prep and has funded teacher centers; and there are undoubtedly others—for example, the city's many publishing firms. Over a dozen corporations have maintained active executive loan programs granting public service sabbaticals to employees to work with EDC or the Urban Coalition, usually for a year or so. Thus, the business community is beginning to see the importance of such participation to protect its economic interest in having the schools become more effective in producing a manpower pool from which it can draw. Obviously, it has a long way to go and needs assistance in knowing what may be the most productive actions to take.

There are several civic organizations as well as businesses that are relatively new to the New York City school reform arena, and the activities of many have been critical in educational change efforts. The Queens Lay Advocacy Service, for example, has been a major force in special education, in ways indicated in chapter 4. It has represented individual students, carried out important studies, served on task forces and commissions thereby influencing policy decisions, and it has actually operated some alternative schools for the handicapped. The Puerto Rican Education and Legal Defense Fund did the legal work in the critical *Aspira of New York v. Board of Education Class Action Suit.* Aspira of New York has been active in this case, in parent training, and other activities. Williamsberg Legal Services, started with OEO funding in 1968, now does legal work on a wide range of issues in education. The Community Service Society has done many studies and much lobbying through its Committee on Education, formed in 1972, and it now has a new technical assistance unit that helps local citizen groups gain better access to agency decision makers and have more influence over their decisions. The New York Civil Liberties Union has been active on student rights projects. And the Educational Priorities Panel has done many studies of the Board of Education's budget process and pressed hard to have funds shifted from headquarters to the schools.

There is a whole new set of citizen advocacy activities around food programs, through the Community Council of New York and Community Service Society. The Citizens Committee for Children is involved in studies and action programs around special education. The Teachers Action

Main Trends in Educational Improvement Efforts 245

Caucus is a vocal group within the teachers union for school reform programs. The Coalition of Associations of Black and Puerto Rican Educators and Supervisors is a newly formed group to protect the jobs of its constituency. And the Public Education Association has now emerged as the most active consumer advocacy agency and does research and engages in action efforts to represent all these citizen groups.

Then there are many new district- and school-based activities. The Community School Boards Association is an example, and though many local groups question its effectiveness at times, it could become an important vehicle in the future to represent district interests. Harlem Parents Union and the United Bronx Parents are other active organizations, both having been in existence long before decentralization.

Thus, despite all the disappointments and failures of past school reform efforts, there remain some of the old groups, working in new modes, with many new ones having joined them. New York City does not suffer, then, from an absence of involved educational interest groups. The question is how they might become more productive and have more of an impact. We discuss that in the next chapter.

Changes Within the Official School System

Turning now to the school system itself, there are many new participants there as well, some of whom have taken initiatives in promoting new programs. The top staff in the Office of Career Education are one example, and we have already described how they were able to leverage federal (Vocational Education Act) funds to develop many pilot programs that later became part of city tax levy funding. The top staff in the Office of Bilingual Education are another example. They have played the same positive entrepreneurial role in seeking state and federal funds and in assisting schools to develop programs.

Other headquarters staff also initiate and/or support innovative programs. The Access Office in the Division of High Schools is one we have referred to several times in this inventory. It oversees the alternative schools, the mini-schools, the programs for the talented, the articulation programs between high schools and colleges, and other developmental activities at the high school level. If the High School Division is to really indicate a commitment to change, it will have to provide much more resources to this office whose director is charged with too many responsibilities for the limited staff that he has. But at least there is such an office, and it does serve as a focal point for developmental activity.

The Deputy Chancellor's office is still another center for efforts at change, this time in management. As we described in chapter 3, the Deputy Chancellor and his staff have produced many reports and introduced many new procedures to improve the management of the schools. The Board of Education had never had the management analysis capability or the technical understanding of the use of computers and management information systems that the Deputy Chancellor and his staff have brought in, with continued prodding and help from the Economic Development Council. The present board and its successor must insist on further support and expansion of these management improvements, if the agency's capacity to deliver services in more cost effective ways is to be enhanced.

The Center for Educational Management, formerly the office that ran Title III programs, provided management assistance to the districts, and has been running management and teacher training programs, is still another initiator of innovative activity. So too is the Learning Cooperative, which was so effective in securing outside private sector funding for new programs in the arts and has stimulated other curriculum developments as well.

Viewed more generally, most agencies develop a small, informal cadre of staff who have been there a long time, know the problems, and constitute a key internal source for innovation. The New York City Board of Education has such a group, some of them old-timers and some relatively new. They must be located and supported by outside private sector agencies in the future. Several are new, minority staff who have moved into top, near top, or key staff positions in such headquarters units as the Deputy Chancellor's Office, the Offices of Bilingual and Career Education, the Division of Community School District Affairs, units responsible for state and federal programs, and the Division of Educational Planning and Support. There are many non-minority people at headquarters as well who constitute an internal resource for change, particularly in the Access Office of the Division of High Schools. For whatever variety of reasons, former Chancellor Harvey Scribner had not drawn extensively on many of these people and that hampered his ability to implement many reform proposals. Whether future Chancellors are insiders or outsiders, these people will have to be drawn on, along with others who will be brought in from the outside.

A related development, in addition to the emergence of new participants, is the playing of new and much more diverse change agent roles by many third party, private agencies. Throughout the 1950s and 60s most reform-minded private agencies and citizen groups either acted as traditional pressure groups, pushing for more services for their constituency, or they came to the educators with a particular kind of expertise, hoped it might make its way into the schools, and were disappointed and disillusioned when it didn't, which was often the case. The programs of the Economic Development Council illustrate some of the possible new roles. Its use of OD techniques in the high schools, helping to stimulate a planning process there and bringing in a variety of new resources, encouraged the development of many new programs. Equally important, it gave many of the educators a sense of hope that they hadn't had in many years. Many of the federally funded programs that involved universities, e.g., Triple T and the Teacher Corps, also encouraged and, in fact, mandated such new roles where the universities would be involved in convening all the main participants, helping them plan for the school, and providing higher education opportunities for those parents, community representatives, and teachers who wanted them.

A classic case of an organization that has assumed new roles and become more effective as a result is the New York Urban Coalition. It has moved from being a strong advocate for community control and from funding action programs in that mode to working within the school system to help schools and districts develop their own new programs.It took several years for the Coalition to get there, and it had many problems on the way in its work on mini-schools, but it is now probably more effective than ever before.

A big problem for the future will be to consolidate as much as possible these private sector agencies so they will become more of a critical mass than had ever developed in the past. Several recent developments seem promising if they continue to develop, first, because they have more political power than any single agency acting alone, and, second, because they also have more expertise and economic resources when acting collectively. The main recent coalitions and consortia have already been described in chapter 4—the Educational Priorities Panel, the Joint Action for Children, Oasis (an association for contracted-out schools), the Education Council that EDC has been putting together, and a recent task force that PEA is setting up to assess the city's many educational change efforts from the perspective of seeing how the educational delivery system can be changed and diversified to be made more cost effective. It is essential that such a coalescing of private sector agencies continue. There is always the danger of a further proliferation of new coalitions that will develop their own vested interests, nullify one anothers' efforts, and thereby undermine the purposes for which they were established—a common New York City pattern that has to be avoided, if at all possible.

Gaps in School Reform Activity

Having reviewed the main trends in educational reform activity, we may now indicate what we see as some of the gaps. Such an assessment must of necessity reflect the author's own diagnosis of the weaknesses of the system, which seems unavoidable. A key theme throughout this summary review is that the delivery system of the schools is deficient, and it is in that context that the following comments about gaps are made. By delivery system we mean particularly the organizational structure of the Board of Education, its management, and the quality of supervision and classroom teaching. In all those respects, there is not nearly enough reform or improvement activity as conditions require, and what there is could probably be more productive.

Looking at the structure and management of the delivery system, there have been some promising beginnings of improvement effort, e.g., all the management consulting work reviewed—but there is a long way to go. A key issue that has still not been adequately addressed is how to make decentralization work better. McKinsey, EDC, Peat, Marwick, and Mitchell, Cresap, McCormick, and Paget, and many other management consultants addressed this issue, but it requires legal remedies and much more political pressure for significant improvements. The legal remedies would have to clarify the respective power of the districts and headquarters much more and, in this author's judgment, give the districts more budgetary, management and educational program powers. Headquarters must function much more as a service center than it has; the districts need much better management; and the community school boards need much better training and resources for their responsibilities. While these are management problems, they have an obvious political component, with many New York City educators most reluctant to have the districts obtain more power or expertise. Thus, during the first six years of decentralization, the school system has taken little initiative on these matters. A study on school decentralization done for the City Charter Revision Commission documents fairly extensively how the central board and headquarters failed to plan ahead and support decentralization, due largely, in the opinion of the authors, to their great reluctance to give up much headquarters power to the districts. This is not to say that decentralization is an answer to the system's problems, but a clearer delineation of powers between headquarters and the districts, as well as much more supportive monitoring and technical assistance from headquarters, might well improve service delivery.

A further area of importance is for headquarters to make budget and resource allocation decisions much more on the basis of systematic and contemporary information regarding what works and what doesn't than it has done in the past. This became a major issue in the spring of 1976, when a coalition of civic groups, the Educational Priorities Panel, charged that the budget process reflected none of these considerations and called instead for a simple repetition of past programs, with no analysis of their merits. Through the assistance of EDC, top school officials held planning sessions in June and July of 1976 to begin to do this, and it remains to be seen how much their work will show in actual budget decisions. We will discuss this issue in greater detail in the final chapter.

The other main parts of the delivery system that need improvement are supervision and classroom teaching. The New York City schools have many outstanding principals and teachers, but the system itself lacks an adequate personnel and licensing system. Responsibility for inadequate teacher training must be placed in the colleges, not the Board of Education, and while there have been improvements, e.g., more field-based internship experiences, more contact between the colleges and the schools, and more inner-city relevant material in education courses, much more should be done in these areas. On the Board of Education's side, it has a Board of Examiners that develops and administers all tests for teachers, supervisors, and administrators. It has been the subject of critical studies for many years, with each recommending that it be abolished and that the tests be drastically changed to include more job relevant items. Reform there has been very slow. A teacher accountability committee was set up many years ago to develop ways of assessing the performance of teachers and schools, but it does not seem to have moved ahead on any significant improvements. Much of its history has been marred by conflicts between the teachers union and member organizations representing citizen interests that the union felt might enact reforms that would threaten teachers' job rights and security.

The same need for better recruitment, training, and performance appraisal exists for principals. There are several efforts underway to improve principals' executive or management skills, but a key problem is the principals association's decision to become unionized to protect its members' job rights, and their desire not to be considered part of management. The work of PEA to change the legal status of principals back to management so that they can be held accountable for what goes on in their schools and the many other programs to train principals in management techniques seem to be moves in the right direction, if the system could be made to respond. Again, the problem is essentially political, and that takes us to our last section, which assesses the various change strategies.

Chapter 7

An Assessment of the Main Reform Strategies and Recommendations for Future Ones

Changing institutions is at best a very complex task, and when they are static public sector agencies like big city school systems, it is even more so. As indicated several times in the inventory, the educational reform movement in America, particularly in big cities, has not been distinguished by many successes. This has resulted in much discouragement, and a top theoretician and historian of the movement, Professor Michael Katz of the University of Toronto, wrote a classic article for the *Harvard Educational Review* in 1969, pronouncing the movement dead. While we don't believe that that is necessarily the case, Katz was clearly reflecting the deep frustration of many who had labored hard and long to change the public schools. Given the limited successes of the past, it is not likely that we will come up with any startling new directions in this concluding chapter. We can, however, pose some of the key dilemnas on which private sector agencies desirous of reform will have to make critical choices.

Part of the problem, in addition to the formidable obstacles to change that big city school sytems pose and to the lack of focus of the movement that has gone from one fad to another, is that we know so little about how to achieve change. There are no established principles, either from social scientists or from social change practitioners. Organizational development (OD) is, as I have indicated, the body of knowledge and technique that has attracted the most recent interest, but it remains bereft of any validated generalizations and constitutes more a body of "true believers" than anything else. It may well be pointed in the right direction, but there is little evidence to indicate that. Furthermore, many directors of OD-type programs tend to strongly resist evaluation and often state that it may take a decade or more before their programs can be adequately assessed. Meanwhile, those people and agencies who desire change have little to go on.

Focus and Locus Strategies

There are many ways to classify the reform strategies reported in this inventory. One is in terms of their primary target or focus. They may concentrate on (1) new educational programs (curricula, methods of instruction), taking the existing delivery system as a given, or trying to make minor, incremental changes in it to accommodate to the new programs; (2) they may focus on the delivery system itself, including its structure, its management procedures, and the recruitment, training, and performance of its staff; or (3) they may include some combination of the two, as in the case of pilot, demonstration programs that are sequestered from mainstream ones to avoid being too encumbered by the agency's bureaucracy. In view of the accumulating evidence on the management deficiencies of big city school bureaucracies, not only in New York but nationally, those future reform efforts that focus mainly on programs will not be that effective. One reason for the limited successes of so many compensatory education programs over the years, though not the only one, has been their poor implementation in school systems with essentially defective managements.

Another way of classifying strategies is in terms not of their focus but their locus. Thus, one can proceed with educational reform in any number of ways: (1) Emphasizing alternative schools outside the traditional classroom or new programs within it; (2) proceeding in a bottom up fashion, starting at the school or district level, at the point of delivery, or in a top down way, starting with the top management and policy-making structure at headquarters and spreading or driving reforms downward from there; and (3) having programs sub-contracted out, as in the case of the alternative schools for the handicapped, or working within the bureaucracy of the school system. One can argue the pros and cons of each of these six choices, though a strong case can certainly be made for the non-traditional ones within each pair—alternative schools, working in a bottom up way (in large part the philosophy of community control advocates) and having private agencies or groups run programs on a contracted-out basis. Rather than think in terms of polarities, however, it is probably much more productive to see how the strategies within each pair of choices can be phased, alternated, or otherwise orchestrated with one another. The ways for doing so have yet to be well developed.

Affiliated and Unaffiliated Strategies

Notwithstanding the importance of these considerations, we focus in this concluding section on a perhaps even more basic question, dealing with the kinds of social change strategies that private sector agencies might best pursue as they search for more productive reform efforts in the future. Stated very simply, there are two polar kinds of change strategies one can follow playing the role of either an affiliated or unaffiliated change agent. In the first instance, one works collaboratively with people in the target agency, in this case, the school board, the educators, and school administrators, providing resources and technical assistance, playing a mediating, third party role in conflicts within the system or in its relations with outside groups and agencies, and generally acting as a catalyst for change. These are essentially the kinds of things that consultants and organizational development specialists do, and increasing numbers of private sector agencies that work with schools have explicitly adopted the technology of OD. The Economic Development Council in its high school renewal program is a classic example of this.

The other strategy is one of working from the outside, in a consumer advocacy and adversarial role, a la Ralph Nader, not in collaboration but rather in conflict with people in the target agency. This strategy may be chosen perhaps in part because of its compatibility with the philosophy and style of the change agent, but perhaps as well based on the judgment that such a power and conflict strategy is the only way to make the target agency responsive to consumer interests and needs. The activities of many citizen groups reported in chapter 4 rely on this strategy.

Again, an effective change strategy doesn't rule out either approach, and the important question is not whether one is in one or the other camp but how the two strategies are orchestrated, sometimes perhaps even in the same organization. The Rockefeller Brothers Fund, for example, has supported many consumer advocacy efforts that come into direct conflict with the school system—e.g., an affiliate of the Queens Lay Advocacy Service, an action program of the United Parents Association, the Educational Priorities Panel's critical assessment of the Board of Education's budget process, and City School News (in collaboration with other sponsors)—while at the same time it gives other grants to programs initiated and run from within the system. The Public Education Association is an example of an organization that has been in a more collaborative mode at some points in its history and in a more adversarial one at others. As reforms it has advocated became incorporated into the schools, it often then became more collaborative to help in their implementation. At other times, when its board and top staff felt the school system was not being responsive to important new ideas, it maintained a more adversarial approach.

Professor Richard Walton of Harvard Business School has written an insightful article on these issues entitled "Two Strategies of Social Change and Their Dilemmas"

(*Journal of Applied and Behavioral Science*, Vol. 1, No. 2, 1965). Applying the principles he develops there to change strategies and the role of the private sector in the New York City schools, I would make the following broad recommendations for future reform efforts. First, it is absolutely essential to work within the system wherever and whenever possible, in collaboration with those board members and educators who have a commitment to change and want to act on it. As I indicated above, there are talented people at all levels within the system. If given the right kinds of support, they would probably be much more assertive and effective than in the past in making the schools work better. The fact that they know the system well, including its past experiences with various reform efforts, makes them an indispensable resource. Furthermore, reform groups have never been successful just attacking the system, without having any positive program or alliances with groups inside. Such a posture often cuts off communication, including access to information that is so necessary for developing any reform strategy.

Some private sector agencies have worked effectively in this mode. The Economic Development Council is one, and the New York Urban Coalition is another. The Coalition pursued a more advocacy posture in its early years when it lobbied for community control and funded community action programs. Since changing over in 1970 to a more collaborative, within-the-system approach, as it first began to promote mini-schools and later to develop school- and district-based planning, it has certainly had more cooperation from the educators. This has resulted, in turn, in the development of many new programs, some of which seem to be working in a way that improves school services to students. The Economic Development Council's renewal program in sixteen high schools has been similarly well received and has resulted in the development of many new educational services there.

This strategy has limits, however. It is easy, when working in such a collaborative mode, to become co-opted by the insiders and have one's programs and resources diluted. This happens not because the target agency staff are necessarily incompetent, uncommitted to change, or otherwise evil, but simply because institutions as systems have various attributes that constitute constraints on change efforts, constraints that people working within the institutions must tolerate or be regarded as too visionary, impractical, or perhaps even irresponsible. The main attributes of the New York City schools in this regard are their strong status quo politics, reflected in defensive actions taken by the educators to protect their jobs, their programs, and their divisions, in the face of demands for change, and their still defective delivery system that blunts reform efforts, even after they have become politically acceptable to the people inside.

This suggests that it is equally essential to sometimes work outside the system and in seeming conflict with it as well on those issues where it has failed to be responsive. Thus, it took a class action suit by Aspira and a ruling by Commissioner Nyquist to make the schools move ahead on more bilingual education and programs for the handicapped. Likewise it took suits and other actions by the New York Civil Liberties Union to get action on student rights; it took concerted political pressure by citizen groups and the mayor to achieve any decentralization; and it took numerous court rulings and citizen protests to get desegregation plans implemented. Collaborative approaches would not have brought initial results in these cases, though they are essential for implementation.

Though advocates for the collaborative strategy argue against these kinds of confrontations and adversarial roles, much change is initiated only as a result of such outside pressure. This is particularly the case when the institution or agency in question is big, quite bureaucratic, involves substantial jobs and other economic interests, and is highly political. Good will, trust, and collaborative relations are sometimes hard to establish in such a situation, and where they are established, after many years of effort, it may take many more before they result in significant institutional change and improved performance. That has yet to happen with any of the collaborative efforts we have described, which is not to urge their abandonment but simply to suggest that they must be balanced with other approaches as well.

Coordinating Strategies

A critical question for future educational reform efforts in New York is how to orchestrate and coordinate both strategies. That can probably be done in any number of ways. One is to continue working outside the system in developing alternative programs, but with the goal of having the system itself adopt them as quickly as possible. The fact that they are started outside may give them more flexibility and a more benign setting in which to develop, allowing them to work out better than if they had been started within the system. Also, their very existence may provide more competition and more consumer options, both of which may provide an incentive for the system itself to develop better services than might otherwise have been the case. The Street Academies and Harlem Prep are examples of such alternative programs that were started outside and later absorbed. There were problems with the absorption, but it has apparently worked out well in many respects. Furthermore, the system might well have been even slower to adopt such alternative schools if they hadn't developed on the outside. It had not taken that much initiative on its own.

One useful way of further orchestrating the inside and outside strategies is to have a division of labor among the various private sector agencies in which some would pursue a power strategy while others would be more collaborative. Professor Richard Walton of Harvard Business School, a key theoretician in this field in much the same sense as Michael Katz is on the educational reform movement, gives many illustrations in his important article mentioned earlier, "Two Strategies of Social Change and Their Dilemnas". He describes how this orchestration can take place, with each set of participants reinforcing the other rather than being polarized. In the civil rights movement, for example, some of the final negotiations with agencies or institutions seen as following racist or discriminatory practices were often made by NAACP or Urban League officials, but they only had bargaining power as a result of initial pressure and militant demonstrations carried out by their local branches and by such groups as CORE and SNCC. Furthermore, it is incorrect to assume, as some of the collaboration advocates do, that pursuing the power strategy from the outside invariably cuts people off from later negotiations with the target agency. As Walton notes: "The substantive gains obtained by the power strategy almost always result in temporary setbacks in terms of the level of friendliness and trust between the groups; but in the somewhat longer run, the result may be better affective relations . . . One reason why more positive attitudes may develop, via the initial power strategy, is that the commitment and self-respect which the Negroes usually demonstrate in pursuing the power strategy may engender respect on the part of the larger white community after the initial heat of conflict has subsided." Walton suggests further, as do many other social scientists, that the collaborative approach to social change is more effective if there is some parity in the power of the parties. That was not the case in relations of blacks to mainstream American institutions, and attempts at OD-type collaborative relations without such power tactics would probably have resulted in fewer gains than took place. There is obviously a need for both, and the trick is to work them together.

There may be much carryover from Walton's analysis of the civil rights movement to school reform activities. The issue in big city school systems is in part one of professional power exercised by the educators against the democratic rights of various client groups. The educators have in the past had a monopoly over definitions of professionalism, and they have had strong stakes in maintaining the status quo, particularly their jobs. They are often in a basic conflict relation to educational consumer groups, and as Walton and others have pointed out, bargaining and power tactics are required in such situations. Advocates of collaboration keep missing this point.

Taking the New York City school budget controversy in this context, the budget process became a big issue in 1975-76 with the drastic fiscal cuts. It is common knowledge that budgets in all institutions, but particularly in the public sector are political, and the politics here was a covert and narrow one, with consumer groups not well represented in the process in contrast to the educators who had much more access to top school decision makers. Many citizen groups felt that too much money was going to unneeded programs at headquarters and not enough to the districts. The Educational Priorities Panel, composed of 16 civic organizations, was formed, and its own independent research raised serious questions regarding the Board's decisions. There was later a big furore over the quality of the Panel's research and the contentiousness of some of its participating members in their testimonies at public hearings, but they had an important effect on school decision makers.

By contrast, the central board asked EDC, its long time management consultant, to help it do some of the same kinds of research that the Panel had done. EDC, working in the collaborative mode, met in private with top school officials and helped them develop ways of reviewing all their operations. It made some of the same general types of recommendations that the Panel had for eliminating or phasing down some headquarters functions and for beginning to set explicit priorities, based at least in part on some attempt to generate systematic cost effectiveness information.

It is unlikely that the central board would have undertaken this exercise had there not been such citizen complaint expressed so publicly. Indeed, the original budget that the board presented to city officials was almost a replica of the previous year's one. Whatever power and leverage EDC has in this process, then, it owes at least in part to the Panel. It is in a role analogous to that of the NAACP or Urban League, negotiating changes with the gatekeepers of mainstream institutions. It is helped in its bargaining power not only by its own collaborative posture but by the more publicly outspoken civic groups in the Panel. More attempts should be made in the future to maintain communications between these two sets of private sector participants.

Consumer Advocacy and Politics

Finally, we want to end by raising a few other key issues that are critical to consider in planning future change efforts. One is the need for active explorations into establishing new educational delivery systems for New York. Numerous national commissions and panels have recommended strongly that the existing public school system in America, particularly at the high school level, does not meet the needs of youth or of the wider society. And these commissions were composed not of militant community activists, by and large, but of educators and social scientists. While we cannot review here all their findings, their essential argument is that the traditional classroom is too confining, too segregated from the rest of society, too action poor for many contemporary youth, and places many of them in too much of a passive, dependency status that they find unpalatable. These commissions urge a vigorous search for alternatives, with the National Panel on High Schools and Adolescent

Education, a commission that the author served on, urging that the concept of the comprehensive high school be replaced by that of a comprehensive education system that includes many agencies in the community—both as learning sites and as vehicles for community service activity for youth. The Public Education Association has now set up a task force to engage in further exploring these ideas in New York City and to develop alternative blue prints for the future, and it has convened many educators and civic leaders in that effort. That work should be supported by many private sector agencies.

A second important strategy would be to follow up on the analyses of the budget process that began in more earnest in 1975-76. Even though they may not know much about education and the public sector, many corporations have considerable expertise in budget analysis and planning, and as taxpayers and consumers of the schools' product—both their graduates and dropouts—these corporations have an enormous economic interest in looking more closely at the process. If several got together and enlisted the assistance of citizen groups for advice on technical education issues, they might well have an important impact. They would be combining an expertise in budget analysis with a political function of having taxpayer and consumer interests much better represented in key education decisions. Furthermore, that process might be extended to collective bargaining relations as well. Those decisions made between the Board of Education and the teachers union deal with up to 75 or 80% of the total expense budget, and consumers have never been well represented in the past. Central board members involved in the bargaining are much more swayed by teachers union pressures than by citizen ones, partly because the latter have never been well articulated. The time has long passed when they should be, and there is no reason why that can't take place, despite the diversity of citizen interests in New York City.

This relates to a point made earlier on building a critical

mass for educational change in New York City. The many consumers of public education must not only become much more active, but they should get together much more than they ever have before. Civic groups have shown signs recently of doing so, and business could protect its economic interests much more effectively than it ever has if it joined in that process.

Finally, a key question for the long term is how one builds into the system a much larger cadre of effective managers. EDC has pressed hard for this, as has the Deputy Chancellor, and what is needed now is strong support to expand on those efforts. This also is a political matter, and it involves primarily the reform of all those civil service and personnel practices in city government that have prevented more lateral entry into middle and higher management positions of people with demonstrated executive competence. Unless that important task is undertaken, many of the needed reforms may not be built into the system and sustained over time.

The underlying theme of all these recommendations is one of consumer advocacy and politics as the directions for the future. Until an informed, powerful, and active constituency for better public education develops in New York City, the schools will continue to pose serious problems for the city's future. The big stumbling block in the past was the diverse definitions of what constitutes better education, but notwithstanding all that diversity, there should be many issues on which civic groups can reach a consensus and begin to make that consensus felt in the schools. The next few years may well determine whether that process will take place.

Appendices

Street Addresses of the Public Schools Cited in the Inventory

Manhattan

Elementary Schools

PS 3
490 Hudson Street
New York, NY 10014

PS 7
160 East 120th Street
New York, NY 10035

PS 9
100 West 84th Street
New York, NY 10024

PS 11
320 West 21st Street
New York, NY 10011

PS 19
185 First Avenue
New York, NY 10003

PS 26
Fort Jay, Governors Island
New York, NY 10004

PS 33
281 9th Avenue
New York, NY 10001

PS 40
319 East 19th Street
New York, NY 10003

PS 41
116 West 11th Street
New York, NY 10011

PS 42
71 Hester Street
New York, NY 10002

PS 50
433 East 100th Street
New York, NY 10029

PS 68
127 East 127th Street
New York, NY 10027

PS 72
131 East 104th Street
New York, NY 10029

PS 75
735 West End Avenue
New York, NY 10024

PS 76
229 West 121st Street
New York, NY 10027

PS 79
55 East 120th Street
New York, NY 10035

PS 83
219 East 109th Street
New York, NY 10029

PS 84
32 West 92nd Street
New York, NY 10025

PS 87
160 West 78th Street
New York, NY 10024

PS 91
198 Forsyth Street
New York, NY 10002

PS 92
222 West 134th Street
New York, NY 10030

PS 96
216 East 120th Street
New York, NY 10035

PS 97
525 East Houston Street
New York, NY 10002

PS 98
512 West 212th Street
New York, NY 10034

PS 101
141 East 111th Street
New York, NY 10029

PS 102
315 East 113th Street
New York, NY 10029

PS 108
1615 Madison Avenue
New York, NY 10029

PS 109
215 East 99th Street
New York, NY 10029

PS 112
535 East 119th Street
New York, NY 10035

PS 113
240 West 113th Street
New York, NY 10026

PS 115
586 West 177th Street
New York, NY 10033

PS 121
232 East 103rd Street
New York, NY 10029

PS 126
80 Catherine Street
New York, NY 10038

PS 134
293 East Broadway
New York, NY 10002

266 Inventory of Educational Improvement Efforts

PS 137
327 Cherry Street
New York, NY 10002

PS 144
134 West 122nd Street
New York, NY 10027

PS 145
150 West 105th Street
New York, NY 10025

PS 146
421 East 106th Street
New York, NY 10029

PS 155
319 East 117th Street
New York, NY 10035

PS 158
1458 York Avenue
New York, NY 10021

PS 163
163 West 97th Street
New York, NY 10025

PS 165
234 West 109th Street
New York, NY 10025

PS 166
132 West 89th Street
New York, NY 10024

PS 171
19 East 103rd Street
New York, NY 10029

PS 179
140 West 102nd Street
New York, NY 10025

PS 183
419 East 66th Street
New York, NY 10021

PS 187
187th Street & Cabrini Blvd.
New York, NY 10040

PS 188
442 East Houston Street
New York, NY 10002

PS 189
2580 Amsterdam Avenue
New York, NY 10040

PS 190
311 East 82nd Street
New York, NY 10028

PS 191
210 West 61st Street
New York, NY 10023

PS 192
500 West 138th Street
New York, NY 10031

PS 198
1700 Third Avenue
New York, NY 10028

PS 199
270 West 70th Street
New York, NY 10023

PS 206
508 East 120th Street
New York, NY 10035

Intermediate and Junior High Schools

JHS 13
1573 Madison Avenue
New York, NY 10029

JHS 17
328 West 48th Street
New York, NY 10036

IS 44
100 West 77th Street
New York, NY 10024

JHS 47
225 East 23rd Street
New York, NY 10010

JHS 52
650 Academy Street
New York, NY 10034

JHS 56
220 Henry Street
New York, NY 10002

IS 82
371 Madison Street
New York, NY 10002

JHS 104
330 East 21st Street
New York, NY 10010

IS 117
240 East 109th Street
New York, NY 10029

JHS 118
154 West 93rd Street
New York, NY 10025

JHS 167
220 East 76th Street
New York, NY 10021

IS 201
2005 Madison Avenue
New York, NY 10035

High Schools

Art & Design
1075 Second Avenue
New York, NY 10022

Benjamin Franklin
East 116th Street & FDR Drive
New York, NY 10029

Charles E. Hughes
351 West 18th Street
New York, NY 10011

George Washington
549 Audubon Avenue
New York, NY 10040

Haaren
899 Tenth Avenue
New York, NY 10019

Julia Richman
317 East 67th Street
New York, NY 10021

268   Inventory of Educational Improvement Efforts

Louis D. Brandeis
145 West 84th Street
New York, NY 10024

Murry Bergtraum
411 Pearl Street
New York, NY 10038

N.Y. Printing
439 West 49th Street
New York, NY 10019

Norman Thomas
111 East 33rd Street
New York, NY 10016

Seward Park
350 Grand Street
New York, NY 10002

Alternative High Schools

Auxiliary Services
198 Forsythe Street
New York, NY 10002

Branch Office of Auxiliary
    Services
65 Court Street
Brooklyn, NY

H.R.A. Executive Internship
    Program
250 Church Street
New York, NY 10013

Harlem Prep
2435 8th Avenue
New York, NY 10030

Lower East Side Prep
169 William Street
New York, NY 10038

Park East
230-34 East 105th Street
New York, NY 10029

Satellite Academy
50 Chambers Street
New York, NY 10007

West Side
257 West 93rd Street
New York, NY 10025

Schools for the Education of Socially Maladjusted and Emotionally Disturbed Children

P-8M
Livingston School
29 King Street
New York, NY 10014

P-58M
Manhattan School
317 West 52nd Street
New York, NY 10019

P-82M
Cyrus W. Field School
371 Madison Street
New York, NY 10002

P-106M
Bellevue Psychiatric Hospital
30th Street & First Avenue
New York, NY 10016

P-169M
Robert F. Kennedy School
110 East 88th Street
New York, NY 10028

P-226M
415 East 88th Street
New York, NY 10028

PS-402M
45 East 81st Street
New York, NY 10028

J-47-M
School for the Deaf
225 East 23rd Street
New York, NY 10010

Bronx

Elementary Schools

PS 2
1363 Fulton Avenue
Bronx, New York 10456

PS 4
1701 Fulton Avenue
Bronx, New York 10457

PS 6
1000 East Tremont Avenue
Bronx, New York 10460

PS 8
3010 Briggs Avenue
Bronx, New York 10458

PS 14
3041 Bruckner Blvd.
Bronx, New York 10461

PS 18
502 Morris Avenue
Bronx, NY 10451

PS 21
715 East 225th Street
Bronx, NY 10466

PS 23
793 East 165th Street
Bronx, NY 10456

PS 24
660 West 236th Street
Bronx, NY 10463

PS 32
690 East 183rd Street
Bronx, NY 10458

PS 37
425 East 145th Street
Bronx, NY 10454

PS 40
568 East 140th Street
Bronx, NY 10454

PS 42
Washington Avenue & Claremont
   Parkway
Bronx, NY 10457

PS 48
1290 Spofford Avenue
Bronx, NY 10474

PS 49
383 East 139th Street
Bronx, NY 10454

PS 51
810 Trinity Avenue
Bronx, NY 10456

PS 54
1241 Intervale Avenue
Bronx, NY 10459

PS 60
888 Stebbins Avenue
Bronx, NY 10459

PS 61
1550 Crotona Park
Bronx, NY 10460

PS 63
1260 Franklin Avenue
Bronx, NY 10456

PS 64
1425 Walton Avenue
Bronx, NY 10452

PS 65
141st Street & Cypress Avenue
Bronx, NY 10454

PS 68
4011 Monticello Avenue
Bronx, NY 10466

PS 71
3040 Roberts Avenue
Bronx, NY 10461

PS 76
900 Adee Avenue
Bronx, NY 10469

PS 77
1250 Ward Avenue
Bronx, NY 10472

PS 87
1955 Bussing Avenue
Bronx, NY 10466

PS 89
980 Mace Avenue
Bronx, NY 10469

PS 92
700 East 179th Street
Bronx, NY 10457

PS 93
1535 Story Avenue
Bronx, NY 10473

PS 97
1375 Mace Avenue
Bronx, NY 10469

PS 99
1180 Stebbins Avenue
Bronx, NY 10459

PS 102
1827 Archer Street
Bronx, NY 10460

PS 103
4125 Carpenter Avenue
Bronx, NY 10466

PS 110
580 Crotona Park South
Bronx, NY 10456

PS 115
East 183rd & Ryer Avenue
Bronx, NY 10458

PS 121
2750 Throop Avenue
Bronx, NY 10469

PS 129
2055 Mapes Avenue
Bronx, NY 10460

PS 134
1330 Bristow Street
Bronx, NY 10459

PS 140
916 Eagle Avenue
Bronx, NY 10456

PS 150
920 East 167th Street
Bronx, NY 10459

PS 152
1007 Evergreen Avenue
Bronx, NY 10472

PS 154
333 East 135th Street
Bronx, NY 10454

PS 160
Hutchinson River Parkway &
　　Einstein Loop
Bronx, NY 10475

PS 185
170 Brown Place
Bronx, NY 10454

PS 198
1180 Tinton Avenue
Bronx, NY 10456

PS 232
930 Soundview Avenue
Bronx, NY 10472

Intermediate and Junior High Schools

IS 38
701 St. Ann's Avenue
Bronx, NY 10455

IS 52
681 Kelly Street
Bronx, NY 10455

JHS 98
1619 Boston Road
Bronx, NY 10460

JHS 117
1865 Morris Avenue
Bronx, NY 10453

JHS 125
1111 Pugsley Avenue
Bronx, NY 10473

JHS 133
1010 Stebbins Avenue
Bronx, NY 10459

Inventory of Educational Improvement Efforts

JHS 136
750 Jennings Street
Bronx, NY 10459

JHS 139
345 Brook Avenue
Bronx, NY 10454

JHS 144
2545 Gunther Avenue
Bronx, NY 10469

IS 145
1000 Teller Avenue
Bronx, NY 10456

JHS 148
3630 Third Avenue
Bronx, NY 10456

IS 155
470 Jackson Avenue
Bronx, NY 10455

JHS 158
800 Home Street
Bronx, NY 10456

IS 184
778 Forest Avenue
Bronx, NY 10456

High Schools

Adlai Stevenson
1980 Lafayette Avenue
Bronx, NY 10473

Alfred E. Smith
333 East 151st Street
Bronx, NY 10451

Grace H. Dodge
2474 Crotona Avenue
Bronx, NY 10458

Harry S. Truman
750 Baychester Avenue
Bronx, NY 10475

Herbert H. Lehman
3000 East Tremont Avenue
Bronx, NY 10461

James Monroe
1300 Boynton Avenue
Bronx, NY 10472

Morris
166th Street & Boston Road
Bronx, NY 10456

Samuel Gompers
455 Southern Blvd.
Bronx, NY 10455

Theodore Roosevelt
500 East Fordham Road
Bronx, NY 10458

Walton
West 195th Street & Reservoir Ave.
Bronx, NY 10468

William H. Taft
240 East 172nd Street
Bronx, NY 10457

Schools for the Education of Socially Maladjusted and Emotionally Disturbed Children

P-205M
Henry Ittleson
5050 Iselin Avenue
Riverdale, NY 10471

P-12X
Lewis & Clark
2555 Trafman Avenue
Bronx, NY 10461

P-186X
Edenwald School
1250 East 229th Street
Bronx, NY 10466

Lt. Joseph Kennedy Jr. Home
1770 Stillwell Avenue
Bronx, NY 10469

Brooklyn

Elementary Schools

PS 3
50 Jefferson Avenue
Brooklyn, NY 11216

PS 10
511 7th Avenue
Brooklyn, NY 11215

PS 11
419 Waverly Avenue
Brooklyn, NY 11238

PS 13
557 Pennsylvania Avenue
Brooklyn, NY 11207

PS 16
157 Wilson Street
Brooklyn, NY 11211

PS 17
208 North 5th Street
Brooklyn, NY 11211

PS 21
180 Chauncey Street
Brooklyn, NY 11233

PS 23
545 Willoughby Avenue
Brooklyn, NY 11206

PS 31
75 Meserole Avenue
Brooklyn, NY 11222

PS 52
2675 East 29th Street
Brooklyn, NY 11235

PS 56
170 Gates Avenue
Brooklyn, NY 11238

PS 63
116 Williams Avenue
Brooklyn, NY 11207

Inventory of Educational Improvement Efforts

PS 76
20 Wyona Street
Brooklyn, NY 11207

PS 84
250 Berry Street
Brooklyn, NY 11222

PS 90
2840 West 12th Street
Brooklyn, NY 11224

PS 91
East New York & Albany Avenue
Brooklyn, NY 11203

PS 99
1120 East 10th Street
Brooklyn, NY 11230

PS 102
211 72nd Street
Brooklyn, NY 11209

PS 105
1031 59th Street
Brooklyn, NY 11219

PS 108
200 Linwood Street
Brooklyn, NY 11208

PS 110
124 Monitor Street
Brooklyn, NY 11222

PS 131
4305 Ft. Hamilton Parkway
Brooklyn, NY 11219

PS 137
121 Saratoga Avenue
Brooklyn, NY 11233

PS 138
801 Park Place
Brooklyn, NY 11216

PS 139
330 Rugby Road
Brooklyn, NY 11226

PS 144
430 Howard Avenue
Brooklyn, NY 11233

PS 147
325 Bushwick Avenue
Brooklyn, NY 11206

PS 149
700 Sutter Avenue
Brooklyn, NY 11207

PS 150
364 Sackman Street
Brooklyn, NY 11212

PS 152
2310 Glenwood Road
Brooklyn, NY 11210

PS 154
11th Avenue & Windsor
Brooklyn, NY 11215

PS 158
400 Ashford Street
Brooklyn, NY 11207

PS 159
2781 Pitkin Avenue
Brooklyn, NY 11208

PS 174
574 Dumont Avenue
Brooklyn, NY 11207

PS 178
2163 Dean Street
Brooklyn, NY 11233

PS 180
16th Avenue & 57th Street
Brooklyn, NY 11204

PS 182
720 Dumont Avenue
Brooklyn, NY 11207

PS 184
273 Newport Street
Brooklyn, NY 11212

PS 188
7601 19th Avenue
Brooklyn, NY 11214

PS 190
590 Sheffield Avenue
Brooklyn, NY 11207

PS 191
1600 Park Place
Brooklyn, NY 11233

PS 192
4715 18th Avenue
Brooklyn, NY 11214

PS 197
1599 East 22nd Street
Brooklyn, NY 11210

PS 199
1100 Elm Avenue
Brooklyn, NY 11214

PS 202
982 Hegeman Avenue
Brooklyn, NY 11207

PS 213
580 Hegeman Avenue
Brooklyn, NY 11207

PS 219
1060 Clarkson Avenue
Brooklyn, NY 11212

PS 225
1075 Ocean View Avenue
Brooklyn, NY 11235

PS 226
6006 23rd Avenue
Brooklyn, NY 11204

PS 236
6302 Avenue U
Brooklyn, NY 11234

PS 238
1633 East 8th Street
Brooklyn, NY 11223

PS 243
1580 Dean Street
Brooklyn, NY 11213

PS 244
Tilden Avenue & 54th Street
Brooklyn, NY 11203

PS 251
1037 East 54th Street
Brooklyn, NY 11234

PS 270
241 Emerson Place
Brooklyn, NY 11205

PS 272
101-24 Seaview Avenue
Brooklyn, NY 11236

PS 273
923 Jerome Street
Brooklyn, NY 11208

PS 274
800 Bushwick Avenue
Brooklyn, NY 11221

PS 279
1070 East 104th Street
Brooklyn, NY 11236

PS 287
50 Navy Street
Brooklyn, NY 11201

PS 298
85 Watkins Street
Brooklyn, NY 11212

PS 307
209 York Street
Brooklyn, NY 11201

PS 312
7103 Avenue T
Brooklyn, NY 11234

PS 321
180 7th Avenue
Brooklyn, NY 11215

PS 327
111 Bristol Street
Brooklyn, NY 11212

PS 328
330 Alabama Avenue
Brooklyn, NY 11207

PS 335
130 Rochester Avenue
Brooklyn, NY 11213

PS 345
111 Berriman Street
Brooklyn, NY 11208

PS 396
110 Chester Street
Brooklyn, NY 11212

PS 397
490 Fenimore Street
Brooklyn, NY 11203

Intermediate and Junior High Schools

JHS 43
1401 Emmons Avenue
Brooklyn, NY 11235

JHS 68
956 East 82nd Street
Brooklyn, NY 11236

JHS 88
544 Seventh Avenue
Brooklyn, NY 11215

IS 96
99 Avenue P
Brooklyn, NY 11204

IS 117
300 Willoughby Avenue
Brooklyn, NY 11205

JHS 126
424 Leonard Street
Brooklyn, NY 11222

IS 171
528 Ridgewood Avenue
Brooklyn, NY 11208

IS 210
188 Rochester Avenue
Brooklyn, NY 11213

JHS 211
1001 East 100th Street
Brooklyn, NY 11236

IS 218
370 Fountain Avenue
Brooklyn, NY 11208

JHS 228
Avenue S & West 4th Street
Brooklyn, NY 11223

JHS 239
2401 Neptune Avenue
Brooklyn, NY 11224

IS 271
1137 Herkimer Street
Brooklyn, NY 11233

JHS 281
8787 24th Avenue
Brooklyn, NY 11214

JHS 285
5909 Beverly Road
Brooklyn, NY 11203

IS 293
1 Butler Street
Brooklyn, NY 11231

JHS 303
501 West Avenue
Brooklyn, NY 11224

High Schools

Abraham Lincoln
Ocean Parkway & West Avenue
Brooklyn, NY 11235

Bay Ridge
4th Avenue & 67th Street
Brooklyn, NY 11220

Boys and Girls
1700 Fulton Street
Brooklyn, NY 11213

Bushwick
400 Irving Avenue
Brooklyn, NY 11227

Clara Barton
901 Classon Avenue
Brooklyn, NY 11225

Eastern District
227 Marcy Avenue
Brooklyn, NY 11211

Edward R. Murrow
1600 Avenue L
Brooklyn, NY 11230

Erasmus Hall
911 Flatbush Avenue
Brooklyn, NY 11226

Fort Hamilton
8301 Shore Road
Brooklyn, NY 11209

Franklin K. Lane
999 Jamaica Avenue
Brooklyn, NY 11208

George Westinghouse
105 Johnson Street
Brooklyn, NY 11201

George W. Wingate
600 Kingston Avenue
Brooklyn, NY 11203

James Madison
3787 Bedford Avenue
Brooklyn, NY 11229

John Dewey
50 Avenue X
Brooklyn, NY 11223

John Jay
237 Seventh Avenue
Brooklyn, NY 11215

Midwood
Bedford Avenue & East 26 St.
Brooklyn, NY 11210

New Utrecht
1601 80th Street
Brooklyn, NY 11214

Prospect Heights
883 Classon Avenue
Brooklyn, NY 11235

Samuel J. Tilden
5800 Tilden Avenue
Brooklyn, NY 11203

Sarah J. Hale
345 Dean Street
Brooklyn, NY 11217

South Shore
6565 Flatlands Avenue
Brooklyn, NY 11236

Thomas Jefferson
Pennsylvania & Dumont Avenues
Brooklyn, NY 11207

William E. Grady
25 Brighton 4 Road
Brooklyn, NY 11235

Alternative High Schools

City-As-School
59 Schermerhorn Street
Brooklyn, NY 11201

H. S. Redirection
315 Berry Street
Brooklyn, NY 11211

Pacific
112 Schermerhorn Street
Brooklyn, NY 11201

P. M.
105 Johnson Street
Brooklyn, NY 11201

Schools for the Education of the Socially Maladjusted and Emotionally Disturbed Children

P-162M
League School and Research
 Center
567 Bronxwood Avenue
Brooklyn, NY 10466

P-85K
Sterling School
510 Clermont Avenue
Brooklyn, NY 11238

P-141K
Vanderbilt School for Girls
227 Sterling Place
Brooklyn, NY 11238

P-368K
Kings County Psychiatric
 Hospital
(G Building)
Brooklyn, New York 11203

P-369K
James Lawrence School
383 State Street
Brooklyn, NY 11217

P-370K
Jim Thorpe School
3000 West 1st Street
Brooklyn, NY 11224

P-371K
Lillian L. Rashkis School
355-37th Street
Brooklyn, NY 11232

PS 401-M
360 -36th Street
Brooklyn, NY 11232

PS 401-K
2675 East 29th Street
Brooklyn, NY 11235

Queens

Elementary Schools

PS 3
108-55 69th Avenue
Forest Hills, NY 11375

PS 12
42-00 72nd Street
Woodside, NY 11377

PS 13
55-01 94th Street
Elmhurst, NY 11373

PS 14
107-91 Otis Avenue
Corona, NY 11368

PS 19
99th Street & Roosevelt Ave.
Corona, NY 11368

PS 22
153-33 Sanford Avenue
Flushing, NY 11355

PS 26
195-02 69th Avenue
Flushing, NY 11365

PS 48
155-02 108th Street
Jamaica, NY 11433

PS 63
90-15 Sutter Avenue
Ozone Park, NY 11417

PS 68
59-09 St. Felix Avenue
Ridgewood, NY 11227

PS 71
62-85 Forest Avenue
Ridgewood, NY 11227

PS 79
15-28 149th Street
Whitestone, NY 11357

PS 87
67-54 80th Street
Middle Village, NY 11379

PS 88
60-85 Catalpa Avenue
Ridgewood, NY 11227

PS 90
86-50 109th Street
Richmond Hill, NY 11418

PS 97
8552 85th Street
Woodhaven, NY 11421

PS 101
2 Russell Place
Forest Hills, NY 11375

PS 112
25-05 37th Avenue
Long Island City, NY 11101

PS 116
107-25 Wren Place
Jamaica, NY 11433

PS 118
190-20 109th Road
Hollis, NY 11412

PS 120
58-01 136th Street
Flushing, NY 11355

PS 133
248-05 86th Street
Bellerose, NY 11426

PS 134
109th Avenue & 203rd Street
Hollis, NY 11412

PS 138
253rd Street & Weller Avenue
Rosedale, NY 11422

PS 150
40-01 43rd Avenue
Long Island City, NY 11104

PS 153
60-02 60th Lane
Maspeth, NY 11378

PS 154
75-02 162nd Street
Flushing, NY 11366

PS 160
109-59 Inwood Street
Jamaica, NY 11435

PS 163
159-01 59th Avenue
Flushing, NY 11365

PS 164
138-01 77th Avenue
Flushing, NY 11367

PS 183
245 Beach 79th Street
Rockaway Beach, NY 11693

PS 187
61-25 Marathon Parkway
Little Neck, NY 11362

PS 188
218-12 Harland Avenue
Flushing, NY 11364

PS 201
65-11 155th Street
Flushing, NY 11367

PS 203
53-11 Springfield Blvd.
Bayside, NY 11364

PS 206
61-21 97th Place
Rego Park, NY 11374

PS 209
16-10 Utopia Parkway
Whitestone, NY 11357

PS 229
67-25 51st Road
Woodside, NY 11377

Intermediate and Junior High Schools

JHS 73
70-02 54th Avenue
Maspeth, NY 11378

JHS 125
46-02 47th Avenue
Woodside, NY 11377

JHS 189
144-80 Barclay Avenue
Flushing, NY 11355

JHS 218
65-21 Main Street
Flushing, NY 11367

JHS 237
46-21 Colden Street
Flushing, NY 11355

High Schools

Andrew Jackson
207-01 116th Avenue
Cambria Heights, NY 11411

August Martin
156-10 Baisley Blvd.
Jamaica, NY 11434

Beach Channel
100-00 Beach Channel Drive
Rockaway Park, NY 11694

Francis Lewis
58-20 Utopia Parkway
Flushing, NY 11365

Grover Cleveland
2127 Himrod Street
Ridgewood, NY 11237

Springfield Gardens
143-10 Springfield Boulevard
Springfield Gardens, NY 11413

Newtown
48-01 90th Street
Elmhurst, NY 11373

William C. Bryant
48-10 31st Avenue
Long Island City, NY 11103

Alternative High School

Middle College
31-10 Thomson Avenue
Long Island City, NY 11101

Schools for the Education of Socially Maladjusted and Emotionally Disturbed Children

P-4Q
Orville Wright School
39-25 Crescent Street
Long Island City, NY 11101

P-75Q
Robert E. Peary School
1666 Hancock Street
Ridgewood, NY 11227

P-9Q
Walter Reed School
58-74 57th Street
Maspeth, NY 11378

P-224Q
(JHS 218Q - Room 236)
65-21 Main Street
Flushing, New York 11367

P-23Q
Lincoln School
138-11 35th Avenue
Flushing, NY 11354

Staten Island

Elementary Schools

PS 3
80 Goff Avenue
Staten Island, NY 10301

PS 13
161 Hylan Blvd.
Staten Island, NY 10305

PS 16
80 Monroe Avenue
Staten Island, NY 10301

PS 19
780 Post Avenue
Staten Island, NY 10310

PS 18
221 Broadway
Staten Island, NY 10310

Intermediate and Junior High Schools

JHS 2
333 Midland Avenue
Staten Island, NY 10306

IS 61
445 Castleton Avenue
Staten Island, NY 10310

High Schools

Curtis
Hamilton Avenue & St. Mark's
    Place
St. George
Staten Island, NY 10306

Ralph McKee
290 St. Mark's Place
Staten Island, NY 10301

Port Richmond
Innis Street and St. Joseph
    Avenue
Staten Island, NY 10302

Susan E. Wagner
1200 Manor Road
Staten Island, NY 10314

Schools for the Education of Socially Maladjusted and Emotionally Disturbed Children

P-25R
St. Michael's Home
1380 Arthur Kill Road
Staten Island, NY 10312

PS-271-R
Richmond - O.T.C.
Prospect & Harvard Avenues
Staten Island, NY 10301